"The Innocent Crusaders"

-An Anzac Story-
Based on the World War 1 Diary Records of
Ralph Edwin DeGaris, OBE MSM

William S DeGaris

Copyright © William S DeGaris, 2007.
All rights asserted by the author.

Second Edition, 2015.

ISBN 978-0-646-48529-4

Sergeant Ralph DeGaris, Cornwall, 1919. (Aged 24 years.)

OBE: MSM   1914-18 Service medals   Gallipoli ANZAC Medal
OBE = Officer of British Empire (1963); MSM = Meritorious Service Medal (1918);
Ralph Edwin DeGaris, OBE, (Medals and Awards).

"The Innocent Crusaders"
Part 1:

Contents:

	Page
Preface	i-xvii
Chapter 1 Leaving Australia.	1
Chapter 2 Getting to Egypt.	10
Chapter 3 Heliopolis Camp, Cairo, Alexandria	17
Chapter 4 Gallipoli.	47
Chapter 5 Recuperation on Malta.	73
Chapter 6 Egypt revisited.	102
Chapter 7 The First Australians in France, 1916.	115
Chapter 8 Armentieres, "The Nursery of France."	134
Chapter 9 From Armentieres to the Somme, Pozieres..	164
Chapter 10 Ypres, Belgium for the first time.	189
Chapter 11 Winter back in the Somme Valley, 1916/17.	204
Chapter 12 On the Somme; Bullecourt, May 1917.	231
Epilogue	246
Bibliography.	251
Index	255
About the Author	258

Front Cover Photo: (Courtesy Margaret Blackwell)

Back row: Herb Harvey, Alan Black, Johnnie Walker, Bill Stewart, Bill Callaghan, Bert Brown, Alec Blackwell
Centre row: Dolphus Kemp, Ted Nunn, Ralph DeGaris, Jack Bruce, Snowy Hill
Front Row: Don Pace, Peter Spence, Jack Ellis

Preface:

Ralph Edwin DeGaris was born in Naracoorte, South Australia in 1895. He attended primary school at Naracoorte. His secondary schooling was at Prince Alfred College, Kent Town, between 1908 and 1911. Ralph was an excellent schoolboy sportsman. He won the Intercollegiate Gold Medal for gymnasium, played in the first eighteen football side for 2 years, 1910-11, and was also a member of the Intercollegiate Athletics team. He was not a good student, and freely admitted this. In a letter he sent to his father in 1911, towards the end of the year, he wrote;

> "Nearly all my exams are over now- only one more to go. I have not done very well in these exams at all; but I have worked hard and luck has been rather against me..."

He then went on to beg his father to allow him to spend one more year at PAC. He was not very convincing in his plea, but typical of Ralph, he was disarmingly honest about his intentions. He wrote;

> "If I were to come back next year, Father, I'll admit it will be mainly a years sport, but I could still take a few subjects namely Wool-classing (School of Mines), Book-keeping, Commercial Arithmetic and a few other commercial subjects.
> I would also have a chance of being;
> -Prefect;
> -On College Committee;
> -In Athletics Team;
> -Captain, Gymnasium;
> -Capt or Vice Capt, Football;

-In Cricket team (Wicket Keeper);
-Obtain Gold Medal (Football);
-Obtain Gold Medal (gymnasium)."

Ralph's father, Lucas, refused to allow Ralph a final luxurious year playing sport for PAC. He brought Ralph home to start work in the Stock and Station Agency business which the family operated in Naracoorte.

Ralph's family was deeply religious. Wesleyan Methodists, they regularly attended Church, and as a family always 3 times on a Sunday. Daily prayers were a ritual. Lucas was a strict disciplinarian. Sometime after 1911, and before 1915, Lucas DeGaris moved to Adelaide, to live firstly at College Park, and later at Gurney Road, Dulwich. Lucas and his wife Anna had Lucas' father, Elisha, living with them. Elisha turned 90 in 1915, and from all accounts he was a bit of a handful for Anna. Elisha died in 1917 while Ralph was away in Europe.

After leaving school in 1911, Ralph joined his older brothers back in the business in Naracoorte. Lucas, who bore his father's Christian name, was the eldest son, followed by Clem, Leo and Ralph (who was the baby of the family). Ralph's sisters were Selena (Auntie Sean, who married Dr Renfrey Gershom Burnard), Amelia (Aunty Mill Fisher, who married Percy Fisher), Beryl (Auntie Beryl, who married Roy Kidman), and Hilda (Auntie Hilda, who married Mr Davey of NSW.) Ralph was the youngest of 8 children, although Anna delivered 10 children. There were twins, younger than Ralph, but who both died soon after birth.

Returning to Naracoorte in 1912, Ralph immersed himself in learning the family business. He also pursued his sporting interests, particularly football and cricket, and was an active member of the Methodist church.

After Federation in 1901, the Defence Act imposed an obligation on all citizens to train and serve in the Citizens Military Force. In South Australia, the universal training scheme of 1911 involved raising the 74th Battalion which stretched from Boothby, (Unley) to the Victorian border, and encompassed Naracoorte and Mount Gambier. Ralph, who had been a member of the P.A.C. Cadet Corp from 1908, joined the Citizens Military Force, and was commissioned as a 2nd Lieutenant in the 24th Light Horse Brigade.

When World War 1 broke out in 1914, little local interest was actually paid to the conflict erupting in Europe. Not many understoodthe reason for the outbreak in hostilities. Most commentators thought the war would be over in a short space of time. Nevertheless, after Britain declared war on Germany in August 1914, the rest of the British Empire and her Dominions, including Australia, were at war. In Australia, volunteers were called for the newly formed Australian Imperial Force. The AIF was to serve overseas in aid of the Mother Country. The entire AIF was and army of volunteers, because service was to take place outside the Commonwealth of Australia, and the permanent Army could not serve outside the Commonwealth. Later in the War, the Government tried to push through two referenda for conscription in 1916 and again in 1917 to allow the Government to force compulsory service. Conscription was defeated at both referenda, the first narrowly, and the second by an overwhelming majority. The AIF Forces remained voluntary. Because of the voluntary nature of the force, the Australians developed a unique character which is hard to define. Perhaps popular author Bryce Courtenay summed it up as succinctly as anyone when he wrote;

> "The Australian recruit, unlike some of his British counterparts, had offered his services voluntarily and he believed this entitled him to a

say in how he should be treated. He was hard put to see how poor rations, confinement to barracks, mindless drills and thirty mile route marches in new boots that chafed and pinched would help him kill Germans more effectively."

Courtenay continued;

"What hadn't been taken into account was that peacetime training in the militia hadn't gone in for much routine drill. Besides, discipline had never been seen as a priority for men playing war games in which they willingly collaborated. (Kyle, R, Pp 128-129)"

Additionally, the first Australian volunteers were the best physical specimens of Australian manhood. They were literally the flower of Australian youth. Five feet six inches was the required minimum height for volunteers, (which was 6 inches taller than the required height for the British serviceman), a minimum chest measurement of 34 inches, and age limits of 18 to 35 years (Butler, A.G., Vol I, P. 20.)

The ANZAC character of the first AIF members has been a formative component of our national psyche. Much has been written about ANZAC mateship, which is the essence of our Aussie character. Searching for the meaning of the "ANZAC spirit," which was essential to the formation of our true national identity, really drew me to reading and re-reading Ralph's diary. He was there on Gallipoli when the legend of Anzac was being indelibly etched on our national character. Through his brief records, Ralph truly articulates that mysterious and incredible experience which encapsulates the ANZAC spirit.

Most of the AIF volunteers did not the reasons for the war. They hated "The Hun," mainly because of the publicity campaign against Germany, but for no other rational reason. The outbreak of war was poorly reported, especially in local newspapers. There was a small single column on the front page of the "Naracoorte Herald," for example, but after the outbreak of hostilities there was precious little editorial space in Ralph's local paper. (Shane E Smith, in his unpublished book, "The Fighting Cavemen," publishes this relatively short editorial. Shane researched all of the Naracoorte Herald newspapers for the era 1914-1918, and confirmed that there was virtually no reporting of the war, nor was there much reporting of the efforts of the 370+ Naracoorte men who enlisted.) The volunteers left their homeland, attacked and defended other homelands, and had only their mates as their source of solace, strength and inspiration. The ANZAC's mateship, their sense of camaraderie, friendship, respect for sound sensible leadership, contempt for unnecessary and pretentious authority, officiousness and pomposity, and above all, a real love of team spirit really defines their corporate character. While we claim this character is still alive in our community, there has been an inevitable and subtle shift away from the spirit of solidarity, called mateship, which defined ANZAC. We are more self-centred now. I venture to suggest our young men of 18 to 24 years would not be as selfless as our AIF men to volunteer to defend "King and Old Blighty" simply because we were asked to do so.

I am proud to say my grandfather played a part in creating the legendary ANZAC spirit. I want my children, my grandchildren, Ralph's other grandchildren and all his descendants to know about his part in creating and preserving the ANZAC tradition.

In March 1915, Ralph enlisted in the new AIF, and entered the Mitcham Camp in SA to start his initial training. He was not yet 20 years of age. He enlisted with two of his closest cobbers, his cousin Eric Kidman and good friend, Alec Blackwell. His other close friend, Harry Schinckel, and Ralph's brother Leo, were at first rejected for service on medical grounds. Harry later joined his mates in France. Leo also served, mainly in Egypt, later in the war. In addition, Ralph's brother in law, Dr Renfrey Burnard, later enlisted and served as a medical officer in France and Belgium, particularly in field hospitals.

As it was Army policy that commissioned officers could not serve overseas until they were at least 21 years of age, Ralph decided to resign his commission in the Citizens Military Force, so he could enlist and go away overseas with his mates.

The boys were assigned to B Section of the 7th Field Ambulance Corps. They were to be stretcher bearers, and ambulancemen in the 7th Field Ambulance Corps. These raw recruits went on to serve with the 2nd AIF Division, 7th Field Ambulance in Egypt, Gallipoli, and later on the Western Front in Europe. All three men returned home after the war. Together for most of the war, they endured one of the bloodiest conflicts in history.

While rummaging through some old books and materials which had been kept by Ralph in an old green single filing cabinet, I found an old "pounds, shillings and pence" ledger book, and some very old, foolscap sized paper with tightly-written single-spaced typed pages.

The ledger book was a record of inventory of the Adelaide warehouse of DeGaris and Co. It did not seem to be very important, until I looked about half way through the book and found, on the reverse side of the ledger-book's pages what turned out to be some 80 pages of handwritten notes. As I read the notes, I realized I was reading a hand-written reconstruction of Ralph's memories of his World War 1 experiences. The notes were based on the letters he sent home to his parents. His mother had kept all his letters. Unfortunately, only three of those letters survive today. The typewritten record is a different record. It is a transcription of the daily diary which Ralph kept. The original diary has been lost. But the transcribed diary is a gem. It is a succinct daily record. Bearing in mind that it was contrary to war regulations (therefore illegal) for soldiers to keep a diary, it is understandable that our soldier's diaries are not lengthy documents. So when you read the original transcriptions, you feel almost a frustration that Ralph has not given enriching detail of his experiences. While reading the two sets of Ralph's personal records, I set about reading some of the historical records so I could understand where Ralph was at various times, and what he and his mates were doing.

During this process, I became engrossed in the story which Ralph had recorded, and so I decided that his story needed to be preserved for the rest of our family, and hopefully for generations to come. I thought that the best way to do this was to merge the two sets of records, the diary record and the recollections based on the letters which he sent home.

Therefore, in Part 1 of this record I have transcribed Ralph's primary diary, in the manner in which Ralph kept that diary, that is, on a daily basis. To this, I have added comments and quotes which Ralph recorded from letters he sent home, and which letters form the basis of the hand-written record in the ledger book. I have tried to be faithful to Ralph's records, and used his language and his descriptions. I have occasionally amended the grammar to make the record a little more reader-friendly.

Research:
In the course of compiling this record, I researched numerous historical facts, records, and personal service files to corroborate

Ralph's records, and in certain circumstances, to augment his record. I have done this because, as I have said previously, due to forbidding War Regulations, and Army directives, the diary records Ralph kept are brief. He makes references to people, and to places which are fleeting, and often disguise the full story. For example, Ralph does not tell us precisely where he was camped in his dug-outs at Gallipoli.

By looking at his diary, the official battalion records, and the official war history records, I was able accurately to place Ralph, and the 7th Field Ambulance at Chailak Dere, a small river running from the Chunuk Bair hill to the sea and north of Anzac Cove. In the month prior to Ralph arriving in Gallipoli in September 1915, Chunuk Bair had been the scene of a courageous New Zealand advance on Turkish positions, and an equally courageous counter-attack led by the legendary Turkish commander, Mustafa Kemal (later Ataturk, the remarkable and beloved first Turkish President) to reclaim the hill.

For details of battles, and the course of the war, I have relied heavily on the works of that genius historian, and major author of the official record of the Australian involvement in World War 1, Captain CEW Bean. His 6 Volume contribution to the 12 volume work on the history of the AIF in World War 1 is universally acknowledged, and I marvel constantly at his remarkable record every time I access it for information. Bean was present at Gallipoli, as an official war correspondent, and on the Western Front after Gallipoli. After the War he revisited all the battlefield sites of Europe and Gallipoli gathering material for his monumental work. He also collected enormous amounts of war memorabilia, including airplanes, tanks, motor vehicles, guns, ammunition, shells and shell casings, from all battlefields of Europe and Turkey, and returned these historical items to

Australia. His collection formed the nucleus of the Australian War Memorial World War 1 collections. I have used Bean's works to give precise dates, times, places, troop movements and battle descriptions. Interestingly, Ralph met Bean while serving in Europe. Bean's brother was an officer (Major) in the Australian Army Medical Corp.

I have also found the works of Colonel A.G. Butler extremely helpful. Butler was the official historian of the Army Medical Service 1914-18. As the 7th Field Ambulance was attached to the Australian Army Medical Corps, and their officers were mainly doctors and surgeons, Butler's two volumes covering Gallipoli and the Western Front have been an invaluable resource.

There are two other works which I have found particularly helpful. Patsy Adam-Smith's work, "The Anzacs," is wonderful. The author spoke with many old diggers, and read some 8,000 personal diaries and letters before writing her book. I think it is much under-rated. Dr Peter Pedersen's work, titled "The Anzacs—Gallipoli to the Western Front" is both a precise chronology of events and a wonderful pictorial record.

The Australian War Memorial and the National Archives have also been valuable sources to locate historical service information about diggers to whom Ralph refers in a casual way throughout his diary. I have been able to research most people to whom Ralph refers, and when I eventually discover who they are, I try and provide a pen picture of those individual's service history. It must have been disheartening and devastating for Ralph to lose so many close friends and acquaintances during the war years.

I have also checked the relevant daily Battalion diaries which are available at the Australian War Memorial. Each Battalion kept a daily diary. They have been valuable tools to verify Ralph's daily record. I hope the references and records I have noted are helpful, and assist in placing Ralph's personal history properly in the overall context of what was actually happening in Egypt, Gallipoli and Europe. Sometimes that context, understandably, is not entirely clear from Ralph's diaries.

References:
I have included a bibliography at the end of the book. The references throughout the work are included, and historical notes, basically using the Harvard reference system. For example, where I refer to a work, it is referred to firstly by author, and if there are two authored works in the bibliography, the different works are referred to either Volume and/or year of publication. That can be accessed from the bibliography. Therefore where I refer to Bean CEW. *"The Official History of Australia in the War of 1914-18, Volume I 'The Story of Anzac,'"(1921) P 208,* it is recorded in the references as *Bean, (1921) Vol. I., P 208*. Patsy Adam-Smith, who has only one work in the Bibliography, will be referred to in the footnotes as *Adam-Smith,(1978) Pp 75-77*. References are bracketed at the time of reference. Footnotes do not readily transfer into digital formats.

The Title:
The book's title, "The Innocent Crusaders," was chosen because during the writing of this book, it struck me as ironic the similarity between the missions of the original religious crusaders, and the mission our young men embarked upon early last century. Both groups willingly volunteered for a military journey thousands of kilometres from home; they were motivated by national leaders calling on their people to defend foreign states from expansionist occupiers; they embarked in an atmosphere of innocence as to the real conditions they would meet on foreign soil; they initially did

not believe they would see any military action; they were progressively disillusioned by the course of the campaigns in which they fought; they spent their formative years slogging in awful conditions, watching their mates being killed and seriously injured.

I have confined this analysis to the troops. The original crusaders, including those led by Peter the Hermit, were seduced by their leaders about the righteousness of their cause. The leaders were generally zealots, or power hungry nationalists. They led their men into awful battles, ostensibly to reclaim the Holy Land for Christianity. They were, however, invaders.

In the case of Ralph and his cobbers, they not only motivated by nationalistic desires, but like the original crusaders, they were all from intensely religious backgrounds.

With the Gallipoli campaign, they were led as invaders into a foreign land, and like the original crusaders at Antioch, met daunting terrain, and almost impregnable defensive conditions. They were certainly not as well led by their English command at Gallipoli, as the Crusaders at Antioch. After a series of bloody battles, the Crusaders eventually took the city. As we know, the latter day crusaders were unsuccessful.

The leadership of our latter day Innocent Crusaders, particularly the British leaders, cared little for the men in the trenches. They, like the Crusader leaders, treated the foot soldier as expendable cannon fodder.

Mercifully, the Australian leaders, particularly Monash and White, and the Canadian leader, Currie, changed the way leaders regarded and respected their men. This only really translated onto the battlefield later in the War.

Ralph and his cobbers were in my opinion, when they left our shores, full of nationalistic zeal, inspired to fight the Hun to protect our way of life, without having any idea of the time this would take, or the shocking conditions and mass murder they would witness in the course of defending the Empire. They voluntarily enrolled in the AIF through a sense of duty. They trusted their leaders that they were required. They were indeed, at the outset, Innocent Crusaders.

Acknowledgements:

I have been helped by some very gracious people in putting this book together. First and foremost, my wife and soul-mate, Lyn has been extraordinarily patient with me. Often when I have climbed into bed in the small wee hours she has lovingly inquired of me, "And where is Grandpa tonight?" I shared all of the terrible stories, and Lyn listened to me as I enthusiastically recounted each new discovery, and each new revelation based on my interpretation of the source materials.

She also forced me back to twenty first century reality day after day. Lyn has read and re-read the transcript and made lots of helpful suggestions about the presentation of the book.

I wish to thank Alec Blackwell's daughter, Margaret Wood, who generously gave her time to talk to me about her Dad, and provided me with photos of Alec, Ralph and the 7th Field Ambulance group. Shane Smith of Naracoorte, who is publishing a work, "Fighting Cavemen" detailing the history of the AIF volunteers from that town, provided me with photos, and other records, including a diary of Ralph's mate Harry Schinckel. The Kidman family, particularly Tania Shaw, Eric Kidman's granddaughter, have also provided me with information. South East author and raconteur, Lois Dean kindly gave me access to photographs and stories about her father, Hubert Meathrel, who served in the 7th Field Ambulance with Ralph. Norman J.

Cleveland, whose uncle served in the 11th Field Ambulance, and won a Military Medal at Ploegsteert Wood on June 16, 1917, was generous with his library of World War 1 literature. Emma Bamford from my office has helped type large portions of the diary, and became absorbed in the story. A renewed acquaintance with my old friend, author and publisher Steve Lewis, has been entirely to my advantage. Steve is generous with his wisdom and advice, and his laconic and laid back manner belies his deep passion for recording our history.

My other office staff, Amanda Pascoe, Wendy Ielasi and Kris Allen have put up with me talking about this project, and helped me immensely. Of course my own family, my mother Norma, brother Richard and sisters Ruth Craig and Louise DeGaris-Boot have generously given their help when I have asked for it, as have extended family including Bob DeGaris and Peter DeGaris. Also I thank those people who read this first draft and provided me with so many valuable suggestions, including Robin Watts, Graeme Gilbertson and Steven Lewis

Finally, I hope that you derive as much pleasure from this little work as I did in writing it. For those of us who knew Ralph, they knew a true gentleman who was a committed Christian, and who rarely said a bad word about anybody. The profound inhumanity which man heaped upon his fellow man and which he witnessed from 1915 to 1918 must have affected him immensely. I have only just begun to really appreciate the gruesome horrors he lived with. But to be subjected to those horrors for such an extended period of time is unfathomable for me. Yet he returned to his community with an unshakably strong set of Christian values, and a strong belief in his country. He was not a drinker, nor a smoker, but I would not call him a wowser either. He was very much a believer in "live and let live." I believe that the ANZAC ethic of mateship and being there for your cobbers defined the way he lived his life.

Having witnessed the carnage and pointless disposal of human life of World War 1, Ralph then endured World War 2, with his two precious sons involved in active service in the RAAF. One, William Sowden DeGaris, (1924-1945) after whom I was named, was killed at barely 21 years of age, "missing in action," flying a Lancaster bomber over Germany, in March of 1945, only 3 months before the cessation of hostilities. The other son, my father, Renfrey Curgenven DeGaris, (1921-2007) returned from active service in the Pacific region with Tuberculosis, and Malaria, and was hospitalized in the infectious diseases ward of Daw's Road military hospital for 2 years.

Ralph, like so many Australians who served, was no war hero, but immediately, and without thought, leapt to serve his country in its perceived hour of need, and subsequently served his country well. For his service he was awarded a Meritorious Service Medal, and he always maintained he was Mentioned in Dispatches, but in fact he was recommended for the Military Medal, which recommendation was not confirmed.

He also endured the pain of seeing his own children enthusiastically jump to defend their nation in the 1939-45 War. In some ways Ralph had a right, perhaps, to express a profound hatred of war. He did not. Nor did he glorify war. It was to him a necessary evil, and the price you occasionally had to pay, as a nation, and a people, for democracy and freedom.

This is the First World War diary record of Sgt. Ralph Edwin DeGaris, of the 7th Field Ambulance, 2nd Division, 1st A.I.F., 1915 to 1918. It's preservation is dedicated to my sisters Ruth and Louise, my brother Richard, my children Shannon, Renee and

Lucas, my nieces and nephews, Sam, Jessica, Sarah, Kate, Anna, Lucy, Matthew and Alex, my grandchildren Griffin, Archer, Finley, Clementine and Savannah, and all Ralph's descendants.

Note on the Primary Diary Source materials:
Presentation:

The two primary sources for this book are **The Diary** which Ralph transcribed from his original war diary. The second primary sources are **Ralph's handwritten notes.** They are referred to as **"Ralph's notes,"** throughout this book.

I have presented **The Diary**, being the typewritten transcribed diary in normal print, basically on a day to day basis, as Ralph recorded his diary. The two primary sources are pictured in the next page after this preface.

All quotes and references to Ralph's notes are referred to as ***Ralph's notes,*** which are *italicized,* to separate those notes from the diary text. I have tried to align the handwritten recollections chronologically, to the diary, and thus I have tried to keep a seamless chronological account using Ralph's two sets of source materials.

To make this text easier to read, I have eliminated footnoting so I have included all historical references, and my personal notes which I think will help the reader, in the text, with the heading ***Historical notes,*** which are also italicisied, chronologically presented, and referenced. The researched references rather than using footnotes have been italicized and noted *"(Ed.)"* indicating they are my notes.

The two primary source materials used to reconstruct this diary record are Ralph's *transcribed diary* and Ralph's *hand-written notes* recorded in an old ledger book. The transcribed diary was typed up by Ralph from his old diary records. The old original diary has been lost. Ralph would have typed the transcription himself, on an Underwood typewriter. He always had a typewriter at home. There are five carbon copies of the transcribed diary. The original typed manuscript, is in reasonable condition. Even though the original is damaged, the carbon copies enabled an accurate reconstruction of the typed diary. This diary forms the major background of this book. It is referred to as **"Diary"** in the book.

The ledger-book is an old warehouse inventory ledger-book. Ralph has used the book to record handwritten notes of his memoirs, based primarily on the letters he sent home.

There are only 3 letters from France from Ralph which survive. They are dated May 18th, 1916, 6th December 1916 and 8th December 1917. All of the early letters are referred to in the body of the text of the book. The ledger-book contains columns of "pounds, shillings and pence" entries. It has inscribed in it, "King William Street Stock at 30-6-1925." I would say the first part of the diary was written by Ralph between 1925 and 1938. When quoting Ralph's memoirs from the ledger-book in the main text of this book, I use text boxes titled **"Ralph's notes."** The ledger book also contains other handwritten notes, including notes Ralph made of his recollections of the Second War. There are also some notes written by Renfrey DeGaris AM, of his early war years, 1942, and some later notes he wrote about electoral systems in about 1990 after he had retired from politics. This old ledger book has been a mine of historical information.

Illustrations:

All photos and illustrations in this book are of low quality. As most of the originals are now almost 100 years old, and taken with very basic "box brownie" type cameras, I hope you will forgive me in publishing with low quality images.

Finally, this second edition has been edited more thoroughly. Thanks to Kris Allen for her painstaking efforts to read and re-read the text, and for all her suggestions

Bill DeGaris
Mount Gambier, 2015.

Chapter One:
Leaving Australia:
April and May 1915:

Ralph's notes:

"Eric, Alec and I enlisted for service with the Australian Forces on 23.4.1915 and sailed overseas per "SS Geelong," leaving the Outer Harbour on May 31st 1915.

I had celebrated my 20th birthday just one month prior to sailing. I was a lad always full of spirit, but we had been brought up in a Christian home. My parents were of the true Puritanical stock, and our whole family had lived in a cloistered atmosphere. Every morning our family would gather for family Prayer. Church 3 times every Sunday was the regular order. It was from this atmosphere of prayer and love that we went overseas to learn, in a very short time, of another mankind. It was a mankind not previously known to us."

"From one extreme element in common with hundreds of thousands of Australian we were thrown headlong into another. One is sometimes apt to question why so many men "went under" to vice of the world, and since returning to Australia have not made good, but the marvel really is that more did not "go under," and that so many who have returned to civil life have made good.

What is to follow in this record is not my impressions now, but is the record taken from my letters which were preserved by my loving home folk. It will be found that there will be little if any reference to the war and the activities in this regard. Some letters are naturally missing and others have been severely dealt with by the censor and in addition as a general rule, the soldier did not write on war experiences, rather he would deliberately avoid any reference to any matter that would add to the anxiety of his loved ones at home.

The first letters are those written from Mitcham camp. As will be seen by the date of enlistment, and date of embarkation, the story in the Mitcham camp was only a short one, but appears by the tone of the letters to have been fairly enjoyable. We were placed in the camp with the B Section of the 7th Field Ambulance amongst a wonderfully fine lot of chaps. Friendships were made in those early camp days which have never been broken. Some were terminated later by the untimely death of some very fine characters.

At time of enlistment, as I was a Lieutenant in the Citizen Forces, but being under 21 I could not then leave Australia with my commission. There were orders that no commissioned officers under 21 years of age were to leave Australia. To get away with my friends was my chief desire and I was also prompted by the belief that the war would be over before I reached the age of 21 years!"

"I therefore decided to resign my commission, and take rank as a private, which I did, so I could go overseas with my mates.

While we were in the Mitcham camp, the first casualty lists were published and the comment on these was, "The casualties are pretty great. But instead of making us less eager, our eagerness is increased. Since the news of the Australians in action has been received the recruiting has risen considerably. Yesterday over 100 recruits presented themselves."

Mitcham letters give very little for me to write about. We were all well inoculated and vaccinated while at Mitcham and had our numbers allotted to us about a fortnight before we sailed.

Leo was first rejected as medically unfit for service before we left Mitcham, and Harry Schinckel also seem to have offered at that time and been rejected. Later in the war, both Leo and Harry were accepted into the Army.

Just before we sailed we had to allot our money. In one letter I advise having made 2/- per day payable to Father. 2/- per day would be defence pay, which would leave 2/- to be drawn in the field."

The Diary:
31/5/1915
We left Outer Harbour, on Monday 31st May, 1915, Father, Hilda, Milly, Luke, and Leo all came down to see us off. Mr. Blackwell came down to see Alec off. Roy Kidman was there also to see us off. A great crowd was down at the Outer Harbour. It was a very inspiring sight.
We put out to sea at about 8.30 pm. I tipped a fellow from the engine room who gratefully accepted, and showed us all over the engine room in the ship. It was very interesting.

Historical note:
Four of Ralph's brothers and sisters came to Adelaide see him off. The others who were not there were Sean, (Mrs Ren Burnard, wife of Dr Renfrey Burnard, who later joined the AIF as a doctor, and was a Captain in the Army Medical Corps; Ren had a part to play later in the romances of Ralph, Harry Schinckel and Eric Kidman), Clem, Beryl (to become Mrs Sydney Kidman). Milly was Mrs Percy Fisher, known to us as Aunty Mill, and Hilda (later Hilda Davey), who moved to Sydney with her husband to raise her family.
Roy Kidman, later Lieutenant Roy Kidman also joined the AIF and served in the Middle East with the 3rd Light Horse Regiment. He won the MC (Military Cross) for gallantry in Es Salt, in April 1918.(Ed.)

Ralph's notes:
"The letters written at sea were most uninteresting, and all much of a muchness. However, it is fair to say that I was chronically seasick for

most of the journey, which lasted from June 1st to June 6th, 1915. Looking back, I would say the food we received on board "HMAT Geelong" was the worst food we had during the whole war."

1/6/1915 to 6/6/1915.

Sea sickness; took little interest in anything. All fellows excited, just arriving at Fremantle. All in hopes of getting ashore and having a walk etc.

("etc" is underlined in the original diary. I guess it was "code" for the fact they were interested in female company whilst ashore!(Ed))

We arrived in Fremantle, and anchored in mid-stream, in the estuary near Fremantle dock. After such a voyage, the troops were anxious to get ashore. All the chaps are talking (only talking) about swimming ashore. There was a splendid reception on shore for the ship. There are fine looking girls, and plenty of chaps in uniform. There were two German boats anchored in the stream.

Historical note:
These were possibly merchant boats in Fremantle, but would have certainly been impounded.(Ed.)

We also saw two of the ships escorts for the first time today.
7/6/15
We are still anchored in the stream. Fellows were slipping down ropes onto boats and going ashore. Two coaling boats were alongside all last night, and fellows were hidden all over the place on them, and although these were searched by officers, scores of chaps got ashore on the coaling vessels.
We eventually pulled ashore to the wharf at about 10 am, and had a great time, but could not get off the boat. Leave was denied.
I had a long conversation with a nice young lady, Kath Samson, who lived at Ellen St, Fremantle. I found that she was related to the Oakes

in Naracoorte, and she also thought she was related to Mrs Goldsworthy. She gave me a memento from Perth, a K.P. badge.

I also had my cap knocked overboard, but recovered it uneventfully.

One chap from the infantry was pushed overboard when we were about 2 chain *(40 metres)* from the dock. He had his full uniform on, and he swam bravely towards the wharf. He began to tire, but was picked up by a motor launch before he got into any real trouble, and he was pulled upon board again.

Ralph's notes:
"The censor was extremely active with our letters, even those sent from the "HMAT Geelong." It seemed as though the officers were over zealous in their work as censors of the Digger's letters. They learned later that the little information allowed through would not after all lose the war, at the same time there was always that doubt present in writing that we may get captured and some information of importance drop into the hands of the enemy. It is quite evident that at least one letter forwarded was destroyed entirely by the censor. It referred to practically the only excitement on the trip over. Quite naturally all the troops were expecting to get ashore at Fremantle, but the authorities would not allow it."

7/6/15 (cont'd)
At about 7.00 pm, the troops "overcame" the officers, and got onto the top deck. They then lowered 2 boats, and those in those boats rowed ashore. About 100 men got ashore through these two boats. The troops rose in a mutiny calling for the officers and especially the colonel. The troops respected the colonel, but did not respect his officers, one in particular.

The Colonel did come up and address the men, and this quietened them for a time; but soon the mob cooked themselves up into a frenzy and threatened absolute mutiny.

John Blackett was the officer against whom the troops showed most spleen, and I can now see John standing in one of the small boats, half lowered with his revolver drawn and the howling mob of men pressing in on the ropes to lower him to the sea. For a considerable time it looked as if anything might happen. I am surprised the mob did not just throw him overboard and into the sea, they were so frenzied.

(Captain John Blackett was hated by the troops on board the transport ship. He was killed in action in France in 1916, and Ralph says in later diaries that Capt. John Blackett was a great field officer, a superb leader of men who always thought of his troops first, and who died highly regarded by his men in the field under his command. (Ed.))

Other officers were seen very little of during this riot. Many of the troops got ashore, some returned before we sailed, but after getting out to sea we found a number were still ashore. The Colonel himself came down again later and tried again to pacify the men and succeeded for a time, but they soon rose again and all hands were up until very late.

Ralph's notes:
"The irreverence of some of the Australian troops to authority is something which later characterizes the ANZAC spirit in the field of battle. They certainly showed their contempt for authority here in Fremantle, even before we have left our own shores.
The situation remained tense the whole night."

8/6/15

The troops were still discontented at not getting leave. The ship pulled a little way upstream at about 10 am, but stopped about a mile away from the dock. We believed that the ruse was to frighten the men who got ashore, and have not yet returned. They say there are about 160 men missing, but I should not think there is that number missing. The New Zealand troops on the *"HMAT Moldavia"* anchored close handy.

We got going in earnest again at about 10.30 am. We have seen nothing of the escort ships all day. It is said that we are going across unescorted as far as Port Said. I cannot believe this. At roll call today, we found about 60 men were missing, all of them from our unit. These men joined their units later, but all were punished with a severe docking of pay, which may, or may not, have been made up again later.

Mitcham Army Barracks: Parade Ground, 1915. (AWM)

Mitcham Army Barracks in 1915.
Designed by Colonel Hill, the open-front barracks were regarded as the very essence of modern army living. (AWM photo)

April 1915.
(Left): The 3 Naracoorte mates who enlisted together, on same day, at the same time, and were assigned consecutive enlistment numbers. L to R: No 3708 Pte. Alec Blackwell, No 3706 Pte. Eric Kidman, No 3707 Pte. Ralph DeGaris. (*Photo; Courtesy Tania Shaw.*)

Chapter Two:
Getting to Egypt:

The Diary:

9/6/15:

Apart from the problems with deserting troops at Fremantle, our disembarkment from Australia was uneventful. We steamed quietly out of Fremantle on June 8th, which was a miserable, rainy day. *"SS Geelong"* was accompanied by two other transport ships, *"SS Botanist"* and the New Zealand troop carrier, *"Moldavia."*

Surprisingly, I was not seasick early on, but plenty of the others were, especially the WA troops we had taken on board.

10-11/6/15:

The ship cruised westward, and on the second day out, we hit a wild storm. The ship rolled like a tin can in a pond. Plates rolled all over the place. With the extraordinary rolling, Eric and I felt sea sick again.

12/6/15:

Church services were held on the way over. The only Padre on board was a Roman Catholic priest, and it annoyed me to be preached at by an RC Priest. The fellows are given no option regarding attending or otherwise. However, the sermon was good on the text, "Without Faith there is no Hope."

A private in our unit conducted a service in the evening, which was also good.

Ralph's notes:
"His name is Dick Campbell. Through his religion he to our knowledge later joined the YMCA and his war career is not known to us. The last we heard of him in the war was after Gallipoli, when he was working in a YMCA hut in Cairo. After the war, he returned to Adelaide and married Molly Craven. Personally I have not seen him

since the war, but he is now a "head man" in Cravens. He will always invite you to have a drink and from what I have been told is apt to think that he would not like to be reminded of the Church services on the "SS Geelong.""

14-16/6/15:

We start to drill on deck, just to keep fit. We drill section by section, and it is really a bit impossible. We also have lectures.

Ralph's notes:

"The letters written at sea made reference to "Lectures." We attended lectures on the way over. The casualty lists on Gallipoli were heavy, but it was evident that venereal disease was seriously adding to the number of Australian (and other troops) unable to join the fighting forces. As a result of these "lectures," our innocence was converted into an almost unbelievable knowledge. Lecture after lecture all dealing with the question of sex. The sordid and filthy condition of Cairo were explained in detail to us. We were inclined to disbelieve what we were told and considered that the conditions were exaggerated, but later we learned that exaggeration would be impossible, so low and filthy and debasing were the lower quarters of Cairo and also other towns in Egypt which we subsequently visited.

A comment passed in our tent at Heliopolis camp the second night we were in Egypt has always remained in my memory. Some one said, "It is the oldest profession in the world, and it is surely showing signs of old age!""

17/6/15:

I was on piquet duty, and did my rosters as they came due. I was a shockingly poor traveller, and the variety of conditions on board did not help me. One night, Eric and I decided to sleep on deck. We wrapped ourselves in a sheet of canvas over the isolation block. It rained heavily during the night, and we both woke up soaking wet.

18/6/15:

It was not all a grind on the way over. We saw lots of flying fish, of all sorts of colours and hues. There were also pods of dolphins, and I remember one large pod of about a thousand animals. It was spectacular. They all seemed to appear above the water at the same time. They did this for hours on end, and only disappeared at night time. This was a first for us country boys, and we enjoyed the sight very much.

19-23/6/15:

Weather varied from hot and calm to heavy tropical rains. We also had high tropical winds and heavy seas, which I found most to my disliking. When we passed over the equator, we were not told, as the crew feared practical jokes from the troops. There was a concert on board tonight, but I was too crook to listen.

We were 19 days without sighting land. I suffered Mal-de-mer, or seasickness whenever the weather was inclement. My state of health was a good barometer to the state of the weather.

23/6/15:

We had a number of measles cases on the way over. At one time we had over 40 cases of measles in the infirmary on board.

The last few days before we sighted land were the roughest of the trip, the wind and the waves being high and stormy.

24/6/15:

We could not attend the concert last night, and tonight, poor old Bill Graves was going to take us out to the canteen for his 25th birthday, but he was so seasick the night out was cancelled.

27/6/15:

Today we experienced the hottest day of the trip. We passed a lot of ships, including 2 cruisers, one of which was French. The French cruiser passed within about half a mile of us. It was dusk, so we did not get a good view of her.

28/6/15:

There was heavy fog today, and the horn is being sounded every few minutes. Apparently the bridge got a message that there was a ship which had run aground inshore of us. We sighted her at about 9-30 am. Unfortunately, the fog prevented us from getting near to her. We all wanted to be involved in her rescue! Another ship, "Sutherland" came to her rescue.

1/7/15:

We have had 3 beautiful days in a row. Today there are five transports traveling close to us. I large ship passed the other way, and it was said she was a German boat which was captured early in the war.

2/7/15:

The scenery was changing now. Land was plainly in sight, and we passed a fine lighthouse on the Egyptian side. The land is mountainous, but it appears as though a big beach runs back to the foot of the hills. In parts the impression is that big sand-drifts run back to the Hills from the beach. The hills appear to be of rock and sand formation. The colours on the hills are superb, although the appearance was very dreary, not like our Australian hills.

We reach Suez at a 1.30pm Saturday, but have anchored out about a mile. There are two French cruisers and one British cruiser handy.

3/7/15:

We are still at Suez, and it is very hot. We will not be allowed to leave the ship until Monday. There are 42 down with measles now.

The natives approach the ship in small dhow rigged boats. They are trying to sell us cigarettes and fruit. When the guards level rifles at them, and warn them away, they are able to have the dhow turned and running with the winds as quickly as can be, waving their hands above their heads and yelling, "No, No, No!!"

We got the papers this morning. The general position of the war seems not to have changed much. Except that it seems likely we will be involved in some fighting before Peace is declared. When we left Fremantle, we did not think it likely any of us would see action.

4/7/15:

This morning we saw two sea planes, Tiger moths with floats. They flew around the ships as if they were inspecting the troops. Also a small boat came quite handy to our ship, and we saw the first white ladies we have seen since Fremantle!

5/7/15:

We disembarked *"SS Geelong"* today. This was the most interesting day we have spent yet. We disembarked at 12 noon, and it took three trains to convey the troops from our ship to Cairo. We were more fortunate being in the first train. The train went right through the main street of Suez. The town is just as we expected, very ancient looking, all houses flat roofed and gypo women walking around with pitchers on their heads, just like of old. The most striking building was the mosque.

(The Masjid Hamza Mosque, named after the Uncle of Mohammed, the Prophet of Islam)(Ed.)

This is outstanding, with its 4 minarets, and beautifully built dome in the centre. The markets in which they sell their good are interesting. When they approached the ship to sell goods to us we quickly learnt they knew something about the art of selling without delivering!!

Ralph's notes:
"At this time, in one of my letters to Grandpa, I wrote, "When the war is over, I will do my best to visit Guernsey, your old home." Little did I know then that before the end of the war I would have spent two leaves in Guernsey."

After leaving Suez, we were stuck alongside the canal for about an hour and a half. There was little irrigation here, and the appearance generally was of a sandy desert. After leaving the canal, we came into a very extensively irrigated land. The growth was magnificent and wonderful to behold. It was amazing to witness the transformation from desert to lush agricultural land. It was hard to credit the desert could provide such fertility for plants such as dates and banana palms, which were seen practically all along the line. These were not as attractive as the green growth near the ground. Mostly I was told it was cotton plant. Some appeared like sorghum, or maize. At all the places at which we stopped the natives came out to the train with water and sweet melons, and when they did come there was a terrible rush. They were cunning commercial operators, and took us down as quickly as we let them.

The most interesting place we passed by was Zag-a-zig, although we really only saw the station there, it was modern and seemed to have up to date facilities.

The irrigation was fantastic, but the methods of pumping water, and the methods of crushing corn were the same as biblical times. It was all done with oxen as the main force for the irrigation pumps, and the grinding mills.

We reached Cairo at about 5.30 pm and still had a 2 mile march to our camp which was
in Heliopolis, an outer suburb of Cairo.

We went into Heliopolis for the first time. The natives are peculiar. They approach you when you sit down for a feed, or for a drink, and embark on conjuring tricks, and tumbling, which is fine, but then they come and ask for a piaster *(100 piastres in an Egyptian dollar. (Ed.))*, as a reward. That is most odd.

Chapter Three:
Heliopolis Camp, Cairo, Alexandria, and initial training:

The Diary:

6/7/15:

Heliopolis, Egypt. The Heliopolis camp is situated just on the eastern outskirts of the city of Heliopolis, and on the other side there is nothing but miles of sand. It is about 6 miles east of Cairo.

A group of us went up to Cairo proper tonight, and we were stunned by the filthy conditions of the place. *(There were tramways running from Heliopolis into Cairo, which was about 6 miles east of Cairo proper. (Ed))*

The city was abominable. The weather was not as bad as we expected. We thought it would be blindingly hot, and unbearable.

Historical notes:
The town was established by the Heliopolis Oasis Company, headed by the Belgian industrialist Baron Empain (Edouard Louis Joseph) beginning in 1905. The Baron, a well known amateur Egyptologist, and prominent European entrepreneur, arrived in Egypt in January 1904, intending to rescue one of his Belgian company's projects in Egypt; the construction of a railway line linking Matariya to Port Said. Despite losing the railway contract to the British, Baron Empain stayed on in Egypt; a decision due to his love of the desert or, more likely, his relationship with Yvette Boghdadli. In ten years, Heliopolis had grown into a respectable sized outer suburb of Cairo.
Australian and New Zealand troops were brought here to Egypt for training and organisation. Units were located in and around Cairo, from Mena, west of Giza, to Heliopolis in the eastern quarter. There was also three large and extensive field hospitals here run by the Australians. They coped with wounded from Gallipoli and later from Europe. (Ed.)

7/7/15:

We drilled for the first time in Egypt today. It was hot, but not as bad as I expected, even doing drills and marching with full packs.

8/7/1915:

We did our first bit of training today in Egypt. We train 6am to 9 am, 11am to 12 noon, then 4.30 pm to 7pm each day.

We saw Doug Ridgeway on the 8th July, while he was convalescing here in Heliopolis, and he told us the most gruesome stories of the war. He has been on the peninsula. He told us that Jim McTavish, Lin Lewis and Tom Northbridge were all killed, and we were mortified with the news. Subsequently we learnt that he was gilding the lily, and that while Jim and Lin were killed, Tom was fine, and doing well.

The buildings in Cairo, particularly the mosques, are beautiful and marvelously built. There is a real contrast between the magnificence of some of the old buildings in Cairo and the filthy debased parts in the poorer suburbs.

The Picture Gardens formed a great part of our early entertainment in Egypt. These are run in conjunction with the hotels in the open air. Pictures were continually screened and the reading was in French and English. No charge is made for entry to the Gardens, but you were of course expected to buy drinks. The seating accommodation was at small tables.

Ralph's notes:
"On days off we go into Cairo, and it is undoubtedly the filthiest and most immoral place you could imagine. We saw some of the most un-

thought of things imaginable. Doug Ridgeway, (then almost a hero in our eyes) said he would show us the sights of Cairo. They were sights, all right. There were things I saw that I never saw again, and never want to see again. A person's mind and heart is laid bare by what he desires to see, read and do. This young man took a great delight in showing us around the lower moral parts of the city, and doubtless did the same thing continuously until he left that city. I can't even now write what we saw that night. Someday I may, but they were so crude and disgusting that I doubt I will want to recall them.

A letter I wrote privately to Clem (Ralph's brother AC DeGaris) dated 13/7/15 deals with my impressions then and as this record is supposed to be my impressions at the time I will quote the letter without any alterations.

'*We have not been in this place long but have been here long enough to know that there can be no dirtier place on the face of God's earth than the lower parts of Cairo. Nothing is too bad for it and anything you may hear can be taken as true. Regarding temptation, there is no such thing in Cairo in this respect, for me anyhow, for if any one ever does go down the ill-reputed quarters and is tempted, well he is just as likely to be tempted in a pig sty. Some of the things that I have seen and heard I would be backwards in telling you, leave alone write about. The population here other than native is French, and that is just about as bad as the native population, and little more attractive. I never thought that anything in this world was as bad, and that any woman, black or white could reach down as low. When I heard all the things first I could not believe them, but I know now that all is true. I don't want you to think that these are the only places in Cairo to which a chap can go, as there are any amount of other good clean and pure entertainments such as pictures etc to be seen in the better quarters.*'"

9/7/15:

For the first time, I am feeling the heat. Mail arrived today, but nothing much for me. I was very disappointed.

Ralph's notes:

"The day when the Australian mail arrives is always the greatest day with our boys. I am sure we are no exception. Letters from home must be a grand thing in any Army, but we used to think it was more so in the Australian Army! I often think about CJ Dennis and "The Sentimental Bloke," and wonder if the Australians were more sentimental than the others, and think that love for home is sentiment. I think the Australian was the most sentimental soldier in the field.

We noticed that the natives have burial customs somewhat different from our own. This was witnessed early in our stay in Egypt. There were only two natives present at the burial. The corpse is carried in a big flat box. They dig a hole about 3 cubic feet and then they tunnel under just so as the corpse can be slipped into it and then they put the earth back over the corpse. The corpse is buried without the coffin. The box can then be used as a coffin many times.

On one route march we went through a newly cut road that probably had been a burial ground for thousands of years. It was a mass of skeletons and bones.

About this time our uniform is changed to knickers and light shirt. This is a great relief, as the heat is sometimes just unbearable."

10/7/15:

I got off at 1 pm today. A group of us go up to Cairo for a look around. Doug Ridgeway takes us on a guided tour. We see things that are just unheard of, which I referred to above. It is a most immoral place.

11/7/15:

Colonel Kendrew took the first services in the church parade on July 11th, 1915. This was more of a welcoming nature. The Colonel looks absolutely exhausted. Afterwards, a group of us walked into Heliopolis for the evening. Shops are open 7 days a week.

12/7/15:

I had a couple of sick days 12th-13th July, and felt especially bad when it was so hot outside. I don't think it was anything but coincidence. We got the first mails on the 12th July.

Ralph's notes:
"The reports from home are great to get. The sales have been excellent, and it looks as though we will have a bumper season. My letter home in response is tinged by homesickness, or at least a deeper appreciation of home and all its love means to me. A full page of this letter is taken praising the family, my home life and all the kindnesses of all at home towards me.
The first letters I received from home remind me that Ren has joined the AIF Medical Corps, and was in training at Mitcham camp."

13/7/15:

Alec Roper came over to see me today. I was very surprised to see him and had a good chat over old times. He has been in Heliopolis camp ever since the first lot came over here.

Alec told us that he had all the bad luck in the world not to be on the Peninsula with the other boys. Later we met several others who said the same, but we learned that most of them courted the bad luck to keep them away from the fighting. I did not see him after Egypt, and do not know if he got back or not.

Ralph's notes:
"No-one says it, but I know they think that perhaps sometimes the braver man may be the one who showed cowardice. Looking back on the whole experience, I now recognise that sometimes when I was frightened and full of fear I was not game enough to admit it, so steeled myself and carried on."

14/7/15:

I was up and going again on Wednesday, and was bucked up by a cable from home, even thought I did not really understand the contents. It was worded:

> *"Cable welcome everything bright here. England will win. We write every week.*
> *Reply DeGaris RVS."*

15/7/15:

Alec Roper went into the hospital today, I think. I called up to have a look at him today and he does not look too good. I am concerned about him. I heard today that Frank White of Millicent was in hospital. We called in to see him. Apparently he is suffering from rheumatism. He has seen service, but not much. I promised my family to look up Jack Laurie. I have no recollection of having seen him here, and I did not see him or hear of him at all in Europe, or anywhere else over here. His war record was far from the best, but I do not know all the facts concerning it.

We went on a route march today, and found it pretty warm.

(Alex McLeod Roper was from Dergholm, near Casterton. He served in the 4th Light Horse Regiment. Frank White owned land on the Belt Road at Millicent, and lived on the property, which is now (2007) owned by Geoff Lowe and his family. Ralph DeGaris bought a paddock from Frank White, which we always called "Whites."(Ed.))

17/7/15:

On July 17th 1915, we shifted our camp to Polygon Camp, Abbassia. *(Polygon Camp was about 4 miles closer to Cairo than the Heliopolis Camp, which was situated about 2 miles east of Heliopolis. Polygon* was west of Heliopolis. (see, Butler, (1933) Vol 1, P 170.) It is more out of the way than the Heliopolis camp. And we have to work harder and longer hours. We are starting at 4.30am each day. We share guard duty at night, and I have done my share, even on Sunday evenings, which meant I missed Church parade.

Ralph's notes:
"I wrote home on this day advising that the 2/- per day pay would not be enough cash to have available. I write to ask that arrangements be made whereby I could draw money through a bank. I foresee the probability of being away from my unit, in which case it was extremely difficult to draw any pay at all.
I had spoken with several chaps who had returned from the Dardanelles, and they had told me that they had not received any money for months, entirely owing to the fact that they were away from their units. I now see that they may have had another objective in view in telling me this, and quite probably they succeeded in their objective, which was to cadge a few shillings off me, and others who sympathized with their plight. They certainly did succeed, if that was their objective, for if I had any money, I shared it. No matter how I am now, in those days I was not mean or tight. I state the money seems to go very quickly in Egypt, and now as I look back, I do not know a place where it did not go quickly, with the one exception of the Peninsula.
I reported home that I was 11 stone 8 pounds, the heaviest weight that I have ever registered up to then. I was feeling wonderfully fit and healthy."

18/7/15:

Today I met a lot of chaps who came from Mitcham Camp, and have just arrived in Egypt. I was on guard duty tonight, so missed the Church parade.

19/7/15:

It is getting hotter and we work harder. We are looking forward to mail, and home mail is now coming through on a more regular basis. I got my second letter from home today and six others by the same mail. I know that I would be as well off as the rest of the boys as regards receiving my letters, once mine started to flow in.

20/7/15:

The CO said today that there was a chance of our getting away to the front in a fortnight or so. We are working hard to become efficient so that we get chosen to go into active service, which is why we are all here. We are working hard so that we will get chosen to go off to the front. It is hot during the days, but getting cooler at nights, which are just beautiful. The sunsets are spectacular.

22/7/15:

I met Barnett, from Reedy Creek, at Heliopolis this evening. I did not know him at first, as he has grown a moustache, and is very fat. He is leaving for the Dardenelles shortly. He told me that Frank White is going back to Australia shortly. I must try and see him before he goes.

23/7/15:

Getting very low in cash, only about 10 piastres left.

24/7/15:

Had a pay day today, which is very welcome. Went to Cairo and had a tip-top dinner at St James. It cost 28 piastres. Alec Blackwell, who has been away at the Hospital for a week or so retuned today and we were pleased to see him. We had missed old Tom very much.

25/7/15: (Sunday)

Had leave from 8 am to 10.30 pm today, and had a magnificent time. Church parade in the morning conducted by a private in the AMC *(Army Medical Corp)*, and it was good. Church was at 6.45 am. 25% of the Unit has leave each Sunday, and today was our turn.

We went to Cairo soon after 8 am. We paid for a guide for the day, and paid him the princely sum of 2.5 piastres, (about sixpence) per head, and made for the pyramids. Sometimes these guides are very good, but some of them we have heard are rooks. At the time, we thought we were fortunate with our guide, and it turned out that we indeed made a good selection.

On the way to the pyramids, we passed through the old section of Cairo. It appeared to me as the biblical part of Cairo. We crossed the Nile in this part of Cairo. It is here that Moses was hidden in the bulrushes.

We arrived at the pyramids in the train from Cairo at about 11.30 am. The rest of the trip was done on camels. This form of transport was quite a novelty for us.

The pyramids are undoubtedly wonderful. We went right through the old Temple, and then inside the pyramids, which are 451 feet high, and covers 11 acres of ground, but this is hard to believe, as it does not look it to me. All told there are 9 pyramids, 3 large and 6 smaller ones. The one we went into (the largest) was built 3,751 years BC. It is known as the pyramid of Cheops. My first impression when looking at the pyramid closely was, "How did they get all those huge rocks up where they are?"

There is a passageway we take in the heart of this pyramid. This is pitch dark passageway, where one could be knifed at any moment. It is about 3 feet wide, and 5 feet high. It runs down in a gentle slope for about 50 yards, and then begins to ascend at a rather big gradient, until you are about half way up the pyramid and in the centre of it. Here is the King's Chamber, where some King is buried, and directly below is the Queen's chamber where the King's wife is buried. This journey into the centre of the pyramid is very trying. It is pitch dark and the candlelight avails but little. I am glad we went in there, but I am not going in there again, thanks.

There was a party of us and we had our photos taken out there on camels, by the Sphinx. The Sphinx is a natural rock, but cut into the peculiar shape it is today. It has the body of a lion, and the face of a man. The back of its head is like that of a woman. It is 115 feet long, 70 feet high and 18 feet broad. We noticed that the nose is missing. Napoleon, some 115 years ago, wished to leave some mark in Egypt by which he would be remembered, so one of the things he did was to break off the Sphinx' nose!

There is a big camp of Tommies (Kitchener's Army) out at Mena, near the pyramids. They say there will be about 40,000 here shortly.

Our guide brought us back and showed us through two mosques which are absolutely beyond words. In Australia we talk about the Melbourne Cathedral, but until you have seen these Mosques you are not in a position to speak. The first one we went to was the Mosque of Sultan Hassan. It is 550 years old, not so spectacular from the outside, but inside was built magnificently, every part artistically finished, carved and set with ivory, gold and silver.

The second Mosque was even better, and almost beyond description. It was the Citadel Mosque. It was built 450 years ago, and has been repaired within the last century. The repair itself cost 150,000 pounds. The doors were very massive and heavily covered with metal, the metallic finish beautifully worked. In places the metal had been torn off by Napoleon's forces, and used by Napoleon to erect monuments to himself. Outside we were shown a cannonball embedded in the wall about six inches. The cannon ball was just a ball shaped piece of iron about 5 inches in diameter. My mind often turned back to that cannonball, which was a comparatively harmless missile, and I ruefully reflected that war science had made such enormous strides over the century which intervened.

One is not allowed to go into the Citadel Mosque with boots on, as the whole thing is offset with beautiful carpet which of itself must have cost thousands. You are provided with special shoes to walk in. The building is supported with huge marble pillars. Every chamber of the mosque is unique, and each as marvelous as the other. The tombs of the holy men were perhaps the best pieces of work there. They cost 17,000 pounds each. The mosque is 170 feet tall, and worked magnificently.

It has been a tiring day, but one I will always remember. We returned to camp just after 11 pm.

Ralph's notes:
"In letters home I referred to other damage which Napoleon did during this time, but in the letter I said I would tell the home folks

about it on my return. What I was referring to I now have no idea, and had no idea when I got home. This type of reference was evidence that we expected to be back home in a very short time!"

26/7/15 to 31/7/15:

We are in intensive training. The troops are in wonderful fettle, and very keen. There is an air of confidence and keen eagerness to be well in the fighting. It is a general desire, not something that I personally crave for. We went on a long route march on the night of the 29th July. One stretcher squad had to go with the infantry and ours (No 5) was chosen. On the 30th July I took my exam for No 4. I think I did alright. Anyhow, our Section, B Section ran rings around the other two sections (A and C Sections). At this time I am a member of the B Section Stretcher Squad.

31/7/15:

Today it was "as hot as billio," but not hot enough to stop us playing a game of football. *(Ralph was a good footballer and a good all-round athlete. He had been full forward in the PAC intercollegiate teams of 1910 and 1911. He was also the gymnastic champion at PAC in 1909, and was in the athletics intercollegiate team in 1911. He played football and cricket regularly at Naracoorte prior to enlisting, and talks about playing Aussie rules football games throughout the war. They also played soccer occasionally).*

We are all in great nick. Alec saw Ray Bills today, and he thinks that he returns to the Dardenelles tomorrow.

I went up to Cairo to send a cable home for money.

At about 7.30pm a group of soldiers, who had some grievance against the lower quarters of Cairo mobbed these filthy places throwing all the furniture out of the houses, and set fire to the furniture. The fires destroyed the furniture, but the fire spread, and six houses caught fire, and were destroyed.

Ralph's notes:
In a letter home to Clem, I wrote,
"Last Good Friday night was the night of the Great Battle of the Wosser. The origination of this I do not know but I believe that the soldiers had good reason for the damage that they did, although there is no doubt but that the mark was overstepped.
The name "Battle of the Wosser" is given because this low and immoral and corrupt part of Cairo is known as the Wosser. Anyhow, as I was not here for that outbreak, I will not try to tell you all that I have heard about it, but will try my best to give you an account of what I saw last Saturday night. The damage done this time was much more extensive than that done in the Battle already referred to. You will doubtless think that the Australian soldiers must be a rough lot as you read what I am going to try to tell you now, but before I start I want you to consider what a state of affairs exists in the "Wosser." You may have got some idea from my last letter to you. Although I am opposed to such direct action and lawlessness and of course would have nothing to do with any action such as this, I do conscientiously believe that good will eventually result, in as much as it has lessened the number of these places, and must put fear into the hearts of the persons controlling these places. The practices carried on in these places are the most filthy and beastly and embrace five or six ways of obtaining a livelihood.
Bill Graves and I had gone into Cairo on Saturday afternoon and after tea went into a Cafe for a drink and listen to an orchestra playing at the Café. We had barely got seated when we heard a crash not far down the street. As a result we rushed out, and looking down the "Wosser" street the first thing that caught my eye was a wardrobe hanging out of a window. In a few moments there was a further crash as this came in contact with the footpath. This sort of thing went on for about half an hour until all the furniture, bedding etc from these places was on the street below. By this time as you may well imagine, the crowd was very large, and consisted mainly of Australian soldiers. The dens in the "Wosser" are all 4 stories high, so that will give you some idea of the crash as the furniture etc was hurled to the ground. The natives are very fearful of the Australians,

and it was amusing to see them scattering in all directions, like mice at the approach of a cat. With all the furniture on the footpath, the mob lit the heap in several places but by the way the flames spread, it would appear that kerosene was in readiness for the purpose of spreading the fire as rapidly as possible. The flames were fairly high and gradually caught on to the lookouts, or balconies, on the second story of the houses. This little balcony affair had just about burned right off and the flames were spreading to the buildings themselves when a motor fire brigade arrived on the scene. After a deal of trouble the brigade got through the mass of soldiers, but before they had time to unroll the hose, they were rushed by the mob and forced to reverse the fire brigade and make themselves scarce. In about half an hour the brigade returned with officers and Military Guard on board and after a few tussles managed to get the brigade into position and fight the fire. Nevertheless, the half hour delay had enabled the fire to get a good hold and very extensively damaged the buildings before the fire was extinguished."

Ralphs's notes:
"There were several suggestions as to the cause of the outbreak of lawlessness. In my letter I said that although the action above was taken mainly by an unruly and drunken crowd of Australians, the outcome would be regarded as a good result.
In fact, the Egyptian Times carried an article a few days later which

read:

'Purification of Cairo:
The occupants of the disorderly houses in the Western end of the Waseh-El-Birka Street, Ezhekieh, are being evicted by the authorities and the landlords have been warned that in future they must not let their houses for immoral purposes.'
So perhaps starting the fire, and the other actions of the 2nd Division soldiers I have described was unruly and illegal, but morally not quite so repugnant.

Historical note:
Ralph notes that he sent a photo home of this scene. The two "Wozzer" incidents are famous, and are recorded in the official records. (See Bean, (1921) Vol 1, P.130, n13.) Bean recounts that

the "Second Battle of the Wozzer," involved the 2nd Division, (which was Ralph's Division). Bean recounts that there was an incident on Good Friday, 1915, (the "First Battle of the Wozzer") and a second incident "some months later." He does not give a clear date of the second incident.

Adam-Smith (p 54) is more definite than Bean, and claimed the second "Battle of the Wazzir"(as she called it) occurred in June. However, Ralph is clearly describing the second incident in his diaries and letters, and he provides a clear date, Saturday 31/07/15.

What Ralph does not explain clearly is the reason the troops behaved the way they did. Adam-Smith, on the other hand, is clear about the reasons for these incidents. The troops were not happy with the way they were treated, including "injuries" suffered in the Haret-el-Wasser, an infamous street of brothels in Cairo. Injuries included physical injuries, such as stabbings, but almost certainly included the "injuries" the men suffered by contracting VD at the brothels, which was a huge problem for the AIF at the time. (There were up to 2,000 VD cases amongst the troops who were living in Egypt at this time. (Butler, (1933) Vol. I, Pp 76-77).) There was no certain cure for VD in those days, (no penicillin) and many VD patients were repatriated to Australia, and, unfortunately subsequently discharged in disgrace. While in Egypt, those who contracted VD were isolated from the rest of the troops and identified with white armbands, which they were compelled to wear. Rather than a "badge of honour" this was treated as an indignation which some of the troops blamed on the brothel-keepers. The troops reacted by attacking the brothels in the Haret-el-Wasser, and extracting some sort of retribution. Bean describes it as not much more than a University 'rag,' but Adam-Smith, and Ralph's accounts make it appear a bit more serious than that!

While Ralph writes home he was an innocent observer, he was right there, he was in the second Division, and he was having a drink with Bill Graves. I wonder if they were a little bit more involved than they let us know? Perhaps his excellent recollection is proof of the fact that he and Bill Graves were observers, as he claimed.(Ed.)

1/8/15 to 9/8/15:

Leave to Cairo was blocked today, 1/8/15. I suspect it was blocked because of the incident yesterday. Apparently things are still pretty willing in Cairo, so leave has been cancelled.

We were granted special leave to go into Cairo on the 2nd. They say that the damage caused by their fellow 2nd Division mates was extensive, but eventually goodwill resulted.

It was Alec's 21st, but because we are all broke, we did not do too much. Alec got a cable today saying that five pounds had been cabled to him. We will have a bang up when this arrives.

I have a bit of a cold on the 3rd August, but it is not really too troublesome. The first anniversary of the war came on the 4th August. And we thought that something would be doing in camp today, but we were disappointed as the usual routine was followed.

The next three days are very hot, and my cold gets a bit worse.

On the 8th August, we heard that Achi Baba had fallen.

(Achi Baba is on the south south-eastern side of the Gallipoli Peninsula. It is on the western side of the Dardenelles as you enter the Dardanelle Strait from the Aegean Sea. It was regarded as an important objective of the Dardanelles campaign.(Ed.))

We also heard that a tremendous lot of wounded were coming in shortly, and the 50 stretcher bearers were to go down to Alexandria to unload the wounded. The Nursing section (Alec included) are opening up a new Hospital in Heliopolis. On the morning of the 9th, the Nursing section moved off to the new Hospital.

(This was the formal opening of the No 1 Field Hospital at the old Palace hotel in Heliopolis. Photo at end of chapter.(Ed.))

We went and had a look at them tonight. They are very comfortable, and ought to have a good time.

10/8/15:

We left for Alexandria today. We left Polygon Camp *(at Abbassia, outside Cairo (Ed)* at 7.00 am and marched into Cairo, where we arrived and were entrained at 9.30 am to travel on to Alexandria. We arrived at Alexandria at 12.30 pm. We were camped at 'A' Camp. It is a great place, and we would have a really good time here if we had any cash. After we had dinner, which was the first meal we had for the day, we broke bounds and wandered around the city. We made first for the sea, and as you would expect, we were not long out of the water. We had a good dip, and went for a walk along the wharf. Two transport ships were just loading for the Dardenelles with Tommies (Field Artillery and Territorials). They all think that the fact of the Field Artillery going is a real good sign. We get very little news of the war.

We saw the *"Teiressias"* in a dry dock being repaired. She was a transport ship and sailed a day or so ahead of the *"Geelong."* She was mined, and they say that she was the cause of our disembarking at Suez. We had a good look at the boat, and saw the damaged and twisted metal at the bottom of the vessel where she hit the mine. The mine caught her amidships. The second mate told us that the boat rose like a cork at the time the mine exploded.

11/8/15:

We get our first real touch of war. We started to unload the two boats which arrived in Alexandria. The boats had mixed Australian, Tommies and New Zealanders injured aboard. We saw many gruesome sights for the first time. The first boat was not a hospital ship, but she had 1020 men on board, with 500 colonials. The next boat had 1300 on board, with about 700 colonials.

(These injured would have been the result of the August advances and charges by the British and Anzac troops along the lines. There were disastrous losses and injuries at The Nek, Lone Pine, and in a number of other charges and battles conducted by the ANZACs during the August offensives. The injured were repatriated mostly to Alexandria, but some were sent direct to England. (Ed.))

The sights were horrific, and awful, and we did not complete our work until about 8.00 pm. We talked to the men, but most were too injured to talk much. I met one lad I knew at College, and had an interesting chat with him. We tried to confirm the news that Achi Baba had fallen. Unfortunately it was not true. The soldiers are saying that the fighting at the Peninsula is fierce, and desperate, and that conditions are not too good there. There have been some heavy casualties, as there has been a push forward by the troops at the peninsula. However, the spirits of the wounded are positive and not too despondent, which surprised me. We are exhausted at the end of the day.

(There were a number of disastrous attacks by the ANZACs during August, which accounts for the shocking casualties repatriated to Alexandria.(Ed.))

12/8/15:

Today we unloaded the *"Tunician"* and the *"Secilia."* There were about 1400 mixed cases. We saw some dreadful wounds. The wounded were, however, in great spirits. After finishing that evening, Bill Graves and I were told to go off to Cairo with a hospital train of wounded. We accompanied the train, and then back to Alexandria after seeing them hospitalised in Cairo. We arrived back at about 3.30 am.

13 & 14/8/15:

We had the 13th off, due to the long day we put in on the 12th. The others were still busy unloading wounded. There was a boat load of Indian wounded unloaded today. We were on deck again on the 14th, and unloaded 1100 wounded from two ships.

This was the first time we came in contact with Indian soldiers. They are described as a fine body of men and reputed as wonderfully good fighters. The Indian soldiers themselves speak very highly of the Australians, while the Indians may have been good fighters, they were not good judges of how long the war will last. An Indian officer gave me the certain prophesy that the Dardenelles would be finished in 15 days, and the Germans would be finished in about 60 days.

15/8/15:

No Church parade today. We went down to the port and loaded a hospital ship bound for England. There were 350 cases loaded out on this ship.

16/8/15:

We went down and unloaded another boat with about 500 cases on board, mostly New Zealanders and Tommies. These cases were perhaps the worst we have seen so far. There we 41 amputations in one ward alone.

The nurses were all Australians, and we had real good chat with them. The boats we have unloaded so far are *"Ascania," "Delta," "Tunisian," "Sicilian," "Seang Choon," "Dongola,"* and those we have loaded with wounded for England are *"Munnan"* and *"Macilici."*

The work of unloading the wounded at Alexandria was continued and we worked to the point of exhaustion.

One thing becomes apparent to us from talking with the wounded, and that is how little the soldier in the field knows of the actual position in warfare.

Ralph's notes:
"I said in a letter home, 'The work and self-sacrifice of the nurses can never be acknowledged to the full. Nurses are needed and I am sure that people in Australia do not realise what a huge part the Nurses are playing in the war.'"

"I wrote home saying, 'From the wounded it is hard to get any definite news of the front. They believe that there has been a general advance and that our forces have succeeded in cutting off supplies to Achi Baba, so now it looks as thought it is just a matter of time.'
I also heard from one of the wounded men that Murray Fowler had been killed. False rumours were always about, especially in these early days of the war. As a matter of fact, Murray saw years of heavy fighting, and returned to Australia after the war."

Historical note:
Ralph states… *"our forces have succeeded in cutting off supplies to Achi Baba…"* which led to the impression the War was all but over!
The Mediterranean Expeditionary Forces (which included the
ANZACs and the Gallipoli forces) never came close to capturing Achi Baba, let alone cut off its supply lines. (Ed.)

16/8/15(cont'd)

We were having trouble with our mail at Alexandria, but did receive a cable enquiring how we were. We presumed the cable was the outcome of the sinking of the transport, *"Royal Edward"* on her way to the Dardenelles, and that they may have thought we were on that ship. We reported back as soon as possible, by cable, that we were all OK and in the highest of spirits.

Life in Alexandria was decidedly happier and cleaner than in Cairo. And our money seemed to go further. While the work here was heavy and at times pitiful and some instances of the shocking wounds we saw caused cold feet amongst some of our party, it really was the most enjoyable of our time in Egypt.

17/08/15:

We received a large Australian mail today. Things in Australia are generally booming in our line of business. This was splendid news to us and bucked us up very considerably. It is quite noticeable in my letters that we are in the highest spirits, despite the depressing and shocking work we are doing, unloading the sick and wounded from the peninsula.

We were paid yesterday, so we all went into Alexandria and had some good fun. We had a splendid 5 course tea. We were told today we were leaving for the front on Sunday.

The next two days were rest days for us.

20/8/15 to 24/8/15:

We unloaded four more ships in these days, which were the *"Euripides,"* with about 700 Tommies, the *"Itonus"* with about 600 Tommies, the *"Dunluce Castle"* with nearly 600 Tommies and the

"*Guildford Castle*" with about 350 casualties, including 100 Australians, I should think.

25/8/15:

We saw 8 armoured cars (Rolls Royces), 13 light Ford transports, 3 Army Service Transports, on the docks. They had all been to the Dardenelles, but were not landed. They were painted all colours. There were two more ships today, *"Ulysses,"* and *"Scotsman."* Also told there were about 2,000 on board. We have unloaded some 9,500 cases since we have been here in Alexandria.

Some have gone back to England, some are in hospitals at Alexandria, and some have been repatriated to Cairo and Heliopolis for treatment.

Historical note:
During August, in all, some 22,400 casualties sick and sounded disembarked at Alexandria and were distributed in nearly equal numbers between Alexandria, and Cairo. There were 4 British hospitals, "among the best in the British Army" which were well equipped to deal with large numbers of wounded. (Butler, AG, (1933), Vol 1, P 399.)
Butler also notes at P 399-400,
> *"The staff at the docks were reinforced from the 2nd Australian Division and the 4th Light Horse Field Ambulances, which, by reason of the fine physique and keenness of the men, worked with two bearers to a stretcher instead of four, and were prominent in the strenuous work done at this, the final "dock" before distribution."*

Ralph was with the 7th Field Ambulance, which was one of the 3 field ambulance units with the 2nd Division. Ralph and his mates therefore helped move about a third of the sick and injured at Alexandria in August 1915.(Ed.)

We worked under an English Major here in Alexandria, and he did his best to convince us to remain there, leave our Units to serve with him in Alexandria. We would not entertain this idea, and after he realized it was no good trying to persuade us otherwise, he said, "Well I have never seen better stretcher bearers and I am very sorry that you are leaving. However you are going where you are most wanted and I know will give a good account of yourselves."

(This view is supported by the Official Record, (see Butler, AG, (1933) Vol 1 P 399 note 13.(Ed.))

Late tonight we received orders to get ready to go back to the Abbassia Camp. We think we are getting ready for the front.

26/8/15:

Left Alexandria today at about noon and arrived at camp at Abbassia at about 4.30 pm. We receive orders to get ready to go to the front. We are excited by this, and preparations are in full swing for our departure. We are conscious that we must uphold the splendid name earned by the Australians in the Gallipoli campaign to date. Everyone we speak to from the front says the same thing about our soldiers. I write home to tell everyone that Alec looks remarkably well, as also does Eric and as regards myself, I cannot say anything about my looks, but I feel prime.

Bill Graves took ill at Alexandria and was in hospital with rheumatism. We were very sorry that Bill would not be with us on Gallipoli.

Ralph's notes:
"I wrote in a letter home, 'Bill is very down in the dumps with rheumatism.'

Bill was never with us in the actual war zone and we were always afterwards of the opinion that the sights at Alexandria had so played on his nerves that he would do all he could not to actually get into the war zone. I firmly believe that Bill was brave enough to be a coward or should I say he had the courage to admit to himself that he was afraid of the consequences. We heard of Bill on several occasions after. Apparently he would do anything to actually keep out of the line. Towards the end of the war, he was a mess orderly in an officer's mess in France, but owing to high casualties he was ordered into the trenches. When he actually got there he proved himself a courageous soldier and his work from then on was always very highly spoken of. I have to say that before he fell ill, there was no better bearer in our Unit than Bill Graves."

27/8/15 to 2/9/15:

We were all medically examined and spent the first couple of days in Abbassia packing up our kits. We were all concerned about Bill Graves, and he had to go before the Medical board. We thought he may have to be repatriated back to Australia.

We had our last Church parade in Egypt on the 29/8/15, and heard that it may not be until next Tuesday until we leave.

We had a full Dress parade on Monday, and found our packs heavy enough.

Had a cable from home on the 1/9/15. I had asked for money, and this was being organised. I cabled that it was not necessary any more, as we were about to disembark. Fortunately it was reply paid.

2/9/15:

We are sleeping in the open as all our tents and everything is packed and ready to go. The advance guard has been chosen, and we really believe we are going to move tomorrow. We still have no official notification, just rumours around the camp.

3/9/15:

At last the day has arrived. We move off and march to the station at Palo de Corta about 2 miles away at about 9.30 am. We left poor old Bill Graves back at the hospital with rheumatism. We do not know what will happen to him, but we are all disappointed he is not with us. We are all highly nervous and excited to be on our way.

We arrive at Alexandria at about 3.15 pm. We move down the docks, and immediately start to load our transport ship, the *"Knight Templar."* First we loaded the horses and then the loaded wagonettes. Everyone is in great spirits. There are 3 boats being loaded with Australians. I don't know the number, but there would be about 6,000 altogether, I should think. We camped over night, and the loading of the transport ships continued the next day. We were ready for departure at about 5.30 pm that afternoon September 4th 1915. We are ready for our trip to Gallipoli. We have about 700 miles to sail before we disembark. Everyone is anxious to get into the war, and there is an air of nervous excitement. As far as we know, we have left unescorted.

Historical note:
The 1/7th Field Ambulance, 2nd Division, First AIF:

The original 1st / 7th Field Ambulance, which was formed in Adelaide and trained in Egypt, consisted of 240 men below commissioned rank, commanded by 14 officers (all doctors except the Captain Quarter-Master.) The 1/7 Field Ambulance was divided into 3 sections, A, B & C sections. Each section was commanded by a Surgeon Major, and comprised 3 Captains, Stretcher bearers, Nursing Aids and Transport drivers. It functioned as a first aid group to serve one combat

Regiment. A Surgeon Lieutenant Colonel commanded the 3 sections, which comprised a Field Ambulance. The 5th, 6th and 7th Field Ambulance provided field medical aid to the 2nd AIF Division, which comprised the 17th, 18th, 19th, 20th, 21st, 22nd, 23rd, 24th, 25th, 26th, 27th, & 28th Battalions and their ancillary units such as machine gunners, Engineers, Pioneers, Signallers, Army service, etc.

In the field the service provided by a Field Ambulance was to carry wounded from the Battalion Aid Posts to Field Ambulance Advance Dressing Stations and then by Ambulance to Casualty Clearing Stations, which were forward of Base Hospitals. Early day transport was by four horse wagons, which were later replaced by motor ambulance. While combat troops were resting and being re-fitted behind the front line, the Field Ambulance provided rest stations with medical services for those not disabled enough to need base Hospital treatment.

Some 678 men served in the 7th Field Ambulance unit, including 44 officers, and 634 other ranks. (Dunn, P.1)

Ralph, Eric and Alec were with the Unit when it was formed. (Ed.)

Palace Hotel, Heliopolis, Egypt, 1915.
The hotel was used as the No 1 Australian Field Hospital during WW1. Ralph worked in and around the hospital at various times during the War. *Photo, AWM.*

Heliopolis Army Camp,
Egypt, 1915. This was the first camp for Ralph's 7th Field Ambulance Unit outside Australia. *Photo, AWM.*

Motor Ambulances: Arriving by rail at Heliopolis. Ralph drove a motorised ambulance in Europe.

Heliopolis, Egypt, May 1915.
The AIF tented camp at Heliopolis. *Photo; AWM.*

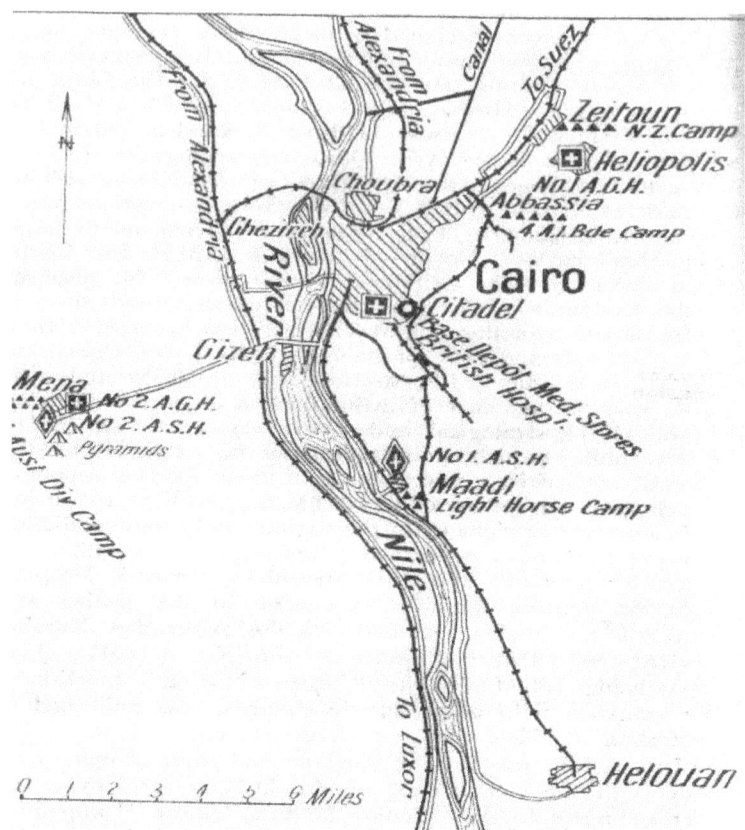

Cairo Egypt and Surrounds, 1915.
Ralph's Unit was originally camped at Heliopolis, but moved to Abbassia Camp for later training. Hospitals are marked with a white cross in a square. There were large numbers of troops trained here before shipping off to Gallipoli or Europe. The New Zealand troops were camped at Zeitoun, north east of Heliopolis.

Harry Schinkel. Joined his 3 mates in France, 1917.

Roy Kidman: Eric's Cousin. Served in the Light Horse in Palestine.

Chapter Four:
Gallipoli:

The Diary:
4/9/15

We boarded the "*Knight Templar*" on the 4th September 1915, bound for the Dardenelles. To see the "*Knight Templar*" pulling out of Alexandria one would think that we had aboard a big crowd of holiday makers. It would be harder to picture a happier crowd of men and I am convinced their keenness was genuine.

5/9/15:

The first day sailing was beautifully calm, and my old nemesis, the mal-de-mer did not bother me. This was a pleasant surprise for me. The next day, the sea was a bit rough, but still I managed to keep away from the rail. I wrote a letter home today, and hope I can get it off.

6/9/15:

Major Stewart left the unit ill just before we sailed for Gallipoli. We were very fond of him. We later found out that he had got that far with another unit before, and he had lost favour. Later he did go the into the field, I think with the 6th Field Ambulance and we met him in France. My later letters may or may not have some further reference to him. The sea was a bit rough today, but I managed to keep off the rail!

7/9/15:

Another beautiful day. So far we have had three days on board ship without me being seasick. Instructions regarding letters have come out so I have had to destroy the one I wrote. Last few days I have had severe pains in my back, and I am afraid of Lumbago. I am trying to doctor it myself, because I don't want to go on sick parade. We arrived at Mudros harbour on the island of Lemnos at sunset, and it was an awesome sight.

(Lemnos is an island situated in the Aegean Sea, about 650 miles from Alexandria, and 60 miles from ANZAC Cove. Imbros is closer, being about 15 miles west of ANZAC Cove. (Ed.))

The harbour was simply full of battleships, destroyers and all sorts of other boats and ships. We took a long time sailing from Alexandria to Lemnos as we steered a zig-zag course all the way. There were threats of submarine attacks. There were German U Boats operating in the area and targeting our shipping.

(There is a brief summary of U boat action in the Mediterranean Sea in Chapter 5. (Ed.)) We anchored at Mudros harbour.

8/9/15:

I am really crook today. I have some sort of fever. There was talk of leaving me at the hospital here, but I objected to that. I was really bad this evening, and was worried I would miss going to the peninsula.

9/9/15:

I am much better this morning. We heard today that one of the other transport ships had been torpedoed, but she did not sink. We believe there were a fair few lives lost, however. Just before we sailed from Alexandria a lot of letters and papers came in.

Felt much worse today at dinner time. I think the heads are thinking of sending me ashore here, but I am not going to stand for that.

10 & 11/9/15:

I am feeling much better again today. Eric joined me in the hospital tonight, and he thinks he has the flu. We are a real lot. No battle witnessed yet, but almost the walking wounded. We are tended on the ship in the hospital quarters.

Next day I am feeling better, but still confined to bed. Eric has been fairly crook, and has a very high temperature all day and into the evening. I am concerned about him.

12/9/15:

Eric went ashore today on account of his high temperature. He will go to the hospital at Mudros. He looks alright, but with his high temperature, they are taking no risks. I am up and although feeling a bit off colour, I am OK really.

Arrival at Gallipoli:

We boarded our transport for Gallipoli from here at about 2.00 pm. It is a small boat, in fact a captured Turkish boat, the *"Osmeneah,"* which is well fitted and clean. There are some Gurkhas on board this boat, about 700 in all. We left Lemnos and as we pulled out we passed a line of battleships and a hospital ship. She looked most majestic. All lights were put out and no smoking allowed. This little transport boat is fast, compared with the *"Knight Templar."*

We caught our first glimpse of the lights at Anzac Cove at about 10.30 pm. We waited out off Anzac Cove for some time. The sound of rifle fire and the crackle of rifles along the ridge woke us to the reality that we were now in a war zone. It was a wonderful sensation. I do not think there is anything akin to fear, even when the splash of stray bullets landing alongside the boat. Then the news that one of our number had been wounded by a stray bullet was further reinforcement for us that this was the real thing.

13/9/15:

Our boat moved as close into the shore as it could reach. We reached our disembarkation point at about 3.30 am. There was lots of quiet action as we worked at getting our stuff up from the hold and into the lighter alongside us. We seemed to take forever getting prepared for our landing, and eventually at about 6.00am we boarded the lighter and came ashore. All night long as we approached the place we heard some heavy firing. We did not suffer any casualties when landing, and we were very, very lucky in this regard. Very few landing crews at Anzac Cove did not suffer dead or wounded on landing. We were told that the Turks can land a shell on the landing place, and that they have the range very accurately. We thank the Lord for the misty rain.

Ralphs' notes:
"A Naval officer loved by all on the Peninsula was in charge of our landing at Anzac Cove. We knew him as Captain Kettle, because he resembles the Captain Kettle!
Ours was the last small boat to berth. We were laughing and joking, full of nervous anticipation. On landing we were greeted by the words, "If Beachy Bill open up you'll soon have that bloody laugh off your faces!"
With plenty of other robust language, he quickly got us landed and on our way. Afterwards I learnt Captain Kettle was killed attending to his work on the beach at Anzac Cove."

Historical note:
The "Captain Kettle" to whom Ralph refers was a popular fiction character, apparently the hero of a few silent movies made in the

Edwardian era, and based on the "Captain Kettle Boys Adventure" books by CJ Cutliffe-Hyne.

"Beachy Bill" was a Turkish battery which bombarded the beach at Anzac Cove. It was reputed to have caused over 1,000 casualties alone on the beach. Bean CEW, (1924) Vol II, P76, says the original battery which caused so much damage was put out of action early in the campaign, and before Ralph arrived. However, "Beachy Bill" was moved, and re-established inland, from where it fired shrapnel shells quite high above the beach. The piles of supplies on the beach apparently afforded quite reasonable protection for the troops which landed subsequent to April 25th. Probably "Beachy Bill" became more of a generic term for the Turkish batteries which were capable of shelling the beach. They did so with great accuracy as the Gallipoli campaign progressed. For example, Corporal Gunter, while on duty at the beach on 2/10/1915, recorded that he "...laid under guns all day; Beachey Bill fired about a dozen on the Beach, got 5 or 6 men..." Cpl Gunter was himself hit by "Beachy Bill" the next day and evacuated (King, J.,(2003) Pp. 190-191). (Ed.)

13/9/15 (cont'd)

The battleships were doing some bombarding of the hills in the background. We were surprised on landing to find the state of the place. A tremendous amount of work had been done. There were piles of provisions on the shore and any amount of ammunition. We are told to get to our dug-outs, and so we do, and make ourselves comfortable. We are in the second Valley from the shore directly behind the landing beach, and on the hill just above us there is a continual sound of rifle fire. Further back we can hear the reports of the bigger guns, but only very occasionally. We are in Shrapnel Valley. Behind us there is a range of hills on which are mounted guns. The Turks try to put these guns out of action and every day there is a duet of noise like that which is going on now. My oath it is a noise and we are just in the position to get full effect of it.

At 9.00 pm we were ordered out of Shrapnel Valley and made for our new quarters. We marched about 4 or 5 miles with full packs through a long sap which is absolutely marvelous to behold. We bivouaced at our new port at about 11.30 pm.

Historical note:
The 2nd Division was in Rest Valley, which was in the northern part of Shrapnel Valley. Although the Field Ambulance units did not stay with their infantry units on Gallipoli, I am sure this is where Ralph was for a few hours. (Ed.)

Ralph's notes:
In a letter home dated 15/9/15, I wrote:

"We landed here at 6.00 am on 13th September. We were to have landed before daybreak, but owing to delay it was well daylight when we landed. Fortunately just as we were landing a misty rain was falling and we got ashore without any casualties. There was one casualty on the boat before we landed. One of the chaps was hit with a stray bullet. There were landing round about us all the time. We were all huddled together on the deck of the boat. On landing at Anzac Cove the first impression one gets is one of marvel that ever a force could land against such adverse circumstances. Really it is far more difficult than ever I had thought talking to the men at Alexandria and Cairo. At Anzac Cove there is only a few yards of beach and a high ridge runs practically straight up from the sea. At the moment on this ridge is a mass of dugouts. Some of them look to be most comfortable. On landing we were taken around into what is known as Shrapnel Valley. This is just behind the first line of hills straight in from Anzac Cove. All through this valley is nothing but dugouts. We made ourselves comfortable in one of these dugouts, and settled down, but we were not there for long as we had orders to be ready to shift our position at 9.00 pm that night. We left Shrapnel Valley at that time to take up our new position.

We marched, I should say, about four miles through a magnificent sap, about 12 feet wide and 6 feet high, absolutely a wonderful piece of work, and in places cut through solid rock. We took up our position, which was on the side of a hill facing the sea, on the ground recently captured form the Turks. Immediately on top of this hill are some of the vacated Turkish trenches, and when you consider that our fellows had to advance over the flat below against such preparation, you get some idea of the wonderful feat that was achieved by our troops. Since arriving here we have spent most of our time in getting our new home comfortable and to a great extent have been successful. Alec and I are in the same dugout, and we contend it is the best of the lot. We do our own cooking and are living very well.

The day we left Lemnos, Eric took ill with a fever and we had to leave him there, but there was nothing serious with him and we are expecting him to join us any day. Our position at the moment is comparatively safe and our view is remarkably fine over the sea. Practically every day the cruisers, destroyers and monitors come in quite close to bombard the Turkish position and guns and explosions literally shake the ground here. We have not started our work in earnest yet, but I expect we will any day now."

14/9/15:

We went to relieve some New Zealanders today, who have been working here. There is heavy artillery fire right against us.

(7th Field Ambulance actually relieved the 4th Field Ambulance (attached to the 1st Division) and the New Zealand Field Ambulance.(Ed))

Historical note:
Ralph does not give an accurate description in his notes or his diary of where this new position was situated on the peninsula. There is no reference to any known ground area on the peninsula.
It is almost certain that Ralph, and his Section B of the 7th Field Ambulance went to Chailak Dere, and established camp between the "field hospitals" which were established there near the beach, and casualty clearing stations nearly a mile inland. I think that his first camp there was higher than the field hospitals near the beach, but not

quite to the two dressing stations which were about a mile inland. The anecdotal and historical evidence which supports this contention is:

- The sap (or trench) that Ralph marvels at is probably the long "SS Sap to no.2 post" described by Bean, (Bean CEW, Vol. II, P 448.) Rest Gully is where the 2nd Division camped on the first night, and the headquarters of the Division was established there. (Bean CEW, Vol. II, P. 809.)
- The headquarters of the 2nd Division Medical Corps was also established at Rest Gully (Butler, (1933) Vol. I, P. 353.)
- Butler, (1933) Vol. I, P 353, records "....the 7th (Field Ambulance) relieved the 4th and New Zealand Field Ambulances." Further, at P307 Butler records the 4th Field Ambulance and the NZ Field Ambulance were operating near No 3 pier in August 1915. This pier is adjacent to the Chailak Dere. (See Butler, (1933) Vol I, map 11 at P. 307.)
- The main Dressing Station, at Chailak Dere was quite close to the beach, and Butler notes that the Field Ambulances were also camped here.
- Ralph later in the diary talks about moving camp on the 5/10/15, when he notes…"Our new camp is much closer to the trenches, practically just behind them." They must have moved higher up the Chailak Dere from the hospital area.
- There were 2 advanced dressing stations, and 2 Evacuation Routes for the wounded which merged about a mile inland upstream on the Chailak Dere. (see Butler, (1933) Vol. I, Map 11, P. 307.) These positions were occupied by Field Ambulance units. I think Ralph was first camped between these and the hospital site.
- Ralph says they were camped "about a mile from the sea" and with a view of the sea. This is where the Evacuation Routes merged, higher on the Chailak Dere.
- Turkish trenches were close by, as described by Ralph.
- By mid August the 4th Field Ambulance was servicing Hill 60, which was north of Chailak Dere, evacuating wounded down to the new pier north of No 3 pier.
- When Eric Kidman was hit by a piece of shrapnel late in September, he was evacuated through No 2 Outpost.

- *When Ralph was diagnosed with Enteric Fever, he says that he also was evacuated "down through No 2 Outpost." No 2 Outpost was just south of Chailak Dere. (Butler, (1933) Volume 1, Map 11, P. 306; Bean CEW (1924) Vol II, P. 448).*

Finally, there are numerous photographs available at the Australian War Memorial, (some available on line at http//cas.awm.gov.au.), which depict the 7th Field Ambulance at Chailak Dere. If, for example, you input and search Chailak Dere, you will find many photos of the 7th Australian Field Ambulance at Chailak Dere (mostly A Section). You will notice in some of these photos the impossible terrain in the higher areas of Chailak Dere, and which is near where Ralph was likely to have camped in his dugout after moving on October 5th 1915. (Ed.)

15/9/15:

We made ourselves quite comfortable in our new quarters. Alec and I are in the same dugout. We find cooking for ourselves a very interesting hobby.

Ralph's notes:

"In my letters home, any descriptions of shelling of our positions had been obliterated by the censor. Many of the Turkish shells could be seen coming through the air and when they exploded 3 or 4 pieces of shell would fly around. I remember the first shell we saw. It landed about 20 yards away from where we were and hardly before the pieces of shell had reached the earth, one of the chaps was there in search of souvenirs.
We were now really in the area of fighting. It was on this second day at Gallipoli which, for the first time, I actually heard a bullet whiz past my head, dangerously close. There were notices all around the trenches and saps telling one not to loiter here, and to run there. After hearing that first bullet, and being constantly in the range of fire and hearing the artillery in action, I always ran when notices, or hearsay from the experienced, suggest that course of action."

Ralph's notes:
"We made the dugout ourselves, and we called it "Mossdera." It is named from the first syllable of Alec's family property, "Mossville," and the last syllable of the DeGaris house in Naracoorte, "Windera." Later, when Eric joined us, the name was changed to include "Netley Park," so the dugout was renamed "Mossnetdera."

The art of cooking for ourselves is one we learn quickly. The staple ration is bully beef, hard concrete-like biscuits, and the almost indigestible bully beef. Occasionally we get rashers of bacon to supplement the diet. The food is not good, but we don't complain. We make porridge from the biscuits, and occasionally make pancakes from the same source. I referred to these pancakes as "delicious" in letters home. Jam is in reasonable supply, but we are frugal with our rations. We preserve the bacon fat in the bully beef tins, and with a piece of string as a wick, make our own candles so we can write our letters at night."

Historical notes:
In fact the food supplied to the men at Gallipoli, and their general diet, was atrocious, despite the Director of Supply and Transport asserting that, "no army had ever had so good and varied a ration." (Butler, AG, (1933) Vol I, P 359, footnote 19.) The Director went on to suggest (seriously) that "the abnormal amount of jam consumed at Anzac might be the cause of the diarrhoea."

Butler, (1933) Vol. I, Chapter XVII, P 341,) describes the progressive disease debacle at Gallipoli. From P 359 onward he deals with the diet issue, and says, "Food was at its worst during the month of August. At the request of the army corps, the issue of fresh meat was stopped during the operations (during August) and was not recommenced till September 14th. For lack of labour, bread and vegetables also were seldom issued; the "rice and milk" alternative was stopped after three days."

Diet, he says, was the major cause of the prevalence of diarrhoea on Gallipoli. Disease became a major issue, and the poor diet was a major influence on the contraction and spread of disease.(Ed.)

16/9/15:

We went up and had a look at some Turkish trenches that were captured in the recent great advance and from here we got a very fine view of a good portion of the battlefield. We could see the wire entanglements in front of the Turkish trenches. Also saw Turkish shrapnel landing in amongst the dugouts in the hill behind ours. Several Tommies were wounded. The sight is a very fine one.

Historical note:
The "great advance" Ralph mentions above must have been the advances, principally made by the New Zealanders when they attacked Chanuk Bair in August, 1915. They very nearly captured the hill, which is the highest point along the Anzac Cove ridge, and to get to it, the New Zealanders advanced up the Chailak Dere valley.
Towards the end of August, Mustafa Kamal (Ataturk) led an inspired counter attack which repulsed the New Zealanders back to the top of the Chailak Dere area.(Ed.)

Ralph's notes:
"We complained of the shortage of writing paper and envelopes. We were limited in the number of letters we were allowed to send home. We were allowed two per mail, and told these must be as short as possible, otherwise the censor would destroy them. In writing on this I state it is a case of, "Choose you this day!"
The sunsets on Gallipoli were exceptionally fine and special comment is made in letters home regarding them. The battleships and hospital ships at sea just finish a glorious picture every evening. I have never seen finer sunsets than those I witnessed on the Peninsula."

17/9/15:

Another quiet day. Things got a bit lively at night. The battleships began a big bombardment at about 6.00 pm. Alec and I have our dugout quite comfortable now.

(Dugouts were just holes in the ground!! Sometimes they were quite elaborate, with sandbags and tents on the outside. However, they were uncomfortable, often vermin ridden, with rats, mice, centipedes and even snakes being a menace to the "diggers" who made them and occupied them.(Ed.))

18/9/15:

A Turkish advance was attempted at about 5.30 pm, but this was repulsed all along the line. For about half an hour bullets were flying in all directions, several landing close to our dugout. No 5 squad had orders to be prepared to be called out on duty, as we were the first squad to be called. However as there were no casualties, we were not called. The Cruisers did some big bombarding, one of which shook parts of the dugouts down by the concussion caused. Got a big budget of letters today, replying to those I sent first from Egypt.

19/9/15:

Fairly quiet today, and there was no church parade. Our big guns and battleships bombarded from about half an hour at about 6.00 pm.

20/9/15: Very quiet day today. We did not do too much. The ships started a heavy bombardment early in the evening, about 7.00 pm.

21/9/15:

Fatigue duty.

22/9/15:

Alec and I are on ration fatigue all morning. Alec and I went down to Anzac Cove in the afternoon to retrieve supplies. I am very tired tonight. Batteries were bombarding all night.

Historical note:
Fatigues are not really well described by Ralph, though he does sometimes say "ration fatigue". Stretcher bearers particularly, when not active did a lot of the fatigue work. This involved sections going

down to the beach and carrying rations, water and supplies up to the hospital stations. There was a large hospital station at Chailak Dere. (See the photos in this Chapter sourced from the AWM.) Water was in critically poor supply. They would have lumped water, in 8 gallon (30 litre) containers from the beach area up to hospital, and to their own section, about 3-4 miles. Fatigue work was rotated through the section.

23/9/15:

Although we are not sappers, we are on pick and shovel duty all day. We are cleaning trenches, and digging dugouts for others. I am tired.

24/9/15:

Today was quiet until early evening. Towards dark the Turks started to land shells dangerously close to our dugouts. I thought we would get hit. One shell landed in the centre of the dugouts occupied by a lot of Tommies, not 30 yards away from our dugouts. Two of them were wounded. This was the first piece of genuine work we have seen, although I was not personally in the stretcher party that brought in the first wounded man. Later, heavy rifle fire was commenced right along the line, and strays were flying everywhere.

Two of our Tommie friends were unfortunate to stop a couple of these bullets, and they were killed. Two Tommies dead, two Tommies injured near us today. We were on high alert, and ready to be called out. We were at the ready when the firing slackened down at about 11 pm. We were lucky not to be hit ourselves, and this action was a bit close for comfort.

25/9/15

We heard today that John Blackett was wounded last night. John is an officer in the 27th Battalion. He was involved in the ugly incident at Fremantle on board *"Geelong."* The troops detested him on the voyage over. However, in action he has become the best loved officer. We heard that there was no more highly regarded and respected officer in the 27th than John. We were dismayed to hear this.

The batteries alongside us are having a duel with the Turks' heavy guns. Shells are landing very close again.

26/9/15:

Typically, the day was quiet, and today was the quietest day we have experienced so far. There was heavy bombardment in the evening.

27/9/15:

Plenty of pick and shovel work today. Heavy rifle fire, and we can hear the bullets whizzing overhead all evening.

28/9/15:

Eric arrived back today. It was great to see him again. He had some great yarns. I am very happy to see old Eric again. The Sergeants could not get any fatigue out of us at all. Another heavy rifle fire tonight, all round. Eric makes digs with us, and shares our dugout. There is great jubilation all round. Anyone would think we had been separated for months instead of just a few days. We write letters home tonight, using our Gallipoli manufactured candles.

29/9/15.

Splendid day today. Visited the 10th.

Historical note:
The 10th Battalion were located north-west of Lone Pine, near the Pimple. (Bean, CEW, (1924) Vol. II, Map 6, P. 150.) The 10th were about 1.5 to 2 miles south from Chailak Dere. (Carlyon, (2001), P 141. (Ed.))

They were in an area heavily laced with trenches and tunnels. Saw some of the finest trenches ever made. They are really fine. There were tunnels running right through the hill into the trench on the other side of the hill. Saw Murray Fowler, Murray Batt, Charles Barclay, Bill Hoggarth, Jack Goddard, and heaps of old College friends.

Historical note:
William Murray Fowler, of Norwood, joined in June 1915, and sailed with the 10th on 23/6/15 on the "SS Borda." He rose to rank of 2nd Lieutenant. Sgt Murray Batt joined in March 1915. Sailed same date and time as Murray Fowler. I cannot find a reference to Charles Barclay, unless Charles was a nickname. There is one Barclay, Joshua Barclay, recorded as a member of 10th Battalion, and would think this is the man referred to. Lieut. Donald Chisholm, 10th Battalion, sailed in August 1915. He was originally from Broken Hill.(Ed.)

These trenches and tunnels impressed us immensely, and we thought they would be impregnable. The pick and shovel work to make these tunnels and trenches is just incredible.

On the way home we met Donald Chisholm and had a good chat. In the evening the boats bombarded the Turkish trenches and simply ploughed the dirt up from their trenches. You could see the dirt flying up everywhere.

We have problems with lice and centipedes. I was bitten a couple of times by centipedes. They probably found our dugouts warm and comfortable.

30/9/15:

On the pick and shovel in the hottest part of the day. In the evening the Turks bombarded right against this position and shells were landing extremely close, but fortunately none here were caught. We are now unprotected by the Red Cross and are now too close to the batteries to fly the Red Cross flag.

Historical note:
Ralph does not describe what he was doing on the "pick and shovel." However he did a lot of this work in Gallipoli. Pick and shovel, or sapping, was trench building. It is more likely though that he was on a sanitary detail. The stretcher-bearers were regarded as the fittest and strongest men of most units, so when they were not engaged in their ambulance duties, they were put on fatigues, assisted sappers to dig trenches, clear trenches after shelling from the Turks, excavate dugouts, and dig pits and toilets for the rest of the unit. Grave digging may also have been part of his duty.(Ed.)

1/10/15:

Quiet day, pick and shovel again. Our position, which is nearly a mile from the sea, makes it all the more welcome when we are allowed to slip down to the sea for a dip. We really appreciate a dip, because lice are already beginning to make themselves a trouble. There is a risk about it, though. The Turks can see us bathing and occasionally they fire on us. An odd casualty occurs, but still we do appreciate having a swim.

There was heavier bombardment in the evening.

Historical note:

The bathing activities on the beach were also reported in diggers diaries and letters, for example, on the 3/10/15, Captain Bill Knox noted, "....one of the RC Padres got his finish while swimming in the water, but the pleasures of a swim always seems to be worth the risk." (King, (2003) P.191). There were constant artillery bombardments by the Turks, also recorded by Captain Knox, who arrived on the Peninsula at the same time as Ralph's unit landed, in September 1915. (King, (2003) P.191, footnote 18. (Ed.))

2/10/15:

This was the most exciting evening we had spent so far on the Peninsula. We had been hard at work most of the day, on pick and shovel work again. Our position was shelled with high explosives and for an hour things were a little too warm. Several chaps had their dugouts simply ruined and two Turkish shells cut their way through the hospital tents. We were all crouched low in our dugouts. Luckily, no-one was hurt.

3/10/15:

Most of the chaps are very busy reconstructing dugouts. Ours was uninjured. We were heavily shelled again tonight. The place is getting pretty hot. The other side of the hill was shelled heavily, and many dugouts we had helped dig today were ruined. Fortunately no-one was injured. Alec had a shell land quite close to him today, and it scared the daylights out of him.

4/10/15:

Rather lively again this morning with shells landing all around us. One landed just alongside the hospital and kills one of the inmates and wounded another. The members of the section are still with the same luck and none get hurt at all. It was the first real actual experience of concentrated shell fire just at our position, and it is frightening.

We have orders to move our position. With the heating up of the shelling, we are happy to be moving tomorrow. We all have to load our packs and leave the old "Mossnetdera" dugout!

5/10/15:

We are shifting to our new position today. Before leaving our old position, we were heavily shelled, but again our luck was prominent. I was in the advance party to our new quarters, and as there was plenty of work to be done. We pick and shoveled a new dugout which needed to be constructed. I can show many blisters for my efforts. Our new home is much closer to the trenches, practically just behind them. When the miles were being loaded at the old place this evening, a high explosive shell landed and landed right in the centre of the remainder of the section who were loading the mules, but again luck was with them and none of them or the mules were hurt. Alec and Eric were in the party left behind. The other chaps returned late this evening and told us of their narrow escape. One shell landed in the door of one of the dugouts, and fortunately the occupants escaped unhurt.

Historical note:
Ralph does not mention it, but there were violent storms and heavy rains at Gallipoli in early October 1915. Charles Bean had a dugout near the beach in Shrapnel Gully. Others recorded that, "....as winter rains undermined his accommodation, Charles Bean (war correspondent) had his dugout moved and rebuilt because where it was it stopped a drain of water..." (King, (2003) Pp.191-193). It must have been terribly uncomfortable with additional burden of storm water in the dugouts.
Bean describes violent storms in early October, culminating in a storm from the south-west so strong that the seas washed over the piers in Anzac Cove. There was severe damage to lighters moored at

the piers at Anzac Cove, and Watson's pier. Watson's pier was badly damaged, with thirty feet of pier being ripped out, and water pipes which carried water to shore being torn away and rendered unusable. This severely affected the water supply to the peninsula, as it was temporarily cut off. (Bean, CEW,(1924) Vol II, P. 836.)
I reckon that due to these early October storms Ralph and his section moved up higher in the Chailak Dere valley, and more towards the Casualty Clearing Station near the Table Top. They used mules to help them, which means they had steep climbs to negotiate. The front line between the Turks and ANZAC forces was at the top of Chailak Dere, just 100 metres or so below Chunuk Bair (the highest hill on the ANZAC front.) The NZ forces nearly captured Chunk Bair, and were repulsed back towards the top of Chailak Dere by Mohamed Kemal (later Ataturk, the first President of Turkey). As the crow flies, this position is just over a mile from the sea. (Ed.)

Ralph's notes:
"News on other fronts drifted through to our lines. In letters home I speak of success in France which we have heard about. Later we realize that very often all the war news we heard at the front was mutilated and distorted, and that we rarely heard bad news."

6/10/15:

We spent most of the day establishing and consolidating our new position. We had a wild night last night, and stray bullets were whizzing overhead all night, but none of us stopped any. Three of a fatigue party (Infantrymen) who were working with us here were wounded by the first shell to come into our camp. I have felt pretty off-colour today.

7/10/15:

Alec, Eric and I had been sleeping in the open last night. We were nearby our "home", just outside the dugout. The night before, Eric and I had been sharing blankets, and I had been bitten by a centipede again. I was woken by Eric complaining that he had been bitten by a centipede. We pulled the blanket down to get the centipede, and on inspection found that he had been hit by a bullet just above the knee, the bullet remaining in the leg. It was about 4 am this morning when he was hit. We took him to the dressing station immediately, and the Major dressed the wound, which he said was not serious. We were told to take him straight down to the beach, and arrange for him to be evacuated on one of the hospital ships.

Eric was very sorry to leave us and we will miss him beyond words. He was wonderful. Alec and I and the two other fellows took him down to the beach which is about a mile from here. We left him at the beach, and believe he will go off to Egypt or Malta.

I was feeling crook all the way going down, and coming back from the beach. I stayed in the dugout, and felt crook all the rest of the day.

8/10/15:

Reported sick and went to A Section Hospital, as ours is not finished yet. Alec is awfully good to me and took the place of one of Section B's men to help lug me to the station.

Historical note:
Ralph does not record the weather that day. But Bean noted that on the 8/10/15 there was a serious storm (Bean, Vol II P 836.) Captain Knox noted the same thing, "..a heavy storm tonight-the heaviest weather since we reached the Peninsula." (King, (2003) P.194.)
So Alec probably lugged Ralph to the hospital through dreadful weather, howling winds, water and mud. (Ed.)

9/10/15;

I am down at the hospital near the beach. I am not at all well. I fear I will be evacuated, which means leaving this place. Alec will be left here by himself.

10/10/15:

I am in the hospital, and not feeling too good. Looks like fever of some sort. There is a lot of illness around at present, and I have been unlucky enough to get a dose. Alec was over to see me each day.

Historical note:
Ralph was one of thousands of sick evacuated from Gallipoli at this time. Butler, (1933) Vol I, Chapter 341, Pp. 341-373, describes what he calls, "The Disease Debacle at Gallipoli." As a result of poor hygiene, fly-borne disease, poor quality food, fatigue amongst long serving troops, illness was just another tragedy. The numbers are staggering. In August 1915, 12,968 sick were evacuated, in September 1915, 22,209 and October 1915, 21,991, so a total of 57,168 sick alone were evacuated in three months. In the same period, 36,844 wounded were evacuated. (Butler, AG, (1933) Vol. I, (see table set out at P. 375.)) (Ed.)

11/10/15:

It was ordered I would evacuate today. I have been diagnosed with a form of enteric fever. Alec came down to see me off. He is now by himself on the Peninsula.

Ralph's notes:
"At the spot on Gallipoli where we stayed for a time, and the very spot where Eric was wounded all of us, or at least a big percentage of our unit contracted a type of enteric fever. It afterwards transpired that this spot was an old Turkish burial ground where the dead had not been buried at a very great depth. With many others I contracted this malady and was admitted to Hospital on the Peninsula for a few days, but fighting the disease there was useless. My temperature

would not come down, and I was feeling sick enough, so I was evacuated, my card recording "enteric fever."
We are loaded onto the small lighters and transported out to the larger ships off shore. I expect I will go to Lemnos. I am very sorry to leave but hope to be back shortly. I came down to No 2 Outpost, and from there was taken out to a hospital ship at about 10 pm.
As we leave, I am sad to leave my mates.
Later, I reflected that "Gallipoli was never re-enacted as far as I was concerned. It was separate entirely from any other experience. We were new. It was our "war honeymoon" and probably that had something to do with it. Nevertheless, we never again saw that magnificent comradeship that existed on the Peninsula. We forged the closest friendships, and our "cobbers" were "cobbers" for life. It was a unique experience.
Lime juice was more in evidence as an issue than Rum. I cannot recall an issue of lime juice anywhere else. When we pulled out of Anzac Cove, I expected to be back at Gallipoli in a week or two.
Little did I know then as I looked back and had my last glimpse of the Cove that this was the last time I would ever see the Peninsula."

Gallipoli, 1915:
Anzac Cove, September 1915. Ralph refers to the build up of supplies on the shore and the dugouts on the hillside. This is the sight which would have been Ralph's first glimpse of Gallipoli. The barges at the pier acted as ferries in and out of the landing area at Anzac cove. *Photo; AWM.*

Gallipoli, 1915:
The dugouts, and marquees of the 7th Field Ambulance at Chailak Dere. This was the ADS. The stretcher bearers lived in the dugouts in the hills, behind the front line. *Photo; AWM.*

Gallipoli, 1915:
Group of 7th Ambulance diggers receiving a mail packet. The boys were keen for news from home. Hood, Hopkins, Frahm, Williams, Holder & Nicholls are identified in this picture. *Photo; AWM.*

7th Field Ambulance, "C" Section. Chailak Dere, Gallipoli, 1915. The Casualty Clearing Station. *Photo AWM.*

Gallipoli, 1915.
7th Field Ambulance Stretcher bearers carrying a wounded man down Chailak Dere to the Field hospital at the beach. *Photo; AWM.*

Gallipoli, 1915. 7th Field Ambulance, 1915
Working in Mule Gully, near Chailak Dere. *Photo; AWM.*

Gallipoli, 1915: Dugouts and tents of the 7th Field Ambulance at Chailak Dere, Ralph's home in September/October, 1915. *Photo; AWM.*

Alec Blackwell, 1915.

Chapter Five:
Recuperation on Malta:

The Diary:
12/10/15

After evacuation from Anzac Cove, we sailed to Lemnos. Our hospital ship arrived in Lemnos this morning, but much to my disappointment, and although I persistently asked the powers that be to let us off here, I was refused permission.

Roy Bice, another B section man, is down with the same thing and is alongside me.

(Sgt G.R. "Roy" Bice was killed in action in France on 29/10/17.(Ed))

We now hope to get to Alexandria as we think we may be able to get back to Gallipoli from there. We remained all day in port, on the Hospital Ship.

13/10/15:

Disappointment today increased when we were told that we are going to Malta. We reckon there will be little hope of getting back from there for a good time. We also reckon it will be ages before we get any letters. We sailed today for Malta. The hospital ship that brought us to Malta was the *"Formosa."*

14/10/15:

One poor chap died in this ward today. The RC Chaplain has gone right through the ward asking all our religions. There was also a chaplain who went through all the patients before they went out of the hospital at No. 2 Outpost.

15/10/15:

We disembarked today in Malta, in Valetta harbour, and I was separated from Roy Bice. I was moved into another transport, a hospital truck, not really an ambulance as such, and I was taken for a long run in Malta. Eventually, I was moved in to the St Davids Hospital, in Valletta, run mainly by Tommies.

16/10/15:

I asked the staff about getting back to the Peninsula. The Doctor said there was no trouble about that. He did not know what he had struck when he found one so anxious to get back to the Peninsula. There are practically all Tommies in this Hospital. I wrote two letters to Australia today, and one to Alec as well. I am the only Australian in this ward. All the sisters are English, and a fine bunch of ladies they are. It had been raining today, all day.

17/10/15:

The Medical Officer marked me down to return by the next boat, but I hear that we must go to Alexandria first so I suppose that will mean delay. Most of the chaps got a mail today, and I can tell you I wished for mine, but there was none there for me.

18/10/15:

Still in this beastly hospital. No word yet when my boat leaves, and I hope it will be soon. The food we get here is awful; I used to get better on the Peninsula. I am bored, and miss my mates.

19/10/15:

Slow days. I am feeling much better, in fact I feel splendid. I am very anxious to get back. I am also longing for my mail. There is a concert down here tonight, but a chap does not feel much like going without a cobber.

20/10/15:

Today is pay day. Because we are in an English hospital, we only get the English soldiers pay of 2/- per week. 2/- per weekly pay is not much, really, but we have no choice. The M.O. is a jolly fine fellow, although the Tommies are treating him as some very austere fellow. He seems to have taken a liking to me as soon as I asked him when I could get back to the Peninsula. Today he asked me to come over to his tent, and he gave me a novel and some late papers to read. He also gave me a nice lot of chocolates. He came into the ward later and said goodbye to me, as he was being relieved. I gave him my name and address and he said that if ever he came to Australia he would look me up. I am very sorry he is going.

21/10/15:

New M.O. on duty today. I am feeling splendid. A lady from the town brought down a big bag of Australian papers sent out by the Australian public, for distribution to the Aussies. One paper I got had Mrs Kirsby's name on it and her address, Geelong. Got a few bulletins and have spent a good day.

22/10/15:

I spent the morning reading the papers I got yesterday. A chap could enjoy himself if he had a bit of money. I would love to buy some silk and send home, but that is out of the question at 2/- per week. To pass the time and help the hospital, I was engaged whitewashing the stone fence surrounding the place.

23/10/15:

Wrote to Coggeshall people today, and wrote a rather long letter. Went into town this evening for a large concert in the big tent set up there. It was great.

Historical note:
"Coggeshall" at Sandringham, Victoria was the home of EC DeGaris, and family. Mary DeGaris gave the Army her calling card when she arrived in UK in 1916, when she inquired about her fiancé, Colin Thomson.
Ralph wrote regularly to his Uncle, and his cousin Mary, and he received letters, books, parcels and money from "Uncle Clem," Mary's father. (Ed.)

24/10/15:

It has been a beautiful day today. Went to church, and it was a good service. Met Sister Hobbs. She was a lady of about 55, and she was an exceptionally fine woman. She took a special interest in me, I expect because I am an Australian. She wrote letters to my Mother, and they evidently kept up a correspondence after this. She is a fine lady.

Ralph's notes:
Ralph, writing about Sister Hobbs, says;
"She never lived to see Australia again. She was invalided to Australia a few years later, (1918) but passed to that great beyond when a few days out of Australian waters."
Historical note:
Sister Hobbs wrote to Ralph and often visited him in Malta after he left St David's Hospital, and was in St Andrews. She also

corresponded with Ralph's mother. (see the letter transcribe at P.64.) She must have been very fond of Ralph.] (Ed.)

25/10/15:

Cabled home today and had the cost deducted from my pay book. They would not allow me to cable for cash. I feel better, and feel that I am putting on weight again.

26/10/15:

There is talk of this hospital shipping out to Serbia.

(Ironically, Serbia is where Dr Mary DeGaris (of "Coggeshall" Sandringham mentioned above)ran a Scottish Women's Field Hospital near the front from July 1917.)(Ed.)

I am beginning to get into the run of things here. The Orderly is taking the Tommies and me up to Valletta tomorrow. It is jolly good of him as he knows that we have no cash.

I am told tonight to get ready to go first thing tomorrow morning, as I may be called at anytime to leave Malta and head back to the Peninsula. That is the first step in the right direction.

27/10/15:

Today I prepared for departure, and could not go to Valletta as arranged, but as it turned out, they did not go to Valletta anyway. I am "standing to" for the day. Got another 2/- pay today.

28/10/15 to 30/10/15:

No further word about leaving. As the Orderly was ill, I took his place and did his duties. It helped to pass the time.

Rained heavily on 29th, and I continued to help around the Hospital, as the orderly is still off on sick leave.

The Orderly, Bob Tunstall, returned to work today, 30/10.15. It was a quiet day, and I am still standing by awaiting orders to disembark. There was a concert in the tent tonight.

31/10/15:

Bob Tunstall and I are arranging to go into Sliema and Valletta tomorrow. I am feeling a bit off colour tonight.

1/11/15:

The trip to Valletta finally takes place. We had a good time in both places. Valletta is a rather decent place. The customs here are quaint, especially the milk delivery system. Mobs of goats are taken around the town. Customers bring out their jugs and approach the milk-maid in charge of the herd. The goat is milked direct into the jug and when that customer is supplied, the mob passes on to the next customer. It is economy to the highest degree, saves on carts and guarantees no dilution. The goats know the round as well as the man, or maid, in charge of the herd.

Tonight, I am still feeling a bit off colour, and may have to report ill tomorrow.

2/11/15:

My temperature is up. M.O. reckons that I lived too high yesterday in Valletta. I am not feeling well. It feels like the enteric fever has returned, but I convince myself that I just ate too much tea the night before.

3/11/15:

I am much better this morning. However, I am warned I am to go into the convalescent camp tonight. I am disappointed as I thought I was going straight back to Gallipoli, but the M.O. says we won't be in the convalescent camp for too long. The convalescent camp is "All Saints," and is alongside the St David's hospital. I am impatient, and not happy about being here at all.

Historical note;
All Saints Camp was a convalescent camp next to St David's Hospital in Valletta. The hospital itself was only used by the most needy patients. All others were shipped to the convalescent camps adjacent to the hospitals. All the hospitals had "tent cities" next to them. When you realise the numbers of ill and wounded going through Malta, you realise that extra tent accommodation would have been essential.
Records show that 2,500 officers and 54,500 troops were treated at Malta during the Gallipoli campaign alone. That is just in the 8 month period from April 1915 to December 1915. (Savona-Ventura, (2005) para. 14.) (Ed.)

4/11/15:

Last night was the worst night I have ever spent. I was eaten alive by fleas. I caught, I think, hundreds of them, but still was literally eaten alive by them. I was so disgusted I washed all my bedding, blankets, sheets pillows, etc in strong disinfectant. I did such a good job it did not dry properly. I had to go to St David's to see if I could get a bed for the night. I decided to go back to All Saints camp as soon as possible. It was the best way to get out of the place and back to the Peninsula.

5/11/15:

Guy Fawkes day today, and it passed uncelebrated. Got a rather decent pay today, £1.1.0. Apparently they give you double pay the first week, and as I was now out of St David's, my pay increased again to Australian pay.

6/11/15:

Bub Tunstall and I went into Valletta again today, and I had a splendid time. I bought a bit of lace and silk, but could not afford much as I had to get my watch mended. I also went to the Wounded Soldiers Club in Valletta, and enquired about Eric, and John Blacket, in the hope they had been shipped to Malta. I was told that neither of them came to Malta. I was disappointed at learning this news. However, I did ascertain that several of our Units are here in Malta somewhere. I will endeavour to find them if I can.

(Eric Kidman was first treated in Gibraltar, then the UK, and eventually shipped back to Alexandria, Egypt where he convalesced.(Ed.))

7/11/15:

I wrote letters all day today. There are a new batch of wounded Tommies coming in to the hospital. Pretty boring day.

8/11/15:

I was told there was a chap from our Unit, Peter Fisken, down at St George's hospital. *(Cpl Peter Fisken served in the 7th Field Ambulance. (Ed.))* I went down there to catch up with him. Peter was with the old B Section until quite recently. I had a good chat and was pleased to hear that old Alec was alright. Peter told me the fever had gone pretty well through the whole mob. I was disappointed he had no mail for me. Peter had some of Roy Bice's mail, which he brought from Gallipoli, as he is somewhere on the island. He had decided that it was too risky to bring my mail with him as well, as they were not certain I was on Malta.

I was pretty glum this afternoon, mainly because of the news that there was no mail for me, and that it was still on the Peninsula.

9/11/15

Down at St. David's nearly all day. Nothing much doing.

10/11/15

Got kicked out of St David's today, and sent back to All Saint's camp, which is awful. Feeling pretty dicky all day.

11/11/15

Still feeling off colour and I am afraid of jaundice.

12/11/15

Not feeling well at all. The sickness seems to have returned with a vengeance. The quack told me I had severe indigestion, and gave me some stuff for it. I thought he was wrong. *(In fact Ralph suffered severe indigestion all his life. He had to sleep in beds which were "propped up" about 20 or 30 cm at the bed-head end. He also took milk of magnesia, and other anti-indigestion tablets all his life. Leo, his brother, always said it was because he was "gassed in the war," but it looks as though it may have started earlier than that!! (Ed.))*

13/11/15

We were warned today that we may be paraded for return to Gallipoli, and I knew that I was doomed to be tossed out as I was as yellow as a chow. We were all lined up for final inspection, as the boat for Gallipoli was leaving at 2.00 pm. The medical officer came along the line and simply looked at us and said to every two of three of us, "Fall out!" This meant you were rejected on medical grounds. Sure enough when he cane to me, I heard those dreaded words, "Fall out!" Candidly, I was very disappointed. Not because I was any hero, but I was genuinely anxious to be back with the boys and to get hold of my Australian mail. It was hopeless trying to put over the bluff, as I had developed jaundice. I was tossed out and sent over to St Andrew's hospital. So I packed my things and moved from All Saints, which is awful anyway. St Andrew's was a very fine place, and much more civilized than St David's and All Saints camp. I am nursed here by a Canadian sister.

Historical Note:
Sister Narrelle Hobbs wrote to Ralph's mother on the 13th November, 1915, from St David's Hospital:
"Dear Mrs DeGaris,
We have had Ralph in this Hospital for quite some time, just sick, but he is quite better now & gone across to the convalescent camp just across the road from here, & comes back to see us just whenever he can.

I thought perhaps you would like to hear from someone who had seen him quite recently, and being an Australian, the only Australian Sister in the camp, I thought I would write and tell you about him, for we are all ever so fond of him, he is a dear boy, the orderly in Ralph's tent adored him & was quite downhearted when Ralph was moved. He will be going back to the Dardenelles one day next week I believe.

Oh, Mrs DeGaris I am so proud of our boys, they are splendid, simply splendid boys, and I have never been as proud of being an Australian as I am now & the way they put up with things & bear their pains and aches, & never grumble. Its just dreadful to see the poor dears coming in from the Hospital ships, just as tired & weary, & sick that they can scarcely walk and then as soon as they begin to feel a little better they are up & doing, helping the orderlies & all sorts of things.

Being the only Australian sister in the camp-there are only five on the island-I feel like the great grandmother of all the Australian boys & they love to have one of their own womenfolk to talk to. I've at least learned more about Australia and the Australian since I came to Malta than I ever knew before & have met some of the finest men I've ever known.

With kindest regards, trusting you will forgive the liberty I have taken in writing to you,

I remain
Yours sincerely
(Sister) Narrelle Hobbes."

14/11/15 to 16/11/15:

I am confined to bed for these three days, and while I feel a little better, my colour is most peculiar. I am as yellow as a sovereign. It is slow going in bed, and I am not allowed up. On Tuesday, 16th, I was allowed up for an hour, but could only last for ¾ of that time. When I took sufficient interest in my health, I grabbed the chart, and noted that my complaint was recorded as "Cholangitis infection," which is probably a flash name for jaundice.

(Cholanagitis is a disease of the bilary tract, characterised by stomach pain, fever and jaundice. It had a high mortality rate in these pre-penicillin times. (Ed.))

17/11/15:

Sister Hobbs, the Australian sister from St. David's, found me and paid me a visit today. She spent some time with me. She also brought me a novel to read. It was good to see her.

18/11/15:

Two visitors today, one was my old orderly from St David's, Bob Tunstall. The other was a Wesleyan Chaplain. The first protestant parson I have seen since leaving Egypt, and I have in no way tried to avoid them. I let him know in no uncertain terms that there was a lack of protestant padres. All the ministers seem to be catholic priests.

19/11/15:

Got out and had a good stroll today. I am feeling much better.

20/11/15:

Very boisterous today, and I am not feeling the best again. This jaundice seems to come and go in waves. I could not even get up and go for a walk.

21/11/15:

Confined to bed all day again. I am sick of it. However, the Canadian sister brought me up a 'Tiser of the 6th October. Got some bonza news from that. Read of Ren's appointment to the Military, and that he was in the Mitcham Military Camp.

("Ren" refers to Dr. Renfrey Gershom Burnard, who was married to Ralph's sister, Selena ("Aunty Sene"). As a medical officer, Dr Ren Burnard was immediately commissioned as a Captain in the 7th Field Ambulance. He served in the Western Front.(Ed.))

22/11/15:

I am on the mend today. I was up all day, and was bucked up by a cable from home, "reply paid." The cable was sent from Naracoorte at 9.45 am, and arrived at the hospital at 8.00 am on the same day!! It raced time by 1 ¾ hours!! This was the first news from home for ages. My happiness is augmented by the news that £5.0.0 is being cabled to me. Cables to and from home became the sole source of news for me, as I did not get any of my letters from home for ages.

I am on a chicken diet. The M.O. offered me a trip to England to convalesce. I refused the offer. Looking back, I wonder how I could have been so foolish to refuse the trip, but I did, in the hope of getting back to Gallipoli and my cobbers.

23/11/15:

Got two letters today. One was from Sister Hobbs at St David's, the other from Roy Bice, who is also on the island in convalescence. I am feeling much better, and my colour has improved markedly.

24/11/15:

I sent a cable home today asking for money.

25/11/15:

Bob Tunstall, the orderly from St David's, is over again. He is a regular visitor, and I like seeing him. He keeps me up to date with things. He brought over some reading matter for me. It is getting very cold now, and winter is starting to set in.

26/11/15:

Received a cable from home, advising money had been sent. That is great news, of course! I have also had quite a long chat with the home people via the cables we have sent back and forth.

27/11/15 to 5/12/15:

I am up and getting about OK now. I am helping the nursing staff, as they are very shorthanded. All the hospitals and the convalescent camps are full, mainly with sick and wounded from Gallipoli. The worst cases are in the main hospitals in Valletta.

I help the nurses taking temperatures, and recording them. Most of the boys here are down with fevers and jaundice type conditions similar to mine.

I help around the wards for the next week, and really don't see too many people except those in the wards. The nurses are wonderful dedicated people.

6/12/15:

Got cable from home today which told me of Alec's illness. They told me that Alec had been evacuated to Alexandria. Cabled to the address given in the cable, and then I wrote a long letter to Alec. At this time I assumed that Alec and Eric would still be together, but I was to learn later that our evacuations from Gallipoli had caused a considerable spread as far as our trio was concerned. Eric had in fact found his way first to Gibraltar, thence to England, a fact I did not learn for some time.

7/12/15:

No reply received from Alec. I expected him to reply to the cable. No word as to where we are going.

8/12/15:

I have heard today that all Australians were going to Egypt. This is good news. I immediately cabled the news home.

9/12/15:

Frank Blackwell called around to see me today. We had a good old chat. Going to see him the first chance I get. I weighed today. I am 11st 12 lbs, the heaviest I have ever been.

(Frank Mead Blackwell was initially with the 3rd Light Horse Regiment, "A" squadron. Like Ralph, he was awarded the MSM and was Mentioned in Dispatches. He was an Adelaide boy. I don't know if he was related in any way to Ralph's cobber, Alec Blackwell, but the embarkation records at the Australian War Museum clearly show they were not brothers.(Ed.))

10/12/15:

Going into Valletta tonight, as I am tired with being penned up.

11/12/15:

I went into Valletta last night. There were crowds of people in the town. I enjoyed myself. Met two of our nursing Sisters and after breaking the news to them that I had broken bounds, I shouted them supper. I became pretty close to one of them, Sister Addison. In fact, I became a sort of star boarder for the nurses. Sister Addison is a Scottish girl, and a real good sort.

It was the wish of every soldier on Malta to be invited into the Sister's Mess for some meals, but this was almost unheard of as English nursing sisters were officers, and not supposed to mix with any but those of Commissioned rank. Anyhow, Sister Addison and I worked out a ruse whereby I was a regular guest at the Sister's Mess for dinner at night. We advertised the fact that I was an adept hand at reading cups, and that I would be pleased to read cups at any time. The first night I was invited, I had to read the cup of the Matron, and one of the other sisters. I told them that two cups were enough for one night. Meantime, Sister Addison was to give me all the information she could concerning the Matron, and the other sister whose cup I was to read.

So I went along to the first dinner fully armed and my cup reading was acclaimed as a wonderful feat. An invitation was promptly given to me for the following night. The two who were to have their cups read the next night were selected. The following day Sister Addison did her part of the work faithfully, and so the cup reading continued with great success. From then on, my stay at St Andrew's was very happy indeed. Sister Addison really spoilt me, as did most of the other nursing staff.

This went on for the balance of my stay at St. Andrew's Hospital, and although I did not dine at the sister's mess every night, it was very frequently.

12/12/15:

Nothing doing today. I worked around the hospital.

St Andrew's is the largest hospital in Malta, and is situated about 5 miles from Valletta, and about ½ mile from the sea. The general surroundings are pretty. The seashore is all ragged rocks. On one side of us is St George Hospital, and on the other St Paul's. Further back still is my old resting place of St David's. In peace time this Hospital was a military barracks, so you will understand that it has been an easy matter to fit it up to be a first class hospital. There are 10 big blocks forming this hospital and each block is able to accommodate 112 patients. So you can see that the hospital is able to take a good number of patients. To each block there are 5 sisters, 4 nurses, as well as 4 male orderlies and 4 Maltese boys to do all the washing up etc. The nurses are Red Cross sisters who mostly have had no previous training, but have voluntarily offered to help in the hospitals. They are mostly from wealthy English families and do their job admirably. They do not hold a commissioned rank. The sisters, however, all hold commissioned rank.

We have breakfast at 7 am, Dinner at 12.45 pm, Tea at 4 pm and supper at 6.30 pm.

13/12/15:

Transferred from T block today to Gymnasisum, the place where convalescents go before leaving, so I expect to leave any day now. Hurry!

14/12/15:

Teamed up with chap named Hatch who went to Wesley College. Played football against him when Princes went to Melbourne in 1910. He is a very fine chap, and we hit it off pretty well.

(William Roy Hatch, bank clerk, joined in Melbourne and embarked for service in October 1915, on HMAT 'Nestor', and served with the 6th Field Ambulance. Like Ralph, he served in Gallipoli and France, and was awarded a Military Medal in 1917.(Ed.)

15/12/15:

Very rough day today, weather terrible. Roy Hatch and I were going into Vallettta, but have had to postpone the trip.

16/12/15:

Pretty miserable day today. We have amused ourselves by making Christmas decorations.

17/12/15:

Rather funny thing happened today. A chap who calls himself a parson, apparently he was a preacher in Victoria, or so he says, calmly returned me a 1/2d in place of a shilling I lent him!

18/12/15:

Having a rather slow time of it. However, things here are not too bad. I spent most of today at the old T Block.

19/12/15:

I cabled home wishing everyone a Merry Christmas. I received word back from Alec that he was recovering, and was quite well. Grand news.

20/12/15:

Roy Bice called to see me today, but unfortunately I was out at the time. I will go down to see him tomorrow.

21/12/15:

I went down to see Roy today. He and two other chaps of our old section have been made orderlies in the new Hospital which has just opened here. They had no choice in the matter. I went into Valletta today with Roy Hatch and Hugh Meathrell, after catching up with Roy Bice. Good word tonight to be prepared to leave for Camp tomorrow.

22/12/15:

Visited Valletta again today with Hatch and Goodfellow (college mate) and had a good time.

(Stuart Charles Goodfellow, served in the 7th Infantry Brigade. He sailed on HMAT "Geelong' 31/5/15. Goodfellow was killed in action 23/4/16 in France, and is buried at Dernancourt, France. The AWM Honour Roll has him listed as "Sturt Charles Goodfellow." (Ed.))

Hatch and I have become great friends.

All the Australians are very wild and disappointed at the way they are being treated. General discontent is felt. This has primarily resulted from being told we are to go to Ghain Tuffieha Camp. It is obviously the worst camp on Malta. It is at the western end of the island, so it is miles from anywhere. Also, we have worked hard decorating St Andrew's, and now it looks as though we will miss Xmas here. That is a real disappointment, because St Andrew's has become a real home away from home for me.

23/12/15:

We arrived at Ghain Tuffieha today at about 12 noon. We are very disappointed with the place. We are determined to leave here first thing tomorrow morning and not return until our funds run out.

24/12/15:

I broke bounds today with Roy, and we went off to Valletta. I spent most of the day in Valletta, and met Frank Blackwell there. We had a cup of tea together. We went out to St Andrew's in the evening, helped the nurses and others with the Christmas decorations and carol singing. We slept at St Andrews the night.

25/12/15:

A splendid Christmas Day, considering we were away from home. It was a most Merry Xmas, and we did well for meals, although we rested on the hospitality of other people. Ended the day with a concert, and finally a ward was turned out and we had a dance. It was quite a night. We were able to stay at St Andrews, the nurses finding us spare beds to sleep in.

26/12/15:

Went back to the "hole" at Ghain Tuffieha this morning. I expected to be brought up to the mat for breaking bounds, and staying away without leave. Nothing was said. Probably because all the Australians regularly break bounds, and go off to Valletta without leave.

27/12/15:

Very quiet. This life does not suit us at all.

28/12/15 to 30/12/15:

Nothing doing at all. It is very quiet here, and the boredom is broken by an occasional walk down along the beach.

31/12/15:

Roy and I went to St Andrew's, at the invitation of Sister Addison and the nurses. They asked us to join them welcome in the New Year there. We spent a very medium evening, but at midnight I was kept busy dodging Medical Officers! We stayed at St Andrew's that night. We welcome in the New Year. 1916.

1916:

1/1/16:

We called to see Don Thompson in Valletta, just to check on my mail. Nothing there for me. We arrived back in Ghain Tuffieha at about 8 pm. Roy and I had photos taken.

(I do not know precisely who Don Thompson was. He was not an Australian serviceman, as far as I can ascertain. It is most likely he worked at the Wounded Soldiers Club in Valletta where the mail, and other information, was disseminated to Australians. Ralph knew him quite well, so he may have also been in charge of sending receiving and delivering cables to and from Australia. (Ed.))
2/1/16:

I got a letter from Katie Blackwell today. I was puzzled to only get this letter but no others. It was addressed to St Andrew's. I was expecting more letters from home, and I am now anxious about them. From Katie's letter I learned that Eric was in England, and I began to "whip the cat" that I had not taken the opportunity to go to England when it was offered to me. Katie also told me that Roy Kidman had sailed a few days before for service abroad.

3/1/16:

Another slow day. I went down to the beach and had a swim.

4/1/16:

I got a letter today from Jean Paris. It was nice of her to write. She wished me a speedy recover from my illness.

5/1/16:

I went into Valletta to tell Don Thompson about the letter received from Naracoorte.

I also had my eyes examined by a specialist, and I am to see our MO today to get the results.

6/1/16:

MO tells me the eye specialist says my eyes are bad, and I am to wear glasses. Glasses are not procurable in Malta, so must go either to Egypt or England to get some. I suppose this means I will be going on the next boat to Egypt. Thank goodness for that!

7/1/16:

Cable home today. They say cables cost nothing and are a gift of the Australian government. We were not allowed to request money, but in my cables, I used to ask my home folk to cable again, and these requests were readily understood as a code to send more money, and they always brought back the desired reply, usually a Fiver at the Bank!

8/1/16:

We broke bounds again, and went into Valletta today. We intend to stay at St Andrew's again tonight.

9/1/16:

I was caught by the Ward Master, and he started to dress me down for "stealing" one of his beds. We would never let on that the nurses were helping us, so after a bit of coaxing, we were let off!!

We arrived back at Camp at about 6 pm.

We learned later that very few Australians were held for any length of time at that hole, Ghain Tuffieha. Roy and I used to report back every few days and the Camp officers used to be satisfied, as they knew it was no use being anything else.

I am really putting on weight, here. I am now 12 st 8 lbs.

10/1/16:

It is a slow day today. I write home, and in this letter describe Malta to the folks at home.

Ralph's notes:

I wrote home from Malta:

"Since being here I have not seen a fence of any kind, except walls of rock. From that you might think that the land is not sub-divided much, but as a matter of fact it is a very rare thing to find any piece of land more than an acre. Most holdings are about ¼ of an acre. At least I don't know whether they are holdings or not but the little patches surrounded by wall fences are mostly about ¼ acre. On these little patches green feed is grown and as you may imagine every inch of the ground is utilized to the full. For instance, there may be about a square foot of earth surrounded by solid rock, well that square foot

is always used. I have been told that this island was nothing but rock at one time but that every ship that came into the harbour had to bring a certain amount of earth and that is how they established cultivation here."

11/1/16:

Roy went out to drill today. I need not go on account of my eyes.

12/1/16:

Beautiful day. I had a good swim today. It is a bonza bathing place.

13/1/16:

Same thing again. I cannot attend drill.

14/1/16:

Very rough day. Raining and very wild. Fortunately it is also pay day.

15/1/16:

Went into Valletta to get photos today.

Ghain Tuffieha is supposed to be our home. It is situated about 10 miles from Valletta and unless you like a good walk, which occasionally we did, it would cost about 10/- to get in and out of Valletta by means of a "garry" (open cab.) So it should be readily understood that trips away from Ghan Tuffieha were really a luxury. The return was delayed as long as possible, for reasons of economy. When driving in the "garrys" the Maltese children would follow for miles doing all manner of acrobatics for the few odd coppers we would throw out to them. These young Maltese seemed to have a super abundance of energy. By contrast, the adult Maltese were the laziest people I have ever seen. The money in use in Malta was the usual English coinage, and things were generally cheap.

While in hospital at St David's, early in my stay on Malta, a Maltese lad "sold" me a coin 1/12 of a penny for sixpence, and I thought I had something to be proud of! I later found out it was a coin practically in daily use in Malta, so if that lad replaced that sixpence he got from me with 72 small copper coins and found 72 equally silly Australians, he would undoubtedly be doing a quite profitable business!

16/1/16:

Went to Church service and heard a good sermon by Presbyterian Chaplain. I found out where Mr McEarchern was living. He is a relative of the Caldwells. I met Tom Schofield today from Balmoral. He is a fine chap.

(Lieutenant Thomas Hallett Schofield, from Telangatuk East, near Hamilton, Victoria, was awarded a Military Cross for bravery in action in France. Ralph says he was very friendly with him in France. Tom Scholfield later became a Member of Federal Parliament, (MHR for Wannon, 1931-40). Malcolm Fraser was later (1955) elected member for the Wannon electorate.(Ed.))

17/1/16:

Letter writing day today. I did get a letter from Ollie Thompson.

18/1/16:

Got a cable from home telling me Ren was in Adelaide, and telling me to call at the bank. I borrowed money to go into Valletta to find that they had not received any money on my account. I called on Mr McEarchern, the relative of Caldwells. He is a jolly fine fellow.

19/1/16:

Nothing much doing. It is beautiful weather.

20/1/16:

Still no more letters from home, and no word from Alec or Eric. I went for a walk along the beach today. The rocks make a very fine sight.

21/1/16:

Another welcome pay day. I was transferred to the Active Service Camp. This is a step in the right direction, and means we are back training again, getting ready for active service. I feel fit and ready to go.

22/1/16:

Paid the usual visit to Valletta. Got the £5 which was cabled from home, and bought a pocket Kodak camera. I went out to the opening of the Hall given to the people of Malta by the Australian government. It was opened by the Governor of the island of Malta. A good concert followed the opening. The Hall is a very fine one. I returned to the camp in a motor car, which is a bit unique.

23/1/16:

I wrote letters today, although I am not getting too many, and that is very frustrating. I heard that the draft would shortly be announced for those returning to Egypt. I hope to be on the list!

24/1/16:

Warned not to leave camp today. I have had too many leaves, authorized and unauthorized, from this wretched place. However, I am hoping that it is because we are about to leave for Egypt.

25/1/16:

I loafed about the camp, waiting for the call to leave for Egypt.

26/1/16:

This was a day of great disappointment, and I have been dumpy all day. The lists came out for Egypt, and neither Roy nor I have been included. Our names are missing.

27/1/16:

Fatigue work instead of drilling today. What a drudge.

28/1/16:

No Australian goes on parade today. We are all on pick and shovel work. The time must be getting close, we are all pretty edgy.

29/1/16:

I went into Valletta again today. It rained very heavily today. I had to arrange for a stop over at St Andrew's. It was too wet to go back to camp.

30/1/16:

Arrived back in camp at 11 am. It was still raining like billio, and so it kept bucketing down. When it rains in Malta, it is really heavy, and often accompanied by ferocious winds. Tonight we were in camp for a change, and our tent went west completely. Roy and I got completely and thoroughly drenched. Such is a soldier's life. We had to bunk in with some unfortunate men who were blessed with two drowned rats!

31/1/16:

Still absolutely pouring today. Very uncomfortable, so I decided to stay in bed all day. I am pretty miserable.

1/2/16:

The camp was fairly swamped today. We got our own tent up with the help of others.

2/2/16:

It was rotten that I slept all day. Did not even get up for breakfast.

3/2/16 & 4/2/16: The same story as yesterday.

5/2/16:

The rain eventually cleared off a bit. Roy and I made a trip into town, and had a good time in Valletta.

6/2/16:

Raining again today. Australians had fatigues instead of church parade. Something is happening, I am sure.

7/2/16:

Raining slightly this morning. Cleared off a bit in the afternoon and we organized a football match. Roy and I played, and we were on the winning side.

8/2/16:

Beautiful day at last! We have been warned again not to leave camp. There is hope we are being moved on, and we are all ready for the orders to disembark.

9/2/16:

I expected we would be going today. We played another footy game, scratch match, and Hatch and I were on the same team again, but lost this game. I played pretty well.

10/2/16:

Definite orders are issued that we are to leave tomorrow. There is great excitement in the camp. While we have been expecting the orders to go, they have come very abruptly. Nevertheless, they are welcome, and we are ready to go. We spent the day in final preparations for disembarkement.

11/2/16:

Had an early breakfast, then we were entrained, after marching six miles. We boarded the *"Borneo"* at about noon. She is a small dirty tub, with only one gun astern. I don't think it would afford much defence to any attack, quite frankly. A British destroyer and French destroyer left with us as escorts. We believe we are on the way to Egypt.

Historical note:
"Borneo" was a leaky old tub. It was about ½ the size of the "Geelong." Or about 4,500 tons. It was a P&O boat, one of the many used during the war as part of the merchant marine servicing the Army for troop movements. It was eventually sold to the Japanese, and it was renamed "Harima maru".

12/2/16:

I have a beastly headache today. I think it is seasickness. The vessel is awful. I note we do not have any destroyer escorts today, and we are not sailing in a straight line. They are changing direction about every half an hour, sometimes less.

13/2/16:

I am still seasick. This boat is a small, evil smelling, slow transport. I stay on deck most of the trip to try and combat my seasickness.

14/2/16:

I feel a bit better today, but nevertheless, I am not venturing down below, for fear such a venture may aggravate my seasickness.

15/2/16:

Rumours are flying around the boat that a submarine was sighted, but we take very little notice of the rumour.

Historical note;
German U Boats regularly patrolled the area from Alexandria to Gallipoli. Submarine warfare was a new thing in World War 1, and submarines caused havoc amongst merchant navy shipping in particular. U Boat action in the Atlantic and around England is well known, but their effectiveness in the Mediterannean is not so well documented. There were two U Boat navies operating from Turkey. They were the German and the small but very efficient Austrian submarine force. The Austrians had a particularly good record with torpedoes, claiming a 75% hit rate. One German commander operating in the Mediterranean sank 23 ships in April/May 1915, and then 54 in July/August 1915. The commander, von Arnauld, only used undersea torpedoes 4 times in his career. Von Arnauld sank his shipping targets mostly with an 88mm deck gun. Von Arnauld (full name, Lothar von Arnauld de la Periere) is still credited as the most successful submariner captain of all time. (Brechtelsbauer, Chapter titled, "The Deadly Mediterannean.")(Ed.)

16/2/16:

We eventually arrived in Alexandria. My, she was a welcome sight for me! I am amazed our journey has taken 5 days, from Malta to here. I think the Romans used to sail the Mediterranean from Malta to Egypt in less time. I am going to check it one day. The trip was tedious. The boat only cruised at about 4 knots, which is ridiculous. If there had been enemy submarines in the area, they could have sunk us without any trouble at all. We were amused by the tactics adopted by the skipper. He 'zig-zagged' the boat, so she never traveled in a straight line towards Alexandria. We thought this highly amusing. It meant to us that an old, slow ship was on the sea for much longer, and therefore more likely to be a target!

Personally, I was not very interested in submarines, being such a bad sailor. The passage was rough, but the tucker was rougher. Owing to the fact that I was cashed up, I was able to use a few shillings to good advantage at the ship's cookhouse.

All up, the *'Borneo'* is a pretty poor excuse for a ship, really.

As we sail into Alexandria, I reflected that our stay on Malta was, on the whole, most enjoyable. I met some wonderfully fine people there, in the forces and in the hospitals. I will never forget the dedicated nurses, particularly Sister Hobbs and Sister Addison. They are fine people. Apart from being separated from Eric and Alec, and missing the friendship and mateship of serving together, the stay in Malta has been a really pleasant part of my life.

Chapter Six:
Egypt Revisited:

Historical note:
The Gallipoli campaign had been a military disaster. One of the most remarkable events of the campaign was the silent evacuation of ANZAC troops from the area in November/December 1915, without the loss of a single man. The brilliant logistical withdrawal was managed by the Australian, General Brudenell White. It was so brilliantly masterminded that the Turks were completely fooled, and had no idea of the operation which was under way to withdraw the ANZAC forces from Anzac Cove.

After evacuation, the troops were evacuated to Egypt to recuperate and re-group. As the sick and wounded who had been evacuated during the campaign recovered, they were shipped back to Egypt to add strength to their old Units. Fresh troops were brought in from Australia, and the difficult task of strengthening and revitalizing the ANZAC forces into front line troops for Europe and the Western Front began.

Those in Ralph's unit (such as his good mate, Jim Godfrey) who were part of the ANZAC evacuations from Gallipoli in November 1915, were already in Egypt when Ralph arrived there in February. Alec had been in the Alexandria hospital, and Eric in Gibraltar, then England.

The 7th Field Ambulance reformed in Egypt, and the Innocent Crusaders were together once again. (Ed.)

The Diary:

16/2/16:

The *"Borneo"* berthed today at Alexandria at day break. We waited on the boat all day, expecting to disembark at any minute, but finally got orders to stay on the boat all night.

17/2/16:

Broke leave, and went into Alexandria this morning. I made enquiries about mail, but could get none. We were loaded onto an open train carriage, and left about 4 pm for Cairo. We arrived in Cairo about 8 pm and were in camp by 9 pm.

18/2/16:

We shifted to Active Service camp at Ghizeh today. The place was as comfortable as camps go. We went for a short route march. When we got back, I made enquiries for the balance of the trio. I learned that Alec had been in this camp, but had rejoined the unit only two days before. The unit, we were informed, was on the Canal. The only news I could find of Eric was the he was having a hard time in England.

Historical note:
Butler, AG, (1933) Vol 1, P 481, (at footnote 13) notes, that on January 1st 1916, 23,500 Australians recovered and recovering casualties were in hospitals, or depots, in England (11,000) in Egypt (10,066), in Malta (2,273) in Mudros (135) and Gibraltar (15). All recovered casualties were shipped out to Egypt for the reforming of units, and to form the new ANZAC corps.

19/2/16:

Went to Heliopolis today. We met the Skuse boys and McPhee, and others from Naracoorte. I am making every effort to get back to my old unit, especially at this time. There is quite a bit of talk about new units being formed.

Historical Note:

There were 3 Skuse boys from Naracoorte who served in the AIF. Edward Skuse and Thomas Skuse were the brothers, and were from a farming family. They gave their mother, Lavinia Skuse, as the nearest relative. The third, Nathaniel Skuse was described as a grocer from Naracoorte. Edward served in the 27th Battalion, and Thomas in the 32 Infantry Battalion. Nathaniel was also in the 27th Battalion. I do not know who "McPhee" is. Perhaps it is Harry McPhee, from Keswick, who served in the 27th Battalion, and who possibly met the

Skuse boys on service. I can find no McPhee from Naracoorte who served in WW1. (Ed.)

20/2/16:

Had a good chat with the old boys from Gallipoli, and got a lot of news.

21/2/16:

Farce of a church service today. Too many men for one service.

21/2/16:

Pay day today, and I drew a good sub. We heard there was no chance of us getting back to our old units. We were all very disappointed.

Historical note:
Because most of the battalions had been decimated at Gallipoli, they were split and re-formed in Egypt from January to March 1916.
For example the South Australian 10th Battalion was "split" to form the 50th, and the 27th was "split" to form the 60th. The generals were working hard to "sell" the re-forming of the battalions to the diggers who had seen battle together, and were reluctant to split up from their mates. (Bean, CEW, (1929) Vol III, Pp 32-68.)
It took all the skill of the battalion commanders to accomplish the splitting of their battalions. (Kearney, R. (2005) at Pp 163-167, records the 10th battalion's reactions, and the skills of Brigadier Sinclair-MacLagan (10th) and Colonel Beevor (50th) in winning the confidence of the old 10th battalion diggers. Beevor told the new recruits joining the old 10th diggers to form the 50th that they were joining a famous battalion, and that nothing but the best men would do. (Kearney, R. (2005) P.167.) (Ed.)

22/2/16:

Alec turned up today. He came from the canal to see us and he is looking great. We had a bonza day together. We made a big gap in the sub I drew yesterday. He holds out very little hope of rejoining the unit. He told me of Katie and Bill's engagement.

(Katie Blackwell and Bill Thompson from Naracoorte. (Ed.))

23/2/16:

Went into the pictures tonight.

24/2/16;

It seems to be a soldiers' motto that while he has money he must make the most of it, and so it was with us, and consequently we went into Cairo again tonight and went to another picture palace. We learnt a good lesson at not trying flash places for tea as we were hit pretty hard.

25/2/16:

We were inspected by a General today. *(Most likely General Birdwood.(Ed.))*

It is rumoured that they are trying to arrange it that we can bet back to our own units. I hope to goodness that is true. Got a cable from home in answer to one I sent last Saturday.

Ralph's notes:
"There have been lots of rumours around that the Hun is being pretty stubborn in Europe. We are being told that after Gallipoli, we are a valuable fighting force for the King and Empire, and that our men are required in Europe. The boys who were on the Peninsula have, in some cases been pretty badly knocked around, but now they are all re-formed and ready again for action. Most of the re-formed battalions have been anxious about losing contact with their mates who they fought alongside in Gallipoli. The brass has had some trouble convincing the men to split up the old friendships, and move into reformed units. The 10th, which took a real punishing in Gallipoli, is being reformed into the 10th and the 50th. This has really caused some consternation here. Some of the old boys have almost been mutinous about it, but eventually, I think with the promise of more action in Europe, they have reluctantly accepted the situation. The new boys from back home have found it quite hard to be accepted by the old hands."

26/2/16:

Went into Cairo this afternoon. Went to No 1 hospital to call on Dave Steele, but he was not there.

(David MacDonald Steele was a doctor who served in the 16th Field Ambulance. He was a highly decorated Army doctor/soldier, having received a MC and bar, and been recommended for the DSO for outstanding gallantry at Ypres. He was from North Adelaide, and went to PAC with Ralph.(Ed.))

We met up with Alec who had heard I was in Cairo. He was based with the unit on the canal. Alec brought with him a letter from mother. The big batch of my mail had again been sent away from the unit, but luckily this one letter had been missed and Alec brought it down to me.

Ralph's notes:
"Just how long I was without mail, and the peculiarity of receiving this letter after such a long spell without news is instanced by this quotation from a letter I wrote home today after reading mother's letter;

> *"Mother made mention of a trip to Penola and on reading the letter through a third time I have come to the conclusion that I must be an uncle once again!"*

I also wrote in this letter,

> *"We are none the wiser now as to what is going to become of us, but it is fairly certain that we cannot rejoin our units. This is really most disappointing, but we must try to take all these things as they come."*

I also referred to Katie and Bill's engagement, and I express the wonder whether we will be back to the wedding, so even at this time we were evidently still half expecting an early ending to the war."

27/2/16:

Getting a bit warmer, so we walked into All Saints Church in Cairo.

28/2/16:

Ray Billo took us to the late theatre tonight, and it was very interesting. Ray is looking splendid and he showed me one of Edith's letters, which was great.

(Ralph refers to him as Ray Billo in his diary. I think it was Raymond Leslie Bills, Stockman, of Laura. He served in the 9th Light Horse Regiment.(Ed))

29/2/16:

Eric returned from England last night. I was greatly surprised to see him in camp this morning. We nearly shook each others arms off. Eric is as big as a house, and we had a great time catching up. Eric later records the meeting as me greeting him with, "Have you got any money, Kidman?" That was not true, as I was quite flush with funds at the time, and not broke! But I guess it does highlight how we relied on our pay, and how we tended to share our money if one of your mates was broke.

1/3/16: *(Ralph records this 'day' as 30th February in his diary!!)*

Eric and I have been together every minute and he has told me heaps of news. We went to Cairo tonight and went to the pictures, but really it was to have a good quiet chat.

2/3/16:

Perce Andrews took Eric and me to the theatre again tonight and we enjoyed it much more that the last time. *(Sgt. Perce Andrews was from Glenelg, and served in the 7th Field Ambulance.(Ed.))* We had supper together afterwards.

3/3/16:

Spent a hot sultry day in camp. We went up to Cairo tonight with Eric and Perce and had a flask tea. I got three more letters today, and was very excited!

One letter was from Mother, and the other was from Harry.

(Undoubtedly Harry Schinckel from Naracoorte. Harold Bismark Schinckel later joined Ralph in Europe, but did not disembark from Adelaide until December 1916. He sailed on HMAT Berrima. Harry joined the 7th Field Ambulance, by request, to be with Ralph, Eric and Alec.(Ed.))

Ralph's notes:
"I wrote home and remarked on the fact that Cairo sees to be much cleaner than before.
A paragraph from the letter gives a little idea of the sentiment of the Army at this time. I wrote;
> "You all seem to have been kept very busy. I often think that you people who are left at home have a much harder time than do we. It will be very difficult for us to settle down to our ordinary life again, but what a pleasure it will be to be once again driving the ponies around the country."

I later learnt that Mother was sending two letters a week, and addressed each differently to make more certain of my receiving at least one of them. It is these little things in life that display our true selves, not necessarily the big spectacular events."

4/3/16:

Orders are out today that we are to join our own units tomorrow or Monday. This seems too good to be true. We have been waiting for this news for ages.

Historical note:
On February 29th, General Birdwood (ANZAC Commanding Officer in Egypt) received warning that the Australian force would be required to begin to move to France. Things were going badly for the Allies in Europe, particularly in Belgium and France.

The Russians, however, had just defeated the Turks in the Battle of Erzerum, which gave the Allies badly needed respite to set free the strategic reserve in Egypt.
So all efforts were put into mobilising the I ANZAC Corp, (1st and 2nd Australian Divisions and the NZ Division) and shipping them off to France. Command of this Corp was resumed by General Birdwood. Gen Godley took command of II ANZAC Corp, which was comprised of the Australian 4th & 5th Divisions. (Butler, AG, (1933) Vol I, Chapter XXII, Pp 482-484: Bean, CEW (1929) Vol III, Pp 1-68.)(Ed.)

5/3/16:

Ray, Eric and I went into St. Andrews Church tonight. One draft has gone to join their units today and we expect to go tomorrow.

6/3/16:

We were drafted out to join our units today. We traveled to the Canal on ordinary trucks, and it was a pretty rough trip. We rejoined our unit near Moascar Camp at about 6 pm. We got a rousing reception, and all the chaps were pleased that we were back. Both Eric and I were terribly excited.

Alec was still looking well. We got a real surprise to find that Alec had turned out to be the hard case of the Unit. His star turn was running the Crown and Anchor boards, and at this he is reputed to have shown a great profit. He certainly had changed quite a lot from when we know him before. The few months of separation seemed to have made a tremendous difference.

Historical note:
After the evacuation of Gallipoli, the AIF units were in large part repatriated to Egypt, to the area around Tel-el-Kebir, Ismailia, Ferry Post (on the Suez Canal) and Moascar, a small town nearby. Anzac Corps headquarters were established under General Godley. With the evacuation of Gallipoli, the Turks were freed to attack Egypt, so the 1st and 2nd Divisions were used to establish a new defensive front for

Egypt, 9 miles east of the Canal. (See, eg, Bean, CEW, (1929) Vol III, Chapter 1, Pp 1-10; Butler, AG, (1933) Vol I, Pp 474-476.)
Moascar Camp, where Ralph joined his old unit, is about 50 miles from Cairo, near Ismailia and about half way between Port Said at the north of the Suez Canal, and Suez to the south.

7/3/16:

We worked at getting the camp straight today. I find it very warm here. We went for a swim, and enjoyed it immensely.

8/3/16:

I got a great back mail today and about 70 letters. I took all day to read them, but did not finish. I was on Guard duty tonight from 1 am to 3 am.

9/3/16:

There are all sorts of rumours about our early departure to service, but nothing official. Colin Thomson came down to see me today. He is now a Sergeant.

Historical note:
Sgt Colin Gordon Thomson was from Mount Stuart Station, Tibboburra, NSW. Colin was engaged to Dr. Mary Clementine DeGaris, Ralph's favourite cousin. Colin served in the 27th Infantry Battalion, an SA based battalion. He sailed to the War with Ralph, Eric and Alec on Geelong, May 1915.
Dr Mary DeGaris was a highly intelligent woman and was only the second woman to graduate from Melbourne University with an MD BS, that is a doctorate, rather than a bachelor of medicine.
When Mary was informed Colin was going to Europe with the AIF, she tried to join the Army Medical Corp, and the Australian Red Cross, as a volunteer doctor, to serve with the armed forces in Europe. They both refused to recruit a woman.
Undeterred, Mary packed her bags and went to the UK, where she worked as a medical officer at the Manor War Hospital, in Epsom,

Surrey. Mary and Ralph corresponded regularly, and saw each other on a number of occasions during the War.
The address, "Coggeshall," Sandringham is the DeGaris address in Melbourne (as it appeared on Mary's calling card,) Mary wrote the War Office to find where Colin was serving in the field.

10/3/16:

The rumours of our departure to England are very generally spoken. I think we must be going there. Headquarters called for those who could drive motors today. I reported that I could drive.

11/3/16:

Got another batch of letters today, rather late ones at that. They contained much of the news I had already read. During the day, we drilled incessantly. We must be getting ready to depart.

12/3/16:

We have been told that General Birdwood is going to inspect us today. The Advance Guard is leaving for England today. I am not quite sure about that, but I believe it is to happen today.

13/3/16:

I am on rations fatigue today. At dinner time everyone was busy at work packing up. There is a real fury of action as we ready ourselves for departure. Tents were all down by 4 pm. We marched to Moascar Railway Station at about 9 tonight and were entrained by about 11 pm. We were not told where we were going.

Historical note:
SS Minneapolis was a passenger ship of the Atlantic Line which was commissioned in 1900. Owned by American interests, she operated under the British flag.
She was commissioned as a troop transport ship during WW I.

SS Minneapolis was sunk on March 23rd 1916, off Malta after being torpedoed by the German U-Boat U35. Minneapolis was on her return voyage to Egypt from Marseilles, France, when she was sunk. It was only 3 days after carrying Ralph and his unit to France! 12 people lost their lives. She was actually quite a stately passenger ship in her day.

14/3/16:

I had a pretty rough sleep last night on the train. We awoke to find ourselves in Alexandria at about 7 am. We embarked the *TSS Minneapolis* at about 8.30 am. We loaded 2,000 troops aboard as well as horses. The ship is about 14,000 tons and has 4.7 inch guns astern. We slept on board in port, and have not been told where we are going.

15/3/16:

We left anchorage at about 7 am. It is very calm and has been all day. The food is excellent. No signs of sea-sickness for me. Most are guessing we are bound for England, but still no official word.

16/3/16:

Reg Dunn was operated on for appendicitis today. Operation was successful, and he is OK. *(Reginald Humble Salisbury Dunn was in the 7th Field Ambulance with Ralph. He died in 1953. It was amazing the number of appendicitis operations were undertaken during the War. Both Eric and Alec suffered appendicitis, and, typically, in these pre-penicillin days, spent long recuperation periods away from the front.(Ed.))*

The sea was fairly rough this afternoon, and I felt a bit queer. I saw John Blacket today and I had a short chat with him.*(Captain John Blackett (7th Infantry Brigade Headquarters) was referred to many times in Ralph's notes. Ralph first refers to him in recording the Fremantle riot incident. Ralph was fond of him, and refers to him as a great officer, well respected by the men. He was killed in action in France on July 4th, 1917.)*

17/3/16:

I wore the stem of a green match in my hat today. I was up before the Major for being absent for Parade. He told us he would let us off with a caution as it was St. Patrick's Day! We passed within sight of Malta today. I was disappointed we did not call in at Malta.

18/3/16:

We were inoculated again today. *(More than likely against Typhoid and paratyphoid by inoculation using the T.A.B. vaccine. (Butler, (1933) Vol I, Pp 487. (Ed.))*

We passed a lot of small islands this morning. John Blacket came down to see me today, and I had a good chat with him. I think he does not look as well as he might. John thinks we will disembark at Marseilles. We cruised past Sardinia tonight.

19/3/16:

We pulled into the port of Marseilles this afternoon. When nearing Marseilles, the sights are very fine. I took a snap or two of the harbour. We pulled into the wharf and off loaded all the baggage. We slept on board tonight. I lost my diary tonight, but L Hansford got it and returned it to me. We had Church parade today, but there were too many for it to do any good for comparatively few could hear anything of the service, as they were too far away.

We are the first Australian troops to land in France.

Dr Mary Clementine DeGaris. MD BS. Mary was Colin Thompson's fiancée. This is her card, presented to the Army in London, when she requested Colin's whereabouts in France.

Chapter Seven:
The First Australians in France, 1916:

The Diary:

20/3/16:

Three other transport ships drew into Marseilles harbour this morning, two of which were Tommies and the other Australian. Orders were given that cameras must be either handed in or sent to someone out of France to keep for us. We arranged to send Alec's, Captain Brownell's and mine to Irwell's today and advised same by letter. Cameras and letter were returned tonight! Capt. Brownell thinks he will keep his camera. We were marched out to camp some miles out of Marseilles. It is a very pretty camp. We tried to get into Marseilles tonight, but failed.

(There were recorded instances of "breakouts" to Marseilles by troops. It was strictly forbidden, however. (see Bean, (1929) Vol III, P 73, fn 3.) (Ed.)

21/3/16:

We were entrained at Marseilles for an unknown destination. Eight of us are in a compartment. We are the first Australian troops to arrive in France, and the locals seem very pleased to see us. It is a very pleasant ride in the French countryside.

Our reception here in France was something that can never really be forgotten. We had read of the French girls rushing and kissing the English troops on arrival early in the war, but while we did not receive such an emotional reception, we could feel that we had come to a country that was genuinely pleased to welcome us.

Ralph's notes:

"We were not long in France before our first casualty was recorded. Australian troops were not satisfied to stay in one carriage. All sorts of stunts to transfer from one carriage of the train to another were resorted to.

Of the many ways of making this transfer that was adopted by one of our "dags," Bombadier Lyons, proved the silliest, and most deadly. While the train was traveling along he would climb to the roof and run along the top until he got to the next carriage. This method was, for a time, easily the most successful way of transferring from one carriage to another. However, the passing of the train under a bridge caught him unawares, and the bridge made no mistake. Poor old "Bombadier" Lyons went west. This gruesome tragedy caused a gloom for a time, but soon everything was as is nothing had happened. As time progressed, these things were taken in the usual course of events, and quite a phrase in France was " C'est la Guerre," or "It's the War!"

We came to get used to all tragedies, failures, shortcomings and even successes being dismissed quickly with this phrase, "C'est la Guerre!""

22/3/16:

I had rather a rough sleep last night but feel pretty good today. The journey is very interesting. We are heading somewhere the other side of Paris. The countryside reminds me much of the South Coast. The French soldiers we have seen are all finely built fellows and the Englishmen seem altogether different people from those we saw in Gallipoli. Things are pretty cheap here after Egypt.

Historical note:
The comment by Ralph (that the Englishmen seem different from those in Gallipoli), is consistent with the historical record. English regular troops were all deployed in Europe. By contrast, the English troops in Gallipoli, by and large, were known as "Kitchener's Army," as they mainly consisted of volunteers, raised in the recruiting drive in the UK masterminded by Lord Kitchener. They were not regular trained soldiers. In fact they poorly trained, poorly

led, and had a reputation of running away from the front leaving the ANZACs to reclaim lost ground against the Turks, often at large cost to the ANZAC troops. In "The Anzacs," Adam-Smith records this poignantly at Pp 98-101. She quotes one of her diary sources thus, "...some of the English regiments that were sent over to reinforce the AIF had no more idea of fighting than kids a year old. Mind you, these were not the regular British Tommy, but part of Kitchener's army....." The record goes on, "...the AIF and NZ's....refused point blank to let the English relieve them in the firing line as on two other occasions where they did, the Englishmen raced them down to the bottom of the hill, as they considered the fire was too hot to hold the trenches. Of course the Australians had to turn around and drive the Turks out of the trenches again....losing a lot of men in so doing....." (Adam-Smith, (1978) P 100). Ralph's grandson, Richard DeGaris, recalled talking to an old Turkish guide on Gallipoli when he visited there. The guide told Richard that the Turks hated the English troops who were at Gallipoli, and had no respect at all for them.

23/3/16:

Spent another rough night last night, but I shan't grumble. Journey is still very interesting. There is a little snow falling today. It is the first time I have seen snow.

I got a little sleep, but was called up about 10.30 pm. It was bitterly cold and we marched through slush and mud for about 6 miles and arrived at camp at about 2.30 am.

Historical note:
The journey from Marseilles to northern France was 58 hours by train. (Bean (1929) Vol III, P 73). The advance staff of the 2nd Division reached Aire (4 miles south west of Hazebrouck) on 22/3/16, only a day prior to Ralph's Unit. (Bean, (1929) Vol III, P 76.)

As for Private Frank Lyons, (No. 3980) (mentioned by Ralph above), he is recorded as having died on 23rd March, 1916. He is buried at Melun North cemetery. His name is on the WW I Roll of Honour. He enlisted in Sydney, and served in the 7*th* Field Ambulance, until his unfortunate death. In Dunn's "Souvenir Booklet of the 7*th* Field Ambulance," Lyons is listed as "XD"- or "Killed Accidentally- 28/3/16". This date is incorrect.(Ed.)

The camp, a rest camp, was at the station at Morbecque, which is some distance out of the town. Some of us were left at the station to guard the baggage. We had to sleep in the open. It was not long before I got to sleep, however!

24/3/16:

When I awoke this morning I was covered in snow. There is snow all over the place. It is about 3 feet deep and it looks just bonza. It is the first snow I have ever seen or experienced. We had a snow fight to keep us warm. It is not half as cold as I would have expected it to be. We were taken to our billets today. We are billeted in an old school in the main street of Morbecque, a small village. We are very comfortable. I wrote to Irwells today, and asked them to send £10.00. I also asked them to cable home for me.

(Morbecque is a small village about 20 miles east of Calais, very near the France-Belgium border, and 60 miles north of Versailles. It is about 2 miles south of Hazebrouk, a larger town of about 10,000 in those days, but over 20,000 today (2007).(Ed.))

(Irwells was a club in London where Australians often stayed when on leave in UK. They also managed funds for Aussies, and managed other affairs for them.(Ed.))

Historical note:
This record in Ralph's diary accords with Bean ,(1929) Vol III, P 76, where he records;
"Lt Col Walker....was directed to the 'rest camp' at the village of Morbecque, two miles short of the country town of Hazebrouck. Leading his battalion with the 7*th* Field Company and the 7*th* Field

Ambulance following behind, Walker found his way to the place, a camp of tents kept standing to accommodate troops who were resting or at the end of a stage of their march. In this the men settled about 2 am. An hour later it began to snow. The men then possessed only one blanket each...."

25/3/16:

Captain Brownell took B Section for a route march of about 2 miles into the town of Hazebrouck, where he dismissed us for an hour. This is a fairly big town of about 10,000 inhabitants and we spent a good hour there.

(Capt (later Major) Herbert Percival Brownell was later awarded a DSO for bravery on 3rd May 1917 at Noreuil. He was listed in his award recommendation as an RMO with the 27th Battalion. He was a medical officer with the 7th Field Ambulance.(Ed.))

Alec and I went round searching to see if we could find anyone who would teach us French. We think we have struck a lady who will take us on. She lives in Morbecque.

I am remembering Grandpa DeGaris today. It is his birthday, 91 years old today. I wrote to him today, and told him I wished to be with him for his 92nd birthday next year. I told the family about the very cold weather we are having here.

26/3/16:

It is still very cold here. There is no church parade today. Alec and I went for our French lesson today. Alec picks it up quite quickly, but I think it is rather hopeless where I am concerned.

27/3/16:

We are inspected by Sir Douglas Haig today *(Also recorded by Bean, CEW (1929) Vol III, P 78.)(Ed.)*. We are still mighty cold. We had been inspected by a French general on the 21st. The 7th Field Ambulance is taking over the Hospital for the English 132nd Field Ambulance. Eric and I are sleeping together. Alec is on night duty in the hospital. Eric took all the blankets.

28/3/16:

I am mess orderly today. Went down to the town and had tea in a butchers shop. Pork chops and sausages went down very well for me.

29/3/16:

Today, we went through a gas demonstration with our helmets on. A cylinder of gas was opened in a trench and we walked up through the trench. The helmets are fearfully uncomfortable to wear, but I suppose one would get used to that. We also had a sniff of the "weeping gas" without goggles on. This made me totally blind for a time. Just the brief sniff we had made our eyes water like anything and made them smart horribly. Lt. Col. Dollman got a bit too close to the trench in which the cylinder of gas was opened and he was partially gassed. He is in our hospital now, and eventually stayed in hospital for some time recovering. It was a great discomfort for the Colonel, but of great amusement to the troops! It is bad luck when we gas one of our own Colonels!

(Lt Col Walter Dollman VD was from Adelaide. He received the "VD" or "Volunteer Decoration" which was awarded to officers with 20 years or more volunteer service in the Citizens Force. The post-nominal "VD' was eventually discontinued, for obvious reasons! In South Africa and Canada, it was renominated as the VRD.)

30/3/16:

Nothing much is doing here today. Tonight I got a photo from home of mother and the girls. It is just great. Eric and I looked at it until the lights were blown out.

31/3/16:

I was put on the water purification job today. It is supposed to be a permanent job. Weather is warming up, and it is most pleasant.

1/4/16:

April Fool's Day. Eric and I caught Alec beautifully. A scratch football match was played today. My finger was a bit sore, so I umpired. Eric was captain of the winning side, but he had his eye slightly cut in the game.

2/4/16:

I got 280 Francs today from Irwells in answer to my request I made of them. Reckon it was jolly fine of them to forward it so soon. Acknowledged receipt of the same by letter today. Church parade today, but as I am on water purification duty I cannot go. It is a most beautiful day. It is rumoured that we will be in the trenches by this day next week.

3/4/16:

Still on the same job, water purification. I packed my camera and sent it off to Irwells. I went down to the village for lunch with Eric and met a Mr. Johnson, a chaplain, who knows Ren *(Dr Ren Burnard)* well. I started to keep a record of all letters I send and receive but I don't know how long it will last. I am wondering how long it will. Another glorious day today, and the chaps have gone for a route march with full packs up.

4/4/16:

Left our Chateau today. We went on a long route march with full packs up. Billeted in a shed tonight. I am feeling a bit tired. Had a good time on the march. My feet are good after the march.

5/4/16:

I am on the water cart fatigue today. We left this morning at about 10.30 for a 6 mile march. As the day went on we found that the 6 miles was a considerably long march. We went through Steenwerke, where we thought we were going to stay and on to Bac St Maur, where we took over some hospital close to the trenches. A party had to go up to the trenches at two points to send the cases down to the hospital. Several wounded have come in already. They say that in 2 days we have marched over 20 miles, and it feels like it! We actually had marched from Morbecque to Fort Rompu. Fort Rompu was a brewery. We worked the front line at Bois Grenier from Fort Rompu.

(They were actually billetted at Fort Rompu, a brewery in, or near Bac St Maur. It is about 4 miles west from Armentieres, 4 or 5 miles south from Steenwerck, and 4 or 5 miles north west of Bois Grenier.)

6/4/16:

Alec was on night duty last night and had a very busy time. There are plenty of wounded coming in. Up through 12 today and over 40 patients have gone through our hands. I think we are the first Australian to get properly to work here. I was sent off to get water first thing this morning. I have to go into Armentieres to get it about four miles away. Armentieres is a big place and is terribly knocked about. There are places still barricaded up with sand bags and very few windows are left unbroken. Still, other than the obvious signs, and the noise of battle, you would hardly know that a war was on. Business is carried on as usual, (mostly by women) in a most unconcerned manner.

This Armentieres front was known as the Nursery of France, as things were apparently very quiet! New troops to France are sent here and to this part of the line to introduce them to conditions in France. When I returned with the water I found that Eric and others had gone up to the trenches. I don't know when they will be back.

Jim Godfrey and I took "French leave" and went half way to Armentieres and saw a vaudeville show, which was not too bad. There is a good bit of rifle and machine gun fire tonight. It reminded me of nights on the peninsula.

(Cpl Jim Godfrey was from Murray Bridge. He served in the 7th Field Ambulance, and remained a lifelong friend of Ralph's. He was a photographer, and he worked at the Murray Bridge Standard newspaper. Jim often wrote to Ralph, and constantly wrote short poetry based on his War experience. Jim was awarded a MM for bravery in action.)

7/4/16:

I went to Armentieres for a walk today. The advanced dressing station where Major Brennan was working was shelled today. As far as we know, there were no casualties. Our infantry are going into the trenches tonight. Alec, Jim Keast, Sid London and I went in to a concert tonight. It was pretty good.

(Major M.C. Brennan was a doctor, and Medical Officer with the 7th Field Ambulance. A.J. Keast, W.S. London, MSM. (Ed.))

Historical note:
"The Nursery of France" - The Armentieres Sector, 1916.
The first area in which the 2nd Division and the 7th Field Ambulance served was around Armentieres. Bois Grenier is to the south of Armentieres, and Fromelles where the first large scale Australian attack took place in July 1916, further south again. Ralph was based at Fort Rompu, a brewery in Bac St Maur, southwest of Armentieres, on the River Lys. Steenwerck, north-west of Armentieres, had a large vehicle repair shop. Estaires, Fleurbaix, and Erquingham are all referred to regularly in the diary. Significant battles occurred at Gris Pot, Bois Grenier, Frommells, Nueve Chappelle and La Bassee during the course of the War. Ypres is in Belgium, about 15-20 kms to the north of Armentieres. Artillery action from July 1916 in this sector was so intense it could be heard distinctly in Kent, Surrey and Essex and, when other sounds were hushed, in the higher parts of London.
The first Australian AIF Casualty Clearing Station was established in the College du Couer Sacre, in Estaires, south west of Armentieres. The second was established in mid June, 1916, in the open fields beside the railway station at Trois Arbes, near Steenwerk. The first ADS's (Advance Dressing Stations) were established closer to the front, one in a disused factory at Bac St Maur, and one at Fort Rompu. Bac St Maur and Fort Rompu received injured from the Bois Grenier line, and the badly injured were transported to Trois Arbes Casualty Clearing Station. (Ed.)

8/4/16

I saw Capt Brownell in Armentieres today. He is temporarily attached to the 27th Battalion.

I did not go into Armentieres for water till late this afternoon. Did particularly nothing all morning. I went out and had a bit of a feed with Alec tonight. The first Australian wounded came in tonight. He was from a Howitzer battery. I got a few Australian papers tonight. Alec got a letter from Perc Andrews. There is very heavy bombardment in the direction of Ypres tonight. Very interesting watching the British planes dodging the German shells this evening. One shell landed close to this hospital.

A severely wounded RAMC officer went through our hand today. His tunic was torn to pieces. Alec and I each got a button, which we hope to keep.

9/4/16:

Sunday, and it looks like there will be no Church parade for us. Our unit is much scattered. Did the same trip to Armentieres this morning and saw nothing of interest. As Alec is on duty in Hospital, I went down town with Sid London. We passed a very nice butcher's shop and in it was a very nice young lady. We were anxious for a good feed, so I went in to the shop, and had the cheek to ask her for some meat, and if she would cook it for us. She explained that it was not the custom to do it, but for some reason she said she would do it for us. They prepared a bonza meal and we had it served up in their dining room. The whole family made us feel quite at home. When we insisted on paying, they wouldn't hear of it.

I got my first letter from home in France today. It was from Uncle Clem.

(E.C. DeGaris. He was Lucas DeGaris' brother, and father of the famous Australian "ratbag," (so described by Dunstan, a Melbourne journalist and author) C.J. DeGaris. Dunstan devoted a chapter of his book, "Ratbags" to CJ DeGaris. Later in 1916 Clem came to live in Guernsey for nearly 2 years. Ralph visited there twice during the war. (Ed.))

10/4/16:

I do the trip to Armentieres every day unless anything out of the ordinary happens. Eric was down today and he seems to be having a great time. Another Australian wounded came in tonight, and I expect we will be getting plenty of them presently. I took Alec down to the butcher's shop with me tonight.

I forgot to say yesterday that they were anxious for us to go down there again. We had a splendid tea and stayed the whole evening. They were all very interested in Australia. We had a splendid time. I am very anxious to see how Alec records this night in his diary.

11/4/16:

It is a dull morning, and it is raining slightly. Alec is not too good today. There is a rumour afloat that all the B Section will come in tomorrow. Hope that Eric is with them. Alec and I are very anxious to see Captain Brownell, and take him off to see our French friends.

12/4/16:

Got wet this morning going into Armentieres. Alec is much better today. We went down to the butcher's shop again tonight and spent a pleasant evening beside a roaring fire. A rich old bachelor was there, and he has taken a keen interest in us, and asked us to go to his place next Sunday. He lives about a kilometre from here, and is a very jolly old chap. We are looking forward to a splendid afternoon with him.

13/14/16

It is still very wintry. I had a letter from Irwells. They had not received the acknowledgment of the 280 francs they sent me, so I wrote another letter to them. Alec was working in the hospital all day.

Some of the B Section have come back, but Eric is not in yet. Alec and I went down to our friends place this evening and had a good evening. An Australian died of wounds here today.

14/4/16:

Still wintry, but had an exceptionally easy day today. I got my pay today, although I was not really in need of it. Eric came back today, with a Charlie Chaplin moustache! Roy Honey's brother who is with the 11th Battalion was admitted to this hospital today. He is only slightly ill.

(I am not sure who "Roy Honey" was. There was no Roy Honey I can find who served in WW 1. They only person with that surname I can find who embarked about the same time as Ralph was Arthur William Honey, who was from Geelong, and who joined with the 7th Battalion, which was used as reinforcements for the 9th and 12th Battalions. He sailed from Melbourne in 29th September 1915. The DeGaris family in Geelong were quite close to Ralph's family, and it could be that Honey were known to him through that contact.(Ed.))

15/4/16:

Cold trip to Armentieres today. I got back to strike the Colonel on his inspection. He went up on condition of carts so I have been busy all the afternoon. Another Australian is in tonight. He is very seriously wounded and they say he can't possibly live.

16/4/16:

There was a Church parade today, but my daily trip to Armentieres prevented me from attending. Alec and I visited the rich old bachelor today, and had a good time. We were taken down to his place by Mme Doucourant. We spent the evening at the Doucourant's. Mrs Doucourant is expecting her husband back from the trenches any day now I am very anxious that we should go down there when he is home.

17/4/16:

Today it is raining. I got wet through going to Armentieres today. On Saturday night last, Germans dropped bombs on Steenwerck, about 4 miles from here. Little damage was done. It was a quiet day for us. We went to the Doucourant's for tea again tonight.

18/4/16:

I received 2 parcels today. One was from home and one from Miss Cameron. Alec and I went to Doucourant's and stayed until 8.00 pm. All the family is very excited about Mr Doucourant arriving that night from Bolougne on "permission" for eight days. I want Alec and I to go down for certain tomorrow night.

We had an Australian in wounded by splinters from his helmet, which evidently saved his life. Eric yarns that he was awakened this evening by rats running away with his boots! In looking through my photos today, I noticed that the one of Mother and the girls is missing. I hope to goodness that is turns up.

19/4/16:

It is a fairly wintry day. I was picked out, with Alec, for this motor drivers job. The rest of our section has gone to the dressing station. Eric has gone with the Major's party to Bois Grenier. Alec and I went to Doucourant's again tonight. We met Mr. Doucourant, and spent a good evening with the family.

20/4/16:

I am off the water cart today! I sat the test for motor driving and I think that I did alright. I was posted to a car tonight, and expect to do a trip or two tomorrow. Alec went out with the Sergeant this afternoon and he got on well with him. My hope is to get on some car. The cars we were tested on today were Talbots.

Ralph's notes:
"There were no Motor Ambulances on the Peninsula, at Gallipoli. However, they were essential in France. At first and for a long time an English Motor Ambulance column was attached to our unit, but a few of us were put on with them. In our unit, there were only three of us who had previously driven a car. We were put on with the Tommy drivers."
(NB. The 7th Field Ambulance had seen Motor Ambulances before, in Egypt. (See photos, P.44.) However, they had not used them before. Ralph had driven motor cars in the course of his father's business in Naracoorte. (Ed.)

I got a batch of old letters today. One late one was from Beryl. It was the first letter she had sent me as Mrs S N Kidman.

21/4/16:

Good Friday. It was spent rather differently than last Good Friday. It was a working day. I went for a couple of trips in one of the cars. I went down to ADMS Steenwerk with the Colonel. I could not go with Alec to Doucourant's tonight, as I was on duty with the car. No hot-cross buns for me!

22/4/16:

It is a wet day today. A couple of Generals were here having a look around the Hospital. I made a couple of trips in the car. I went to the Barrier Dressing Station tonight. Took the corporal, and one of the Tommy drivers down town for tea tonight.

(General Legge and General Walker were the Australian generals in command. However, the French General, General Joffre also inspected Australian troops in about mid April. (Bean, CEW (1929) Vol III, P. 113). Typical of the ANZAC that he could remember the rank of the officer, but the name was not important!(Ed.))

23/4/16: (Sunday):

There was no church parade. I received beautiful mail today, nearly all from Naracoorte. There were 18 letters in all.

There are plenty of aeroplanes around today. It is very interesting watching them being fired upon. I saw one British aeroplane go down, but it landed on our lines. A German one was also brought down and fell near Armentieres. Alec and I went to Doucourant's this evening. Plenty of the chaps saw us tonight, all "tres jealous!" Went to Bois Grenier tonight.

24/4/16:

Bonza weather today. Alec went through his motor driving test and passed. He went to Baillieu this afternoon and had a good time. Alec also went to Bois Grenier tonight. When I was there last night it was the first time I had heard bullets whistling around me since leaving Gallipoli.

Historical Note:
Bois Grenier was right at the front line. When Ralph talks about going the Bois Grenier, it was work, not play! (See the maps in Bean, CEW (1929) Vol III, Map 4, Pp. 104.)(Ed.)

25/4/16:

Another bonny day. Went to Croix du Bac and Erquinghem in the car and had a good time. Went to Bois Grenier tonight. Things are fairly quiet. Eric returned tonight.

26/4/16:

Another simply bonny day. The weather seems to be taking up now. The cars we have been driving with are leaving today and we have another convoy here now, consisting of 5 Daimlers and 2 Fords. These have two Tommy drivers each so we don't know what is going to happen. Alec has gone out in one of the Daimlers to Streaky Bacon near Bois Grenier. I expect Alec will be away for a week.

Eric and I went for a walk this evening. There is very heavy bombardment going on tonight.

Historical note:
Barlette Farm, was near Fleurbaix, south of Armentieres, and just west of Bois Grenier, (see map P. 91) was heavily shelled by the Germans on this evening, (Bean, (1929) Vol III, P. 139). It was about 2-3 miles from Bac St Maur where Ralph was billeted.

27/4/16:

Another rather hot day. I spent a very lazy day since the new convoy has arrived. We have not been allotted to any car. We had a good few wounded cases in today but mostly of our own doing. An Officer in bomb school not far from here was showing the men what not to do when he did it, and the bomb exploded, killing himself, and seriously wounding others around him. Perhaps it was a godsend to him that he was killed. Erquinhem is about 2 miles from here on the main road to Armentieres. *(Erquinghem is about half way between Bac St Maur and Armentieres. So I am sure Ralph was billeted at Bac St Maur at this time.(Ed.))*

The 6th Field Ambulance is there and were shelled today. They were having to send their cases to us. The casualties caused by the shelling of Erquinhem today were one Australian killed, 4 civilian children killed and three wounded. Alec was in today from Streaky Bacon, and he is having a grand time out there. There was supposed to have been a slight gas attack last night, but we felt nothing of it. Several civilians felt it here. We went down to Ducourant's tonight. Eric would not come down with me. Heard today that Captain Brownell was going to be attached permanently to the 27th Battalion. I hope to goodness that is not true.

Our chaps are making the best of the opportunities of the brewery here, and today a good many were a long way gone. We have now over twelve months service to our names, so we are getting to be quite old warriors. Things are rather quiet tonight. There is only medium rifle and machine gun fire.

28/4/16:

Last night at about 11.30 pm we were all awakened by the gas alarm. In two shakes we all had our helmets over our heads and we did look weird sights! We had only had the helmets on a few minutes when we heard there was no need for immediate alarm. A very heavy fire commenced. It was easily the heaviest we have yet had. We all had orders to get dressed but we did no have to stay up long as things eased up in an hour or two.

All sorts of rumours are afloat as to what was really doing last night. We have heard nothing upon which we can rely.

We have had another lazy day today, so I wrote a few letters. Eric and I went down to the YMCA tonight and had a good evening playing draughts. Sgt. Major Croft was promoted to Warrant Officer today and has got the other Sergeants well drunk tonight on the strength of it. Leave to England has started and one from this unit is to go every third day. Alec has not been in today.

29/4/16:

Another warm day and speaking generally a quiet one. A nice little mail today was very welcome. Alec came in today and I had a good chat with him. He is having a splendid time. I bought a few luxuries to commemorate my 21st tomorrow. Went down to Ducourant's tonight and spent a good evening. We had tea there. English drivers have taken over our cars today, so I expect that is the end of driving the cars, as far as we are concerned.

30/4/16:

My 21st birthday today. I have spent a most pleasant day. I went to Armentieres on duty this morning and got back just in time for dinner. Eric and I had a very nice little dinner and Alec came in soon after and stopped until 8 pm. There was a Church parade this afternoon, and had a really good service. The three of us had a splendid tea and together spent a splendid day.

The spring green leaves are all coming out on the trees now and everything looks just beautiful.

Chapter Eight:
The Western Front, 1916; Armentieres, "The Nursery of France:"

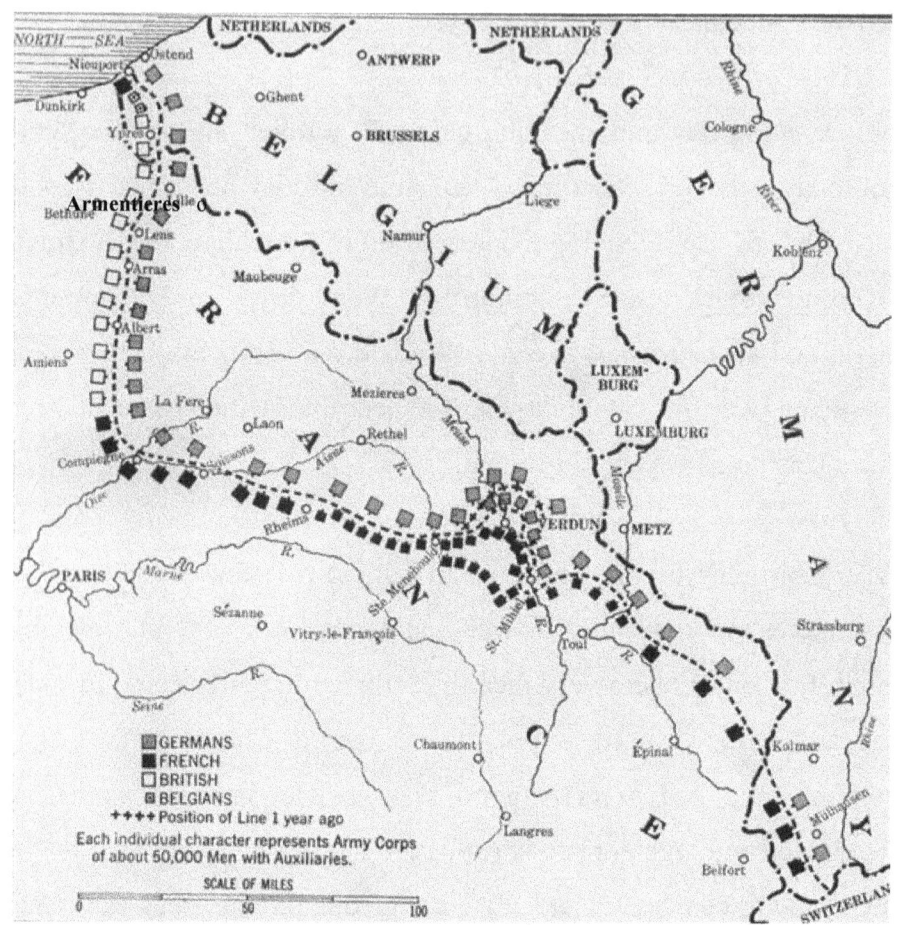

Troop positions on the Western Front, 1916.
The Australian 2nd Division was based around Armentiers, between Lille and Ypres, Belgium. They were with British troops here. This section of the line had been relatively quite in the early part of 1916. By contrast, the French had been taking a pounding around Verdun, and morale amongst French troops was low. Armentieres was regarded as a "low risk area," but that all changed as 1916 progressed. In May 1916, the artillery action increased on both sides,

due to a lifting of restrictions by the British, and the corresponding response by the Germans to the increasing Allied artillery action.

The Diary:
1/5/1916

Another beautiful day today. The Germans were bombarding the railway station just a few minutes walk from here. They have sent over quite a number of shells and have done a little damage, but only two people were wounded. Doucourant's shop got the benefit of a portion of one of the shells but only a little damage was done to their dwelling and no one was hurt. Alec came in today. He goes into the office to do clerical work for about a month. Eric and I were each allotted to a Stretcher Squad today.

2/5/1916

I am on duty in the receiving room. Jim Godfrey, who has been away with mumps returned today.

(Cpl R.J. (Jim) Godfrey, from Murray Bridge, was a close friend of Ralph's. They kept in contact all their lives. Jim won a MM in France.(Ed.))

A couple of wounded in, neither very serious. Alec is in the Orderly room doing clerical work. Capt. Brownell back today just to visit us had a nice chat with him. Generally speaking it has been a quiet day. Alec, Eric and I went down to Doucourant's tonight and spent a pleasant evening. They now have two Australian Officers staying there now who pay 40 francs per week for their cooking. The highest English Officers have ever given them is 10 francs. Heard today that they were making this place an Artillery Headquarters as well as a hospital, so I expect that means the Red Cross must come down.

3/5/1916

I went to Armentiers with water carts this morning and cleaned up the carts in the afternoon. Some nasty wounds came in today. Four chaps were caught by a bomb late tonight, all very serious. Good deal of firing by both sides.

4/5/1916

Today was rather too warm for my liking. Three of us drivers were told to go off down to the 2nd Australian Drivers Motor Transport Headquarters for another test. I think I did fairly well. The Officer who tested us was a great chap and treated us very well. Alec could not come down with us today as he was in the office. Alec and I went down to Doucourants at their invitation to us to have tea. We had a splendid tea and a good evening. The inhabitants of Bac St Maur must soon be thinking seriously of leaving this place. It is fairly quiet tonight. Saw plenty of N.Z. troops today.

Historical note:
Fort Rompu where Ralph was based at this time, was a brewery. It is near Bac St Maur, is a small village about 4 miles south west of Armentiers, on the Rivers Lys. The town was about 3 or 4 miles from the front line, and had been heavily shelled by the Germans. Within five miles of Armentiers, along the westerly flow of the River Lys lies Erquinghem, Sailly, Bac St Maur, and to the south, closer to the front line, Fleurbaix. Bois Grenier, about 2 miles east of Fleurbaix, was then right at the front line.(Ed.))

Ralph's notes:
"The motor driving tests were most amusing. The job of motor ambulance driver was naturally a job well sought after and fellows

who hardly knew the differential from the front axle put in for the job. I well remember one driver who put the car into reverse instead of first gear and backed like a shot out of a gun straight across the cook house knocking 3 dishes of stew over, much to the disgust of the hungry troops. Needless to say this man did not pass his test. The language of the cook will have to be left to your imagination. Apparently I did reasonably well in the driving tests conducted by a visiting English Officer.

My letter home on this day discloses quite a coincidence regarding this officer. When he took my name he said "DeGaris, was that your sister that was recently married?" He had evidently read of the wedding of Beryl (DeGaris) and Sydney Kidman in one of the recent Australian papers, and he told me it was in the Adelaide Advertiser."

5/5/1916

Very close heat today. I went to Armentiers this morning, and wen down as far as Erquinghem *(About 2 miles west of Armentiers, along the southern side of the River Lys.(Ed.))* We were instructed to stop for a time as Germans were shelling the road further on. One officer of 22nd Battalion had been killed on the road just before. I developed a few old films tonight. There was very heavy German bombardment tonight. Have just been fallen in and we have been warned to have Gas helmets handy tonight.

6/5/1916

Last night was easily the busiest night we have yet had. The bombardment referred to last night made a mess of our trenches and caused us many casualties.

Well over 50 wounded passed through our hands. The Germans (it appears) visited one portion of our trench but did not remain there long, although they say that the Germans took a few of our chaps prisoners. The wounded tell us that the enemy casualties must have been heavier than ours. All the casualties that passed through our hands were of the 20th Battalion. Further along the line the Germans (it is said) attacked the 28th Battalion but they were met half way and were out-matched. But as to the truth of this we do not know as the 28th Battalion casualties are going through the 6th Field Ambulance. I have been on receiving room duty today and there has been a good bit of work doing. The different reports one hears of last night's affair are very conflicting but it seems fairly evident that the whole thing was a German success. Their whole object seems to have been to capture our trench Mortars and it appears they were successful in capturing 2 of the small type but the larger one was guarded by Machine Gunners who it is said are recommended for the V.C. It is also rumored that a few of our chaps were taken prisoners but they were all wounded men. Our Artillery seems to be slow in getting into action but when they did open out it appears that they did wonderful work, and some say that the German casualties were heavier than ours. As far as we can hear there have been 30 of our chaps buried today. Wounded and nervous breakdowns as a result of last night must number about 60.

Historical note:
Bean, CEW,(1929) Vol III, P 208 noted that from the 5th May 1916, the Armentieres sector became slightly "livelier." He says the main reason was the raising of the restriction on use of artillery ammunition. The "daily allowance" was trebled.
The action Ralph records on May 5th 1916, near Armentiers, is also described in detail by Bean, CEW, (1929) Vol III, Pp. 198-205.
The 20th Battalion in fact lost 4 officers, and 91 men killed or wounded, in addition to 11 taken prisoner. This accords with Ralph's

diary records. Other units (including the 28th Battalion), lost 25 men killed or wounded.

Ralph talks of a VC being recommended, but it must have been "trench talk" as no Australian VC's were awarded for action on 5/5/1916.

7/5/1916

No church parade. It was a quiet day. Alec and I went down to Doucourants this evening and had a good time. Expect a mail but none came to light. Heard today that the wires connecting our trenches where yesterday's bombardment took place are the Artillery communication lines, which were cut, and that accounts for the Artillery's slowness in getting into action.

8/5/1916

It is B Section chaps turn for Bois Grenier this week, so that we of the B. Section who have not been chosen are in for a week's rest. We deserve it, we have been working hard.

I started the week's rest well having done nothing but read a book which came in the last Sandringham parcel. Eric and I went down to the Y.M.C.A. concert there tonight and it was not half bad. In this morning's paper, Germans claim capture of 2 trench Mortars, but the British Official Report has nothing of it.

("Coggeshall" as mentioned previously, was the mansion in Sandringham, Victoria, which EC DeGaris bought in 1909. He had moved to Melbourne leaving his dried fruit business the hands of his precocious son, CJ DeGaris. Later in 1916, EC and his wife Elizabeth moved to Guernsey to live.)

Historical note:
It was not unusual for "bad news" to be suppressed from the troops. Keeping morale high among front line troops is a major task for the

commanding officers. This German victory was important to them and their troops. It is recorded in the German records.
Bean, (1929) Vol III, P.205, Quotes the German Regimental Records from the Reichsarchiv, in which the Germans claimed, "......the left patrol captured two trench-mortars which were standing on the parados ready to fire, and had been abandoned by their crew. These were thrown over the parapet and brought back into our (German) trenches." (Ed.)

9/5/1916

Very rough day and fairly cold. Doing practically nothing all day. Finished book received from Sandringham and enjoyed every word of it. Doubtless a very solid book although I did not agree with everything in it. Found it very interesting and well worth reading. Name of the book was *"The Second Sighter's Daughter"* by G.B. Burgin. (I have just put this in because I may want to get the book on my return). Went out to the Advance Dressing Station tonight with the Adjutant, and returned at about 11 pm.

10/5/1916

For the last few nights I have been doing my best to catch the rats that carry my boots away. Needless to say all the other chaps think it a great joke and in the mornings when we inspect and find none they don't allow me to forget it. Well, last night the scene was changed and to my own, as well as others surprise, one rat was drowned in the water below. For the purpose I have stolen Grandpa's old patents. We are in hopes of increasing the number of our victims tonight.

Ralph's notes:
"At Fort Rompu we made our just acquaintances with rats – and before we left France we became quite used to them. The most objectionable behaviour was their running over us while we slept. At

Fort Rompu I experimented with a rat trap, originally made by Grandpa, with marked success. But later we took less notice of a few rats. We just learnt to live with them!"

Historical note:
Rats and vermin were a massive problem. It is wildly understated in Ralph's diary. Rats would search for food through clothing and all other parts of the soldier's kit. While the boys slept, the rats would take things, such as clothing and boots, and move them. Body lice were another massive problem for the troops.
The "rat trap" referred to was an old bucket and wood contraption which was an effective device for catching rats and mice. Anyone who knew Ralph would know that his mechanical skills were almost non-existent, so to set up such a device which actually worked would have been a surprise to all of us!!

A quiet morning, a few letters in but none for us yet. I got some parcels. Beer strike seems to have eased a little but still some of the confirmed beer drinkers are cutting their noses to spite their faces. Although only a small thing, it gives us the idea of the brains that are behind such occurrences. A chap through our hands tonight with one arm and one leg amputated.

11/5/1916

A very nice day and an exceptionally quiet one. As usual, there is nothing much to report. I heard today that Roy Koster died. He left the unit with suspected Meningitis.

(Frank Roy Koster, No 3676, of Norwood, died 24/4/1916, aged 22, and in the official record was listed as having died of "sickness." Roy was a member of the 7th Field Ambulance, and left Adelaide with Ralph's Unit.(Ed.))

A few more of our would-be motor drivers were tested today. They think that they did very well. Alec, Eric, Roy Angel and I were the

"Scabs" of a unit strike today. The Brewery Proprietors here have made a presentation to the unit of 2 barrels of good old beer per week. For some unknown reason (as far as we know, to spite the Officers) the chaps had decided not to draw their daily allowance. Mainly to show that the mob would not rule us, we went over and drew ours and we were not at all surprised to be hooted for it. Alec and I went over the Ducourants this evening and had a good time.

12/5/1916

Another quiet day. I saw a P.M. on a chap who died in the hospital last night. A chap who went into the hospital with shell shock last night later rushed out and threw himself under a car and is now in a critical condition.

Nice little mail today.

13/5/1916

The chap who threw himself under the car today died this morning. It was another quiet day. Alec and I went down to Ducourants this evening. B. Section came from the ADS. tonight and A Section went out. B Section was exceptionally rowdy.

(ADS = Advance Dressing Station. These were near the front line, and were virtually first aid hospital areas to dress wounded and have them ready for repatriation away from the front lines to the Casualty Clearing Stations in Estaires and Steenwerck.(Ed.))

14/5/1916

I am on water cart fatigue today. Went into Armentiers. There was a church parade here this afternoon by C. of E. Chaplan. The others seem to have turned us down completely. The longer one is in the Army the more evident this becomes. A very nice afternoon.

15/5/1916

I went into Armentiers this morning. Then I went to Bailleul this afternoon in a car. It is a nice place fairly large. We had a good tea here tonight. I bought three small peaches for one franc each (10d). The Officers whose quarters are just below ours are very happy tonight. The Colonel goes on his leave tomorrow night; expect this is a kind of final flutter for him.

16/5/1916

The Officers happiness did not subside until the early hours of the morning. The Colonel has gone on his leave tonight. I have done practically nothing all day. Alec is out of the office and went up for his Motor driving test today.

17/5/1916

No exception to other days with regard to work done. I had a couple of trips out in the Ambulance. I also got a nice mail today and one parcel from Beryl. I also got heaps of old mail.

Historical note:
The Motor Ambulances were run by the Motor Tranport Divisions in the British Army, not the Field Ambulance Corp. As this same system was adopted by the ANZAC Corps, Ralph was attached to the 2nd Motor Transport Division while he drove Ambulances with the 7th Field Ambulance.
Ralph's record with Australian War Museum shows he served with the 2nd Motor Transport Division, but his primary Unit was the 7th Field Ambulance, and he was seconded, if you like, to the Motor Transport Division in order to preserve the British way of Army personell management.
Ralph was also deployed to drive Officers from headquarters to battlegrounds, (he usually refers to this work as "on the cars") and also other general driving, ie delivering medical supplies and drugs to the Casualty Clearing Stations, and Advanced Dressing Stations.

18/5/1916

I heard today that Alec had passed his driving test and was marked "good." The Major is making a splendid Officer in Command in the Colonel's absence. A fairly quiet day. There has been a slight bombardment down La Basse way tonight. *(La Bassee is about 15 miles south of Armentiers.(Ed.))*

Historical note:
On 18th May 1916, Ralph answered a letter he had recently received from his father, which evidently suggested that when Ralph returned to Australia the DeGaris Stock and Station Agency business may open a branch in Mount Gambier, with Eric and Ralph appointed to run the branch. Ralph responded;

> "Since being away my mind has been continually on the business and future work of the firm, and I don't think we can claim a grip on the South-east (which we do hold) until we have an active and live branch at the Mount. There would be needed a shrewd businessman and with a deal of experience. As far as this latter part is concerned, I cannot answer for Eric, you people will decide that. Being honest, father, I often think that I do not know as much about the management of the business as I should. The chances have been mine right through, but I have not taken them.
> There is one thing that I am determined to do when I return and that is to settle down to solid work.
> We are all tip top. The weather is just beautiful now."

When Ralph did return, a branch of the firm was established in Mount Gambier, with Ralph's eldest brother Lucas appointed as manager. Ralph established a branch in Millicent, in 1920, and Leo established a branch in Penola. Clem was appointed as the Manager of the Naracoorte branch.

19/5/1916

It was a quiet morning. I had to escort a chap back to his unit at Jesus Farm this afternoon; he was under arrest for desertion. It was about 7 mile walk. While I was away this afternoon a few shrapnel shells came over and made a few holes in our billet and a couple of holes through one of the cars.

20/5/1916

I was posted on cars again today. I gave hand in cleaning one this morning. I drove to Beoschepe about 5 miles the other side of Bailluel this afternoon, with a chap for a special hospital. *(Bailluel is about 10 miles north-east of Armentiers, and a couple of miles east of Messines. (Ed.))*

21/5/1916

On pick and shovel all day today and can show some blisters as a result. We are making an emergency dressing room and a safety trench in case of shell fire. Alec and I were told to take over driving the Daimler car at the Advanced Dressing Station (Streaky Bacon). Alec and I only expected to be on the same car for about a week. Came to Streaky Bacon tonight, and took over car. We are not allowed to shift in day time as we are too close to the trenches. All our work is to be done at night.

22/5/1916

I am writing today's diary up tonight at tea time as I am expecting to be exceptionally busy tonight. All the chaps here are standing to, and there are rumours of a German attack tonight. We are very close to Bois Grenier where Eric is. He was down to see us today. Alec and I have been working on the car all day today and have her looking fairly decent. She was passed over to us in a very poor state. Germans have been sending a few strings of sausages over to us today but none have come too close to us yet.

("Strings of sausages" – shell bombardment.(Ed.))

23/5/1916

Nothing came of all the talk of a German attack last night as we slept right through with out being disturbed. We spent a fairly busy day at working on the car. Eric was over to see us today from Bois Grenier. Did one fairly long trip tonight and the car ran very nicely.

24/5/1916

After late night I did not rise this morning till about 11 o'clock. Cleaned car up a bit but otherwise spent a very lazy day.

25/5/1916

Returned to Headquarters late tonight after having spent another rather lazy day. Out at old Streaky Bacon we have had a great time. We are doing our own cooking so naturally living pretty high.

26/5/1916

Busy day Alec and I had a good few runs for patients today. I took the Major to Eclairs this afternoon. I met the Colonel at Steenwerk Station at midnight. We also had a patient on board for D.R.S. but could not find the place.

27/5/1916:

Had a very busy time cleaning up car as place was inspected by some General today. I had a couple of runs to Jesus Farm this afternoon. I transported two serious accident cases, both shot up badly. Alec is not feeling too bright tonight.

(The General would have been either of General Gough, or General Rawlinson, both British commanders in the field.)

28/5/1916

Last night or early this morning Alec took a bad turn and so this morning he reported on medical parade, and was sent to the hospital. I have felt very doubtful about him all day. I had a fairly busy day and took the car to Estaires for inspection this morning. The officer in charge was very pleased with it. I took an officer to Bailluel this afternoon and had a splendid run. Did not feel like staying in Bailluel as I thought Alec might have to be evacuated. Alec was evacuated for appendicitis at about 7.30 this evening. I could not go to Bailluel with him as I had the ration car for Bois Grenier. Eric went.

Alec was disappointed that he had to leave and was worrying because he thought he would not be able to get back with us, but the Major very kindly gave him a special note asking the officer in charge of Alec's convalescence to send him straight back to the unit when he was well. I have been feeling wretched all the evening. I tried to write letters to Mrs. Blackwell to tell her of Alec's illness.

29/5/1916

I spent morning working on the car. This afternoon, I went down to Bailluel for drugs. I went to the hospital to enquire after Alec, but he had been evacuated to base before I got there and they could not tell me where the base was.

Ralph's notes:
"One instance occurred while we were at Fort Rompu which was most pathetic. A Pommy was admitted to our hospital and when he was told he had V.D. (venereal disease) he said it was impossible: he

was laughed at by all present; it was something we had all heard before. He was further pressed and it transpired that he was a married man who had just returned from England on leave: I firmly believe he had been home to his wife but she had not been faithful to him: and as the truth dawned on him tears rolled down that poor man's face as if he were a little child. The next day, he escaped the hospital, and was reported at the front line, where he went over the top of the trenches, charged into no man's land and was shot by a sniper."

30/5/1916

I made a trip to Boeschepe today, about 15 miles away. I took Captain Strachan and Captain Culpin, and had splendid run. The car went like a bird. I also made a trip to Bailluel. It is rather muddy and the car in a bit of a mess. I celebrated the anniversary of our leaving Australia last night. Out of 66 who left together, 27 attended.

We had a grand gathering and our thoughts were well home for the evening.

31/5/1916

The car is in a dirty state, and also has a puncture, so I spent a busy day straightening her up; only a couple of short trips.

1/6/1916

Another fairly slack day. Andy Fisher and Bill Hughes inspected the troops today, but being on the motors today, I could not be there.

(Prime Minister WM (Billy) Hughes, and the Australian High Commissioner in London, and former Prime Minister, Andrew Fisher. They inspected the troops near Fleurbaix, right on the front lines. Bean, (1929) Vol III, P 471, recounts the speech Hughes gave to the troops while standing on a wagon in an orchard.(Ed.))

1/6/1916:

One of our Observation Balloons broke away from its moorings tonight and drifted over towards the German lines. The observers got out by means of a parachute. The Germans opened fire on the balloon and after wasting a lot of ammunition, destroyed it.

One of our horses had his leg broken tonight through a kick in his leg from another horse, and of course he was shot.

Ralph's notes:
"Observation balloons come in for comment in my early letters from France. These were dotted all along the front watching the activities behind the enemy line – they were attached to a lorry by a steel cable, which on occasions broke or came adrift – in which case the balloon would go up and up until it disappeared from view. This occurred on one occasion when we were at Fort Rompu, as there is reference to it in my early letters. In these cases when the balloons were shot or shelled, or if the broke away from moorings, the observers descended by means of parachute, something I had never seen before."

2/6/1916:

At midday the Major came and told me he wanted this car for a long run today; and so he did. The Colonel and Major wanted to go to St. Omer. *(St Omer is about 10 miles west of Bailluel. A Field Hospital was established there.(Ed.))* We went via Hazebrouck and returned via Cassel and Bailluel. Drawing into Cassel was one of the prettiest sights I have ever seen. We passed an aeroplane on a lorry which, while not broken, was severely bent. Arrived back home at about 10.30pm.

3/6/1916

Today was the slackest day since being on duty with the car. The drivers dug a pit today to inspect and repair the underneath parts of the cars. I expected a mail today but none came.

4/6/1916

I have had another slack day. Our car is on duty, but no work to do. The Church parade was conducted by a Church of England Chaplain (Very High Churchman). I am getting just about tired of waiting for a Chaplain of our own denomination to come here and give us a service. It seems much to me that our church is going to the pack, but perhaps I am a little rash. Tonight I am going out on the ration car, I gave the Corporal a drive and unavoidably a drunken soldier came in contact with our mud guard. Other than the drunken soldier being very severely shaken, very little damage was done to the chap. We brought him in here and he has been admitted to the hospital.

ced*Ralph's notes:*ced

"Methodist Church parades are again in for criticism, and in a letter of early June I refer to a service conducted by a very high churchman (Church of England) and I express the opinion that I might see at least one of our own men before the war ends."

ced*Historical note:*ced
*As a devout protestant, Ralph's frustration with not seeing a
Methodist padre in the field is borne out by the statistics.
In the British Army, by 1918 there were 3,475 chaplains who had
enrolled, all volunteers, divided as follows; Church of England,
1,985;
Roman Catholic, 649;
Presbyterian, 303;
Wesleyan, 256;
Baptists Congregationalists, Methodists, 251;
Jewish, 16;
Welsh Calvinists 10;
Salvation Army, 5.*
Total: *3,475*
(Source; Bickersteth, (1995) Introduction, P xi.)

By comparison, only 386 Chaplains of all denominations served in the First AIF. No wonder Ralph complained so bitterly about the lack of spiritual support for the Anzacs.
(Source; www.members.pcug.org.au:) also see; "Statistics of the Military Effort of the British Empire During the Great War, 1914 - 1920," London, The War Office. ISBN 0 948130 14 8)

5/6/1916

I spent today over the pit with the car. I had letter from Alec, who had not been operated on when he wrote. It was just great to see his writing he seemed to be in very high spirits. The 7th Field Ambulance boys are giving a concert down at the Y.M.C.A. tonight.

6/6/1916

The concert was a great success the Colonel and the Major were down there. A wet day. Nothing doing, only a few papers arrived.

7/6/1916

Another quiet day. One of the cars fell in our newly made pit today, but no damage was done. I am on the ration car tonight. After returning from Bois Grenier, I had a trip with a patient. Got up late today and other than clean the car I have done nothing.

8/6/1916

Nothing at all doing. Driving all the more difficult with the mud.

9/6/1916

Eric had a letter from Alec today; it was written after the operation and it was a great relief to know it was over and as far as Alec knew, it was successful. Nothing in the way of trips to report. Things generally quiet along this part of the front.

10/6/1916

Nice mail in today; it was great to get word from home.

11/6/1916

No church parade today. A few more letters came in, including one from Alec. He is getting along fine, I think. Very wet day, so I had the car over the pit again.

12/6/1916

Another beastly wet day. Did Bailluel trip today and Bois Grenier tonight. Car ran nicely but the roads are in a fearful state, a terrible lot of ammunition going up tonight, which made driving all the more difficult.

13/6/1916

The car was in an awful state, mainly due to the roads being so badly bombed up, and muddy. It was our turn to go down for inspection, but after traveling 8 miles they did not even look at her.

14/6/1916

Still raining but nevertheless we spend the day cleaning the car. At 11.00 tonight all time is to be advanced 1 Hour. Perhaps we can get a drop on the Germans getting up an hour earlier. *(Daylight saving jokes in 1916! (Ed.))*

15/6/1916

Had a trip to St. Omer today with 3 Officers on board including a Colonel. Splendid run, got back at midnight. St. Omer is a very nice place.

16/6/1916

Nothing doing, feeling fairly tired today. I am the second car on duty tonight, but don't expect anything will be doing. I had a bonza letter from Alec today. I also had a photo of Mother and the girls returned to me today. Did one trip this evening to Steenwerk with the Major. He is going on leave to England tomorrow morning and I have to take him to the Steenwerk Station.

17/6/1916

Last night was one of the most exciting nights we have yet had. Soon after being in bed we heard reports very close of rifles. It seems that the Guards here had seen a man attempting to cut the wires connecting up with the Artillery Headquarters and as a result a chase ensued, and a few shots fired, but no capture was made. We had hardly settled down after that bit of excitement, when the Gas alarm went. This time the alarm was dinkum and the Gas very strong; and as a result of this there were two Ambulances told to proceed off to our Advanced Dressing Station, and our car was one. We had hardly returned from Bois Grenier when it was time to take the Major to Steenwerk, so you see we did not get much sleep. All the brass on the car that we had done looking so good was tainted by the gas. We all had our helmets on for three quarters of an hour. The horses were showing signs that the gas was slaying *(staying?)* on them. Slept a good deal of the day; did ration car tonight. I am due to do the Hospital "inspection run" tomorrow.

(There were gas alarms sounded in each village. Some were church bells, (Estaires) some were horns. In Bac St Maur, it was a steam siren. Later, the English Claxon horn was used throughout the Western Front.(Ed))

18/6/1916

It has been a very slack day. Good church service in memory of Lord Kitchener. B Section have gone out to Bois Grenier today; Eric has gone out; the Colonel and Eric at it today; Eric very annoyed.

(Lord Kitchener died when the HMS Hampshire struck a mine laid by the German U Boat, U-75, at Scapa Flow, off the Orkney Islands. He was on a secret diplomatic mission to Russia when the incident occurred.(Ed.))

19/6/1916

Heavy bombardment last night and another Gas alarm but nothing came of it. Spent day cleaning up car. Otherwise nothing doing. Had a letter from Alec who was in Scotland convalescing, and is doing well. Another "inspection run" today.

Ralph's notes:
"As had been the case before our arrival in Egypt we were subjected to quite a number of lectures during the voyage from Egypt to France. Lectures to the troops dealt with all manner of things, but especially with the question again of Venereal Disease. Health "parades" for inspection to find if any trace of this disease was showing were regularly held and today a man looks back on those 'parades' as, to say the least – most undignified. We were paraded, naked, and inspected by the medical staff. Anybody ordered to "fall out" was immediately treated as in disgrace.
In France we were told that this disease was nearly as big an enemy to our troops as was the German Army.
A man detected with the disease was questioned fully as to the source of contagion, then the unfortunate girl was located in an "inspection run" and taken to a "hospital," which was really a prison, for the duration of the war. Such was one of the main methods adopted in France to control this disease. Seldom would there be any difficulty in extracting the information from the Soldier but finding the girl was always a difficult task.
Probably a general history of an average case might be worth recording. The patient comes into our hospital with the disease; he is diagnosed, then interrogated; he discloses the place where he

contracted it: a motor Ambulance (and I often had this job) goes around to the local police station to pick up a French Gendarme to do the "inspection run." The patient is then collected, and off we all go to search for the girl from whom the disease was contracted.

Once the house is identified, the leader of the Party enters the house with the Gendarme, and one by one the girls are paraded before us. However, never in my experience was the contact girl paraded first up. At the conclusion of the first inspection, the Madame would say the girls paraded were all the girls in her place: the soldier disagrees, and a general search of the whole premises was carried out. Usually the poor girl was found hiding away in some corner weeping her very eyes out. She was then forced out into the waiting Ambulance and we carted her off to the so called hospital. In fact it was a prison term for the girl, for the remainder of the war."

20/6/1916

Practically nothing doing. Our Artillery very active tonight.

21/6/1916

Another slack day. Did ration car trip to Bois Grenier today, and saw Eric. The artillery is supposed to have caught the Germans changing over last night causing heavy casualties.

22/6/1916

Nothing to report. I had a good game of footy tonight. Germans shelling a place not far from here.

Historical note:
There was a lot of football, soccer and cricket played while the troops were on relief from the front line. Note that they played "footy" even though the Germans were shelling a place not far away. (Ed.))

23/6/1916

Been very busy on car. Heavy thunderstorms and rain tonight.

24/6/1916

Rather a slack day, more heavy Artillery fire tonight. We are expecting to be called out at anytime since these night bombardments started.

25/6/1916

No church parade. Had a trip down to Estaires today. Our artillery is going a million tonight.

26/6/1916

I was called out at 4.00 am this morning. Our chaps had raided the German trenches again. We had about 14 casualties in all, but the raid was most successful. I had the pleasant job of bringing in three wounded Square Heads in this car. They were finely built chaps and showed no signs of shortage of food and clothing. I managed to get a button off one of their tunics which I hope to keep. The German casualties were heavy last night. The remainder of the day has been quiet, except for the excitement of a lovely mail.

27/6/1916

I spent rather an exciting night last night. I was the ration car to Bois Grenier, but was detained for an hour on the road as the German Artillery fire made the roads almost impassable. After the bombarding slackened we made on for Bois Grenier.

We suffered a lot of casualties, so I was on duty all night and I am now very tired. Driving along the road the second time the Germans were shelling and on return our Artillery opened up. It was hard to say which was worse.

Ralph's notes:

"On 27th of June 1916 we had our first taste of real Artillery action on the western front – it was a great change to the activity in this respect on the Peninsula and at first we thought it was devastating and could never get worse: but it did."

28/6/1916

I went down to Estaires today for car inspection. Did the Bois Grenier run again tonight. It was very dark. Had the Colonel and a Major on board.

29/6/1916

Midday today we received orders to be ready to shift at a moments notice. I took the advance party to the Dressing Station tonight. Our Headquarters are at Bailluel and the Dressing Stations are about 12 miles away on the opposite side of Armentiers to where we have been. I returned to Fort Rompu tonight at about 10.30 pm.

(Bailluel is north of Armentiers, and closer to Messines and Ypres in Belgium.(Ed.))

30/6/1916

My car told to report to the A.D.S., and I had any amount of work. I have been going all day and night. The Artillery have been bombarding all day. It has been fairly depressing as the Germans have not replied.

1/7/1916

The German Artillery guns are having their turn today. I did not finish yesterday; it was a continuous job until 3am today. We have spent another busy day and far too exciting. The road at one turn from here to Romarin was being shelled; the road was blown about to billio; one shell was dangerously close to us when driving in Romarin. There was a big bombardment further South tonight.

(Romarin (French for "Rosemary") is a small village about 2-3 miles north of Armentiers. This bombardment is covered by Bean, ((1929) Vol III, P. 284-285 and Pp. 302-303). Germans struck back at the ANZAC troops in two places, one against the 14th Battalion, the other at the Epinette Salient, held by NZ forces.(Ed.))

2/7/1916

Only one trip last night and slack this morning. I did a couple of trips this afternoon. The Artillery here has opened up most violently. The squareheads only seem to be sending over about one shell to our 20 or so.

3/7/1916

The Artillery activity did not cease till the early hours. Had a rather exciting trip down to the batteries at 2 o'clock this morning. I did a couple of trips to Romarin this morning.

(This heavy shelling would have been at or near Bois Grenier.(Ed.))

4/7/1916

Only had one trip last night and am having a fairly slack day today. We have had one rather exciting trip, as the road was being shelled again. We arrested a Tommy chap tonight and turned him in. He is supposed to have been a spy, but have not heard result yet.

(Spying was alive and well. Local French who were German sympathisers, and defecters were caught, and sometimes shot on the spot.)

5/7/1916

One trip with two badly wounded cases last night. The arrest turned out to be a mistake and the old Tommy suspected of being a spy has returned to his lot. I did three or four trips today. Expect to go to Bailluel for a bath tomorrow as all the chaps are 'Chatty' again. We expect to come out again tonight.

Ralph's notes:
"Early in July 1916 (July 6th) we left Fort Rompu. Our stay at the Brewery (for such was Fort Rompu) had been a very happy one. An Australian unit with free access to a French Brewery should at least be happy! But at one stage when the Brewery authorities objected to the free access they introduced rationing and only, gave a barrel of "old beer" a day to the troops. A number of the unit objected, quite unreasonably, we thought, to the rationing and thus there ensued a 'beer strike' that was eventually broken by the 'workers' of the Unit, led by Eric and me, and Roy Angel. (see Diary, 11/5/16.)
Anyhow, the Armentiers front had served to introduce us to France, and quite candidly we liked the introduction. The French people were appreciated by us and we appeared to be very welcome amongst them. We were welcome in French homes and generally were treated handsomely."

6/7/1916

Did not get called out at all last night. That is a record. I left for Bailluel soon after 10 this morning. This car has been relieved from A.D.S., much to my disappointment. I am to go to Headquarters at Bailluel.

Arrived in Bailluel in time for dinner; had a couple of short runs about town. Saw old Capt. Brownell today. He paid a special visit to see me and tell me of poor old John Blacket's death. He was killed a few days ago by shell. Capt. Brownell speaks in the very highest terms of John and says he was well liked, practically adored, by all his men. His last action was wholly characteristic of him. It appears that the Officers were in the mess when the trenches were being shelled; and as was his custom John made for the trenches to be with his men. On his way there he met a man without a shell helmet on. John insisted on the man taking his own helmet and he (John) walked on in his ordinary hat. He had barely moved when the shell came that killed him. His death was instantaneous. Capt. Brownell, was the first man to arrive on the scene and from the report of the men his work was marvelous.

The shell that killed John also killed another Officer, wounded a third and killed a batman. General and sincere regret is felt on both sides. It is ironic that the men who helped in the riots in opposition to John will now sincerely mourn his loss, and agree that no better soldier was ever killed. I also heard today of the death of Perce Jackson. He had risen to be a Captain in the 28th Battalion.

Historical note:
Blacket's death is noted in the Official History. Bean, CEW, (1929) Vol III, (in footnotes at P.327), records;
   "On the afternoon of July 4 the enemy opened a hurricane bombardment on the trenches of the 27th Battalion, killing Captain J.W. Blacket (of Kent Town South Australia) Lieutenant W.W. Hosking (of Norwood, SA,) and several men." Hosking was the other officer referred to by Ralph.
Captain Percy Jackson, died 31/5/16 near Armentiers. His Roll of Honour card indicates he was born in Daylesford, Victoria, but prior to the AIF he had served in the Citizens Military Force, in the "Penola Coy." He joined the AIF in SA.

7/7/1916:

Did a few short runs around Bailleul today, and also one long one. I saw Capt. Brownell again, with the 27th Battalion. He told me of the death of George Davies. George had just returned from a raid when a shell struck him. Capt. Brownell spoke very highly of George.

(Lance Corporal George Campbell Davies, MM, Killed 29th June 1916, and buried in La Plus Douve cemetery in Belgium. Davies was from Adelaide, and was at school (PAC) with Ralph.(Ed.))

Gas Mask:
The Germans breached the Geneva Convention when they resorted to chemical warfare, unleashing mustard gas, phosgene and other deadly gases. The Allies responded, also launching gas attacks. This is a German gas mask, souvenired by Eric Kidman. The tin mask container has directions on how to use the mask, written in German. At right is Eric's hip flask, probably for rum rations.

France 1916: *7th Field Ambulance in Flanders. This is an ADS. The Stretcher-bearers and horse-drawn ambulances brought wounded from the front, and the motor ambulances took the serious cases to the Casualty Clearing Stations. (Vaulx-Bullecourt Road). Photo: AWM.*

France 1916;
The front outside Bois Grenier where 2nd Division fought. Note the two field war graves to the left of the photo. *Photo; AWM.*

France June 1st, 1916: *Australian PM, Billy Hughes, with Australian High Commissioner to the UK Andrew Fisher inspecting 1st Brigade troops on June 1st 1916. Ralph missed this parade, but recorded that the inspection took place. Photo; AWM.*

Chapter Nine:
Moving from Armentieres:
The Battle of the Somme and Pozieres:

The Diary:

8/7/1916

We heard today that we have to move, so things have been busy. Left Bailluel at 2 pm went as far as Borre where we are staying for the night. We had a look through a very nice Church tonight. The Statuary is just wonderful. There is a shell hole right in the centre of the building and has caught the pipes of the organ. Had to go back to Bailluel with one of the Officers so I did not get back to Borre until midnight.

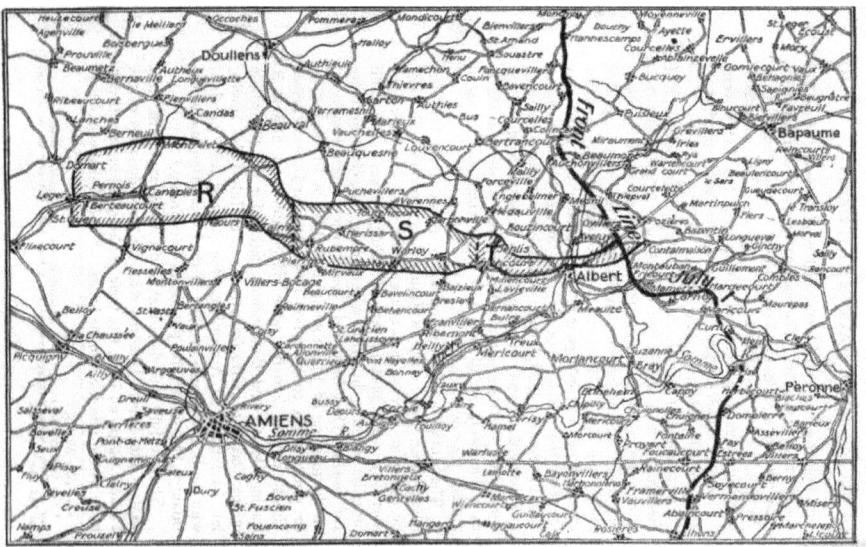

Amiens-Albert sector, Somme Valley, July 1916.
This map of the Amiens sector show the Somme River at Amiens, and the Front Line was it was when Ralph's unit moved there in mid July. The battle of Frommelles (south of Armentieres) raged from the 9th July to 20th July. The 5th Division was involved there. The 1st and 2nd Divisions had been moving to the Somme area. The 1st was based at Doullens, North of Ameins, the 2nd at Longueau, just SE of Amiens.

The Areas 'R' 'S' & 'T' on the map were designated rest areas for the troops coming out of the front line. Casualty Clearing Stations were at Warloy & Rubempre, in the 'S' sector. Pozieres is NE of Albert, on the Bapaume-Ameins road. Amiens was regarded then as a "miniature Paris." The people of Picardy at first seemed unwelcoming, but despite the often appalling conditions provided for the billets, there sprang up a strong mutual affection and admiration for the ANZACs. Most of the towns Ralph mentions in his diary can be found on this map of the Somme Valley.

9/7/1916

Left Borre at 11am this morning, and ran through Hazebrouk and Ebblinghem. *(Ebblinghem is a small town half way between St Omer and Hazebrouk. There is a small Military Cemetery at Ebblinghem.(Ed.))* Had a good run. Tonight had to go back to Erquinghem to collect three men.

10/7/1916

Remained at a billet at Ebblinghem until late this afternoon. I had one run and then to Wizernes *(South of St Omer, about 4 miles(Ed.))* (where the chaps entrain tomorrow) and then I went back to Ebblinghem where we stayed the night. The chaps had several games of footy this afternoon.

11/7/1916

There was chaos as the infantry units marched off at 6 am today. We were all up at 4 am. Only two cars went into the station with the Officers' luggage; my car did not go. I left Ebblinghem at about 9.30 this morning to meet supply at Sylvestre. *(St Sylvestre Cappell, north of Hazebrouk. (Ed.))* Left Sylvestre at about 2 pm had splendid run making Abbeville tonight. *(Abbeville is 85-95 Km south west of Hazebrouk, and 40 kms north west of Amiens. (Ed.))*

Most glorious roads and scenery.

Historical note:
At this time, there were over 100,000 ANZAC troops in the Armentieres sector. 21,650 were from the 2nd Division, which was Ralph's Division. (Source; Bean, (1929) Vol. III, p 306.) The troops moving from Ebblinghem this morning were on their way to Armentieres, and Fromelles (about 3 Kilometres south of Armentieres.) The 5th Australian Division was part of the Fromelles offensive and the Division was crippled by its losses at Fromelles. On one day, July 19th 1916, the Australian 5th Division alone lost 5,533 officers and men. (Bean, CEW, (1929) Vol III, p 442). Leaving out WW II, more Aussies died on this day than in all other military conflicts combined in which Australians were involved. (Ed.)

12/7/1916

Left Abbeville at 8.30 am. We made Picquigny for dinner. *(Dinner to him was lunch! Picquiny is only about 5 kms out of Armeins, about 30-35 Kms from Abbeville.(Ed.))* We remained in Picquigny awaiting orders until about midnight, when orders came to move on to Vaux to join the ambulance unit, which we did. We left the remainder of the supply column at Picquigny. Picquigny is a fine little place and the few hours spent there were most enjoyable. The old ladies have a grand opinion (at present) of the Australians. We were one of the first Australians to arrive there, so we got a good reception.

13/7/1916: *(written as Thursday July 12th)*

With the old boys again. They have had a fairly tough time of it at the front, but look fairly good on it.

I saw the 27th Battalion on the road today. I saw Nic, Nat and Ted Skuse, as well as Harry Lynn. All looking fairly medium.

(Harry Lynn worked at DeGaris, Sons and Co Ltd., and resumed his employment with the firm after the war. Harry subsequently joined Goldsborough Mort & Co., and was a legendary stock agent in the South East during the 20's and 30's. I suspect it was an understatement that they looked "fairly medium." These men had been at Frommelles, and they were lucky enough to have gotten out alive. The AIF had its first heavy casualties at Frommelles. These men had a terrible time and would have been much worse than, "medium" I suspect.)

14/7/1916: *(written as Friday 13th July)*

I made a trip to the 27th Battalion to collect patients again today. Saw Nic and others again. Harry Lynn is a Sergeant now. When I was down at St. Sauvoir today, I bought a dog for 2 francs, which we have called Picquigny.

15/7/1916: *(written as Saturday 14th July)*

I have had a fairly bad day today. Went down to Longpre this morning, to St. Ouen this afternoon and tonight to Berteacourt with the Major, returning at about 2am. There was an air raid on Amiens tonight and when we passed the aerodrome, all our plane sheds were lit up and landing lights ready for our planes, which had gone after the Germans.

16/7/1916: *(written as Sunday 15th July)*

Drove up to Longpre again this morning, and back to Amiens and Corbie this afternoon. Amiens is some city and we spent a splendid hour there.

17/7/1916: *(written as Monday 16th July)*

Went to Longpre this morning for patients. Drove back to Amiens this afternoon. Had an hour or so there and a good look around.

18/7/1916 *(written as Tuesday 17th July)*

Same trips as yesterday. Had a jolly good day. Sent some views home.

19/7/1916

Another repetition of yesterday except for a trip to Amiens tonight. The car is running splendidly.

20/7/1916

Had a grand day today. Orders were received to move, but one car had to take an officer from each Field Ambulance, the 5th, 6th, and 7th. Mine was the lucky car again. We left at 7.00 am taking Major Brennan from this unit, and picking up the Colonel of the 5th and a Captain of the 6th. We went to Albert via Amiens, and from there to the trenches which had recently been captured from the Germans. I rejoined the unit this evening at Herissart taking route via Corbie, where we had tea.

(Major Brennan was a Medical Officer with the 7th Field Ambulance. The German Front Line had been about a mile east of Albert. The Allies had pushed this line back about another mile during the early part of July 1916, east of Contalmaison, and Pozieres. Herrisart is 20 kms west of Albert, 20 kms north of Amiens. It was in the centre of an area about 25 miles by 5 miles which was a designated rest and training area for the I Anzac Corps. On the map at the beginning of this chapter, it is in the centre of the 'S' sector. Corbie is about 10 kms east of Amiens, Herrisart 20 Kms due north. So it was not a direct route taken.)(Ed.)

21/7/1916

Had a trip to Amiens today with cases. Spent an enjoyable afternoon in Amiens.

22/7/1916

Trip to Beauval today. *(About 25 Kms north of Amiens.)* I think we will evacuate all cases there now. Order to move again tonight. We arrived here (Contay*(About 5 kilometres east of Herrisart, near Warloy, and 15 Kilometres west of Albert.))* at about midnight. Terrific bombardments going along the whole front.

(Bean, CEW, (1929) Vol III, Pp 494-557: Chapter XV "The Taking of Pozieres." This was the beginning of the assault on Pozieres. The Australian 1st Division was heavily involved at Pozieres. The AIF losses were dreadful.(Ed.))

23/7/1916

Trip to Puchevilliers today. *(Just a couple of Kilometres north of Herrisart.)* Saw a lot of our first division chaps: they charged last night and did splendidly. Every body is very jubilant.

Historical note:
The 1st Division was part of the force which captured Pozieres. The fierce fighting in July and August 1916 at Pozieres reduced the town to a mud heap. There was virtually nothing left standing at all; not one building was left standing; not one tree. The town, which had been occupied by the Germans, was literally shelled out of existence. They may have been jubilant, but despite their jubilation, the 1st Division lost 5,285 Officers and men at Pozieres.

24/7/1916

I did a trip today with patients. Good many of our wounded arriving in at the C.C.S.

(C.C.S.: Casualty Clearing Station, or Regimental Aid Posts. These were the closest first aid and medical units to the front. From here, the most seriously wounded were take to Advanced Dressing Stations.(Ed.))

25/7/1916

I did a trip to Doullens today with Major Anderson. *(Captain Arthur Anderson, AAMC, promoted to Major in the field.)* Doullens is a very fair place, reminds me a little of Bailluel.

Historical note:
About 20 miles north of Amiens, on the Amiens-St. Omer road. In early July, 1916, the Australian 1st Division was based here, and the 2nd Division at Longueau and Saleux, a few miles south-east and south-west respectively of Doullens. (Bean,CEW, (1929) Vol III, Pp 448-449.(Ed.))

26/7/1916

On returning to Doullens today we found that the others had moved on so we had to follow. Plenty of guns about. Today, when at Beauval, I ran into Captain Cohen, my old M.O. in St. Andrews Hospital on Malta. He was jolly good and I was very pleased to see him again. He is now in the 77th British Field Ambulance.

27/7/1916

I struck the run to Beauval again today. Germans been sending a few shells over today, but they have been at a respectable distance. Orders were given for us to move up to the line tonight. This car told off for duty back at Head Quarters, and I was disappointed, as I thought I could get to the Advanced Dressing Station for work. Late tonight, had a run to Vandencourt, and did not get back to Albert till late. The Stretcher Bearers had moved up to the front. Eric was with them.

(This is phrase is often repeated in Ralph's diary. "Told off" means ordered to do a specific task, rather than the meaning it has today, ie "told off" as in scolded or reprimanded.)

Historical note:
There was a Corps Collecting Station at Vandencourt, which was between Warloy and Contay, 15kms west of Albert. Sometimes referred to as Vandencourt Wood. Lightly wounded soldiers were taken here and from here cleared back to their units. It was also a "camp" site for troops travelling to and from the front around Albert. The headquarters for the 2nd Infantry Brigade were here. General Birdwood addressed the 2nd Division here after there first tour at Pozieres. (Bean, CEW (1929) Vol III, P 600, Plate 46. (Ed.))

28/7/1916

Moved back to Headquarters at Vadencourt this morning. Have been going hard all day. Had a trip to Doullens as well.

29/7/1916

It has been a very slack day. I have been very despondent, watching all our wounded coming in from the frontlines. Not only is seeing the wounded upsetting, but hearing of cobbers who have been wounded or killed is pretty depressing.

I heard that poor old Bert Mallet had been killed, and Jim Keast had been wounded.

(L/Cpl Albert Percy Mallett served with the 7th Field Ambulance Medical Corps. He died on 28/7/16. He was born in Guernsey, and his parents were listed as living at Hartland Vinery, in Guernsey when he enrolled. He was living in Australia in Semaphore, when the War broke out. He would have had a connection with Ralph, whose grandfather, Elisha DeGaris, had emigrated from Guernsey to Australia in 1848. He was with Ralph's unit which left Outer Harbour on the SS Geelong, May 31st, 1915. A.J.(Jim) Keast, who served with the 7th Field Ambulance as a stretcher bearer.(Ed.))

30/7/1916

Another slack day. Fortunately, only a few wounded are coming in today. Carlsson, of our section being of the few who was wounded. The 2nd Division in their charge did not do too well. They are supposed to have another try tonight. Major Russell is here with us for a short time.

(Pte Arthur Florentin Carlsson, 3826, who served with 7th Field Ambulance with Ralph. 2nd Division held the Plateau close in front of Pozieres village. They were engaged now in active trench warfare. Major Kenneth Russell, Australian Medical Corps. (Ed.))

31/7/1916

It was a very slack day for me today, and there was practically nothing doing for us last night.

1/8/1916

It is still slack. Our artillery is not so active now. We had another quiet night last night. I received a grand mail tonight and wrote several letters.

Ralph's notes:
"Before we went into Pozieres we seemed certain of an early peace by our letters, but from memory we were not so confident after coming out. Our spirits were apparently very high before going in at Pozieres, for in one letter I wrote;
> "Alec will have to get a move on if he wishes to rejoin us before peace is declared".

About this time I had received good news of Alec's recovery from his illness. He was in England and his cable home gives in a very few words the spirit of the A.I.F. The cable he sent home and to which I refer was worded as follows:
> "Physically strong, financially weak. Alec". (Ed.)

Casualty Clearance Lines at Pozieres, July & August 1916.

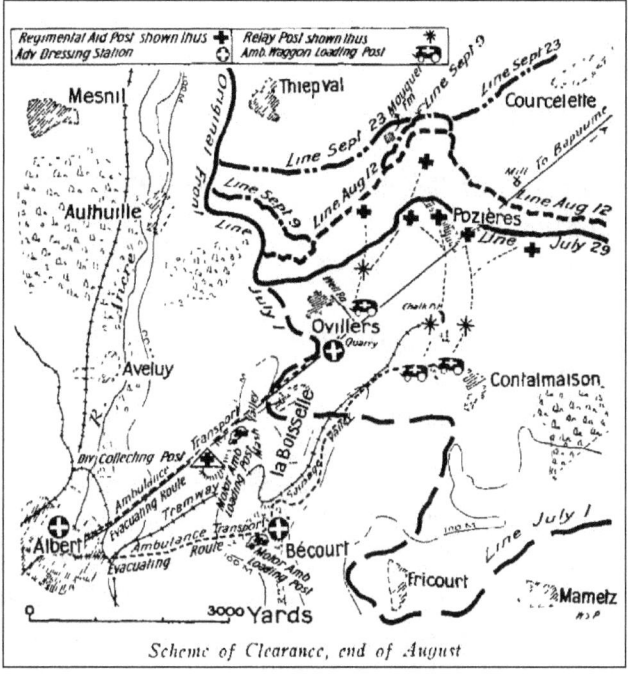

Scheme of Clearance, end of August

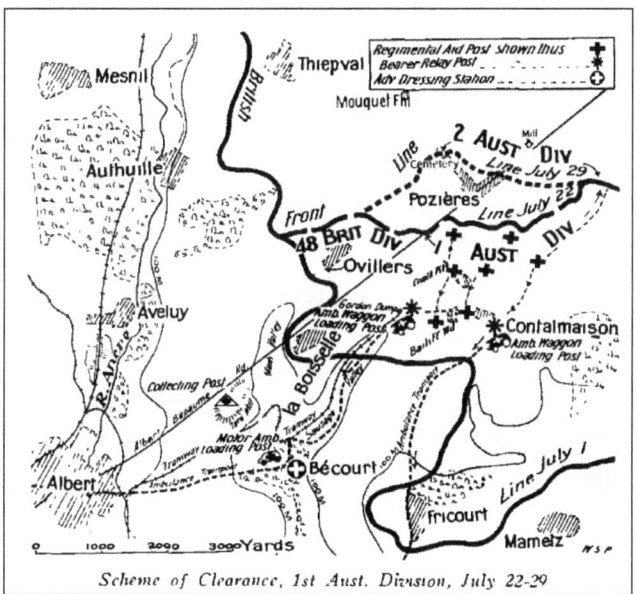

Scheme of Clearance, 1st Aust. Division, July 22-29

(Maps reproduced from Butler, AG, (1940), Vol II, Pp 57 & 62.)

Historical Note:
Casualties were cleared from the front by stretcher bearers to Regimental Aid Posts, then through to the Advanced Dressing Stations. Becourt was the main ADS for the 1st and 2nd divisions at Pozieres.
Ralph was frequently at Becourt, where the 7th field ambulance operated out of the Becourt Chateau.
Clearances from the Chalk Pit was by tramway as well as Motor Ambulance.
Ralph operated in the Becourt, Contalmaison, Chalk Pit area in July and August 1916.
The Casualty Clearance systems changed as a result of the progress of battle. These two diagrams illustrate the differences in the clearance of casualties from the Pozieres fields as the Australian's front line progressed northward. Note the motor ambulance points are moving north along the Bapaume Road, as the front progresses. Ralph drove along the Bapaume road to Albert, and also out of Becourt to Albert, and Vadencourt, further to the west of Albert. The road was subject to heavy shelling. (Ed.)

2/8/1916

Our 50th Battalion camped up very close today. I went up there this morning. I saw Bill Hoggarth, who is a Lieutenant now. I also saw Ken McEwin and others. I went over to the 50th again tonight, and met Harry Thompson who is a Lieutenant in that Battalion. I had a chat with him.

(Lt William Paton Hoggarth was eventually killed in action, April 2nd, 1917. No.3062, Ken McEwin, served with the 50th Battalion in France.(Ed.))

Historical note:
The 50th Battalion had been formed in Egypt, January 1916 by "splitting" the old 10th Battalion. 13 officers and 490 other men from the 10th were taken into the new 50th. Both battalions were made up

to battle strength with new re-inforcements. *The 10th had been badly knocked about in Gallipoli, suffering 150 killed, 538 wounded and 23 missing-in-action. In January 1916, the 10th was first made up to strength of 977, then "divided" to form the 10th and 50th Battalions. (Kearney, R, (2005) Pp 160-167.) So the 50th, like the old 10th, was composed mainly of South Australians.*

3/8/1916

I am fairly busy again today. I was told off as a relief at the Advanced Dressing Station today. I went out tonight to the front.

Historical note:
This wildly understates what was happening at this time. The 1st Division had captured Pozieres on 23 July. The 2nd Division took over and mounted 2 further attacks on July 29th, which were unsuccessful and then on 2nd August, resulting in seizure of German positions beyond Pozieres. The Germans retaliated with fierce shelling, and when the 2nd Division was relieved on 6th August, in only 12 days of fighting, had suffered 6,848 casualties, with 5 of its Battalions suffering losses of between 600-700 men. (see Bean, CEW (1946), P 258; and Kearney, R, (2005) P. 190.) Ralph was part of the unit moving the wounded. He was working right at the front, recovering wounded, bringing them through "Sausage Valley," and back to the Becourt Wood ADS. The road was awful. It had been heavily shelled, and was a nightmare of thick mud after any rain.

4/8/1916

There was a very heavy artillery bombardment last night, but little more doing. I had very little sleep as we were "standing to," expecting our chaps to charge. Our A.D.S. is in Becourt Wood, which is a good position. Peter Spense (another Driver, who we call "Spensey,") is on duty tonight.

(Pte Peter Spence, (no. 6581), Driver, K Supply Column, seconded to the 7th Field Ambulance, 1917.(Ed.))

Historical note:

Becourt Wood is 2 kilometres west of Albert. It is at the southern end of "Sausage Valley," which was the main access route for Australian troops moving in and out of the main Pozieres lines. Bean describes it in this way;

> *"Troops passing through this area by day were immediately struck by the fact that it was flayed of most of its former covering of grass, the white chalk-earth or red-brown soil showing bare, and crossed in every direction by dusty tracks; the outline of the trenches and of the old shell holes were worn down by recent bombardments, and by the feet of thousands of men."(Bean CEW, (1929) Vol. III, P 473-474.)(Ed))*

5/8/1916

Spensey had a fairly busy night. I took over from him at 6 am this morning. I have had a very busy day. Our chaps advanced last night. They took two lines trenches. There was plenty of shelling along the roads tonight. Albert is being heavily bombarded. Johnny Walker ran into weeping gas from shells on our last trip (Ne Bonne).

(There were over 120 John Walker's who enlisted from Australia. Our man was No 2323 John Russell Walker, a driver originally with 3rd Division, seconded to 7th Field Ambulance, 1917. He appears in Alec Blackwell's photo of the 7th Australian Field Ambulance at Xmas 1917 featured on the front cover of this book.)

6/8/1916

Spensey left this morning with slight shell shock. Callaghan was put on with me in place of Spensey. Callaghan is on duty today. There are a few shells lobbing around our resting quarters tonight. Our chaps came out tonight and the boys marched passed here; I was awfully pleased to see old Eric with them. None of them had a wash or a shave for a few days so they looked a rough mob.

(Pte. William Edward Callagan, MM (No. 3648). Originally with K Supply Column, 2nd Division, and seconded to the 7th Field Ambulance. (See front cover photo). Callaghan won the MM for gallantry and bravery on the Menin Road, outside Ypres, in October 1917.(Ed))

Historical note:
Eric was a Stretcher Bearer, and would have been working right at the front. The stretcher bearers really did see the very worst of conditions, often venturing into the dangerous "no man's land" to retrieve wounded comrades.
Bean, CEW, (Vol III, Pp 518-519) summarises their role thus,
> "The stretcher-bearers were moved by an inward desire to show to the combatant troops that they shared the worst dangers....and drew on themselves the special admiration of their mates;"

Having been through the battles at Pozieres, it is no wonder they looked a "rough mob." Ralph and Eric probably did not have enough time to have a decent chat.

7/8/1916

On duty today and had a busy time. Chap wounded by shrapnel in front of one of our cars in which I happened to be at the time. I also bent the bumper-bar of the car tonight. I ran into a piece of timber that had fallen off a load.

8/8/1916

In workshop today having bumper-bar straightened on the car. I arrived back at Albert at about tea time. Cally was on duty tonight.

9/8/1916

Fairly busy today. Heard that Nic Thompson and Colin Thomson had been killed. Hope to goodness it is not true. Our chaps advanced a bit last night.

(Pte Nicholas Thompson died on 28th July 1916 at Pozieres. More about Colin Thomson, who was Dr. Mary DeGaris' fiancée, later in this diary.(Ed.))

10/8/1916

I was off duty today. I went for a stroll around Albert. I saw Nat Skuse and Harry Lynn. It's a fact about Nic Thomson being killed. It is just wretched. There were plenty of shells around our sleeping quarters tonight in Albert.

11/8/1916

I had a very slack day. Our chaps are still advancing, with less casualties than at first advance.

12/8/1916

Another slack day for me. However, there was a very sudden bombardment tonight. Our chaps did more good work and took two more lines of trenches with, few casualties. I received a bonza mail tonight.

13/8/1916

Still rather slack here in Albert. The bombardments seemed to have ceased a little. Fritz is lobbing some Iron Rations here tonight.

Some motor drivers were wounded tonight, Peter Spence of our lot being one. Lots of the cars have holes in them, but so far our old bus is unmarked. I ran across Mc Cutcheon, of Lucindale, the other night. Had a chat on old times.

(Pte Peter Spence, No 6581. Driver with the Australian Motor Transport Unit. Pte Arthur Donald McCutcheon, whose father was a Methodist Clergyman.(Ed.))

14/8/1916

Slightly more busy today. Roads very slippery as it has been showery. I had to follow the 4th Brigade on a march tonight. Rather exciting in its own way; plenty of great circles etc.

15/8/1916

Another rather slack day. I forgot to put in a few days ago that the King was somewhere about these parts. He did not pay a personal visit, but we can say that we heard some of the cheering.

(King George V was in the area around the 7th August 1916. He spoke with Australian troops at Warloy, on 7th August, on the way to the front. (Bean, Vol III, P 488 (photo); & Pp 727-725)(Ed.))

16/8/1916

Heard tonight that Eric had received a stripe. Saw poor old Bert Mallet's grave tonight.

(L/Cpl Albert Mallett, No 3649 is buried in the France 430 Albert Cemetry Extension. Ralph was billeted at Albert at this time. Albert is only 2-3 miles from Pozieres.(Ed.))

17/8/1916

Things getting busier again last night. Our boys advanced again. The Germans are shelling Albert tonight.

(Bean, (1929) Vol III, Pp. 774-782. The Aussies, including the 10th Battalion, were involved in the infamous push to Mouquet Farm, (known as "Moo-cow Farm" by the ANZACs.), north of Pozieres. German artillery meantime concentrated on shelling Albert, where Ralph was now billeted.)

18/8/1916

I spent the majority of day sleeping. I needed to catch up on some rest. I have been absolutely exhausted. I went for a walk round Albert later in the afternoon.

19/8/1916

Fairly busy today, but nothing startling. The best news is that Colin Thomson was not killed only wounded, and I hope this is true. We are now evacuating all cases from Becourt Wood to Warloy; previously we used to evacuate some to Puchvilliers.

20/8/1916

It was slack again today, but am very tired as I had very little sleep last night. Heavy bombardment tonight.

21/8/1916

A fleet of about 20 taubes came over this morning dropping bombs. Luckily none came too close to here; but a good many casualties were caused round about. One bomb killed 11 and wounded 23, besides many horses. I had a fairly busy day. Seventh Field Ambulance takes over Becourt Wood Advanced Dressing Station tonight.

Historical note:
Taubes *were early German war planes. There were three named Taubes; the Kondor Taube, a machine, with a tiny 100 hp Mercedes engine; the Krieger Taube a pre-war designed plane with a sleek cigar-shaped fuselage, and the Jeannin Taube (sometimes called the Rumpler Taube) which was a scouting plane. (Nott, P 316.) "Taube" literally means "Dove." The original Taube was made in 1910 as a scout plane and was a slow, unarmed 2 seater monoplane. It looked like a dove. It was used until late 1916.*
Ralph refers to bomb-carrying planes as taubes, and Harry Schinckel refers to taubes in his diary right through 1917 and 1918. The term was used generically to describe enemy aircraft. The Rumpler Taube was manufactured by Rumpler, was a bi-plane which carried 2 pilots,

a machine gun, and about 250 lbs (110 kgs) of bombs, which were dropped by hand.

22/8/1916

I am still very busy and am feeling sleepy today, through lack of sleep. We are working shorthanded now as a number of the Ambulances have been called away. The 2nd Division has taken over the front from the 1st Division again. The 1st Division took Mouquet Farm before being relieved.

23/8/1916

There is plenty of work doing. I saw Eric today at Becourt Wood, as our bearers are at present in reserve. I had a good old chat with Eric. I have missed not being with him. I also saw Murray Batt today. *(Pte Murray McHarg Batt, No. 2109. 10th Infantry Battalion, 1-8 re-inforcements. Sailed with the 1-8th re-inforcements on the HMAT Borda, June 1915. The 10th was a legendary SA Battalion.(Ed.))* He is looking well. Last night I had a puncture, but owing to Albert being shelled I was forced to run on flat tyre for about 500 yards, which I have to report, as the tube is slightly damaged.

24/8/1916

Not so much doing today. This afternoon I had a good long run with Major Bean and his brother the Official War Correspondent. The run was very interesting. Captain Charles Bean was on Gallipoli, and has seen most of the war to date. Major Bean is a medical man.

The Germans are shelling our quarters again tonight.

(Major Bean was CEW Bean's brother, Major JWB Bean, Medical Officer, AAMC. He was a specialist anaesthetist. Charles Bean of

course was the legendary historian, and Official War correspondent, Captain CEW Bean. His work is constantly referred to in this history.(Ed.))

25/8/1916

It was a slack day today. The report I sent in yesterday about the tube was hardly satisfactory for the Tommy Officer in charge of our own convoy. I have made out another with a few more details and should this not do him I am going to a higher man. A chap gets full of these chaps who take every word you say as a lie.

Anyhow I am personally handling this report into the O.C. of the Convoy and then we will see how things go.

26/8/1916

Went in to see the O.C. of the Convoy today, and after a few words from me, he changed his tune, and at the end could not have been nicer. It is still raining and we are fairly busy.

Expect to leave this part of the line altogether shortly. Our bearers went up to the trenches again today. They are having a bad time of it. Very heavy casualties, not enough bearers and ambulances to cope. Couple in with shell-shock, not physically injured, just nervous breakdowns.

Historical note:
The action to capture Mouquet Farm, north of Pozieres continued until the end of August. There were heavy ANZAC casualties, especially for the 10th Battalion, which was part of the 3rd Brigade. The organisation of evacuation of wounded from the front failed badly during this stage of the battle. The distance between the front line and the RAP's, which were about a mile south of Pozieres, so 2 miles from the front, was too great. The 7th Field Ambulance, together with the 5th 6th and 12th had relieved the 3rd at Becourt Wood. The

evacuation of the seriously wounded from Becourt was by Motor Ambulances to the CCS's at Warloy, and Puchvilliers, whereas the "walking wounded" were sent to Vadencourt and cleared there. Ralph would have been working long shifts driving the Motor Ambulance from Becourt Wood to the Casualty Clearing Stations, (also called Regimental Aid Posts on the casualty clearance maps on P.127.)
(Also see Bean, CEW,(1929) Vol III, Pp 704, footnote 15. (Ed.))

Historical note:
Ralph refers to "shell-shock" a couple of times. (Eg, 6/8/16, Peter Spence suffered "...slight shell shock..." The condition was only starting to be recognised as a specific medical problem in the field, in about August of 1916 at the Battle of the Somme, as Colonel AG Butler records:
"Close to the junction of the lorry switch with the main Albert Road, in the fine grounds of the Chateau Vadencourt, the 2nd Field Ambulance built up a rest station which was to serve the Australian troops under many and varied circumstances.
On July 27th the 7th Field Ambulance (Lieut.-Colonel R. B. Huxtable) formed a Corps
Rest Station in the field near by in order to minimise the evacuation of light casualties from the Reserve Army's zone. During the period July 2nd-16th August, (excluding 1,112 cases of sickness,) 7,183 casualties passed through this unit. Analysis of the returns reveals as the outstanding feature of the experience the emergence, as a major medical problem of the war (as it was to be of the peace), of the condition then known as "shell-shock." The term had been in use for some time and was loosely applied to all cases of physical and mental breakdown within the battle zone without apparent wound. It had become indeed a diagnostic shibboleth and an open sesame to the Base.
Its importance in these operations is shown by the following figures of cases admitted to this unit during the 1st Division's offensive, July 22nd-26th :-

Admissions	July 22	July 23	July 24	July 25	July 26
Shell Shock	11	31.	72	205	57
Walking wounded ..	43	687	180	730	18

(Reference: Butler, AG, (1940) Vol II, P. 72)

27/8/1916

Heard today that old Dave West was slightly wounded; he had volunteered to go up in to the front in charge of the bearers. I have been rather slack today. Callaghan overdid his 24 hours considerably, so think I may be allowed to remain here all night.

(Pte David West No 16671 served with the 7th Field Ambulance. He was killed in action, 28/9/1917.(Ed.))

28/8/1916

One trip to Becourt Woods, but only to get Officers' luggage, as we are moving out today. I moved with the Ambulance to Warloy tonight.

Ralph's notes:
"It was hectic for me. At this time, I was driving both officer transport vehicles, and Motor Ambulances. I was posted to the 2nd Motor Transport Division, because that is the way the Tommies did things. But mostly I am with the 7th Field Ambulance boys."

[**Author's note:** *I note on Ralph's war record that he is listed as serving with the 2nd Motor Transport Division, attached to the 7th Field Ambulance. Often Ralph had temporary postings to other Field Ambulance units to drive Motor Ambulances.*]

29/8/1916

Told off to the 6th. Brigade today. Moved as far as Rubempre with them and then took some officers to Amiens. Did not get back to our boys, who had moved to Toutencourt, until after 11pm.

30/8/1916

I went off to the 6th Brigade again today. They moved as far as Bonneville. Our own boys are billeted just close to Bonneville so I joined them up again tonight.

(Bonneville, France, is actually near Switzerland. This is more likely to be Bernaville, about 5 miles west of Doullens, and just outside to the RST zone established by the ANZAC Corps around the Albert-Herrisart-Berteaucourt corridor. (Bean, CEW, (1929), Vol III, Map at P 450)(Ed.))

31/8/1916

I went round the 6th Brigade Battalions today, but nothing startling to report.

1/9/1916

I am on Battalion duty again today, and was called out late last night. Made a special run to Rubempre this afternoon. I had two beautiful blow outs.

2/9/1916

On duty with the Battalions again this morning. Nothing else to report.

3/9/1916

One more again today, I am on duty with the Battalions. Took Capt. Kenny ahead in my bus. All the boys arrived at our new home Longuevillette at about 2 pm. Met John Blacket's brother today, and had a chat with him. I gave him my condolences, and told him I thought John a fine leader, who was well respected by his troops. It was a sad moment. He belongs to the 7th Brigade, but is now working with the 6th Brigade.

(Captain John Kenny, AAMC, later promoted to Major. Lieut Joseph Arnold Blacket, John Blacket's brother was also killed in action, on 10th June, 1918.(Ed.))

4/9/1916

One trip to Donleus and Beauval. Got into a little extra slippery place, but managed to get out again. Went mushrooming today and got some beauties. I have commandeered an old dames stove to cook them for our supper tonight.

France, 1916:
The Chateau at Becourt Wood which the 7th Field Ambulance used as an Advance Dressing Station for wounded from Pozieres and Mouquet Farm. Only about 2 miles from Pozieres. Photo; AWM.

Taube: *A German Taube ("dove") reconnaissance aircraft captured by the French, 1914.*

Pozieres 1916
The landscape of a previously wooded area near Pozieres, devastated by constant artillery action.
The effects of constant shelling on the landscape. The remains of Pozieres township is in the middle part of the picture! Anzacs used the shell holes for protection.

Chapter Ten:

From the Somme to Belgium:
Working at Ypres for the first time:

Historical note:
The effects of the battle at Pozieres on the AIF was such that the forces were withdrawn from the Somme to take over from the Canadians at Ypres. The 2nd Division were located near the Menin Road; the 1st and 4th Divisions further west. The movement of troops here was more for rest and recuperation in a quiet sector than for intense battle. There were only three series of raids undertaken around Ypres in September to October 1916. The main task of the ANZAC corps seems to have been focussed on repairing and improving the trenches and winter quarters for troops around Ypres. These works were undertaken with great zest. Deep tunnelling of dugouts was done; broken down parapets were repaired; wires were repaired; trenches were "duck-boarded" to provide better access; drainage works were completed; a light-railway system was constructed, and it was screened to conceal avenues of approach. (Bean, CEW, (1929) Vol III, Pp 877-881.)

The troops stayed in the Ypres sector until recalled to the Somme Valley in mid-October 1916. It was a relatively quite time for the German troops as well. Their command had also transferred tired division to Ypres. They were short of shells and ammunitions.

In October, the ANZAC divisions were transferred back to the Somme, and the last Battle of the Somme, at Flers, was conducted with the oncoming winter, to be one of the most vicious winters in Europe for 40 years, a major factor in the increasing discomfort of the Western Front for all troops.(Ed.)

The Diary:

5/9/1916

What a great feed last night and am none the worse for it now. I left on direct journey for the North at 7am. I picked up the Convoy at Puchvillers and steered North via Donleus, St. Pol, and Hazebrouk. We arrived here at about 5pm after a wet, but good run. It looks as if we will see Ypres now.

6/9/1916

I spent the morning about cars doing maintenance. We made ourselves scarce this afternoon and saw town. Popperinghe is not half a bad place. The people about here are great and just about all speak English splendidly.

(Popperinghe is about 6 miles south of Ypres. It was right on the main front line between Armentieres and Ypres. (Ed.))

7/9/1916

I cleaned up cars this morning. I joined up with the boys this afternoon. They were camped about 2 miles from where we were. They are all well.

8/9/1916

Couple of trips but nothing startling doing, as far as I can tell. I took Captain Hamilton and 6 others (including Eric) to Steewoorke tonight. I got back at about midnight. I don't know what they have gone there for.

9/9/1916

Eric was made Corporal today. I did one trip, but nothing much doing.

10/9/1916

Another slack day for me. I spent it cleaning up.

11/9/1916

I heard today that it is quite right about Colin Thomson being killed. I am pretty down about it, especially after hearing that it was not true about a week ago.

12/9/1916

It is raining slightly today. I only did one trip this morning. I had a letter I had written to Clemmie yesterday returned, as Colin's death is still not officially announced.

Historical note:
Sgt Colin Gordon Thomson (No 467) was engaged to Dr Mary Clementine DeGaris. Colin enlisted from Tibbobura, NSW and served in the 27th Battalion. The family affectionately knew Mary as "Clemmie." Mary was the surgeon/doctor at the Tibboburra Hospital where she and Colin met. Colin was the eldest child of Agnes Thompson, who was a widow. Colin ran the station after his father's untimely death.
Colin Thomson was killed at Pozieres, on the night of 4th-5th August 1916.
He was mentioned in dispatches for
> *"continuing to lead and fight until overcome through loss of blood, and was killed while being recovered from the field." (Ref: AWM, Canberra.)*

Ralph was initially told Colin had not been killed, but when the news was confirmed, he wrote to Clemmie, to tell her what he had been told about Colin's death, particularly that he had died bravely, but regulations did not permit Ralph to write to her at this time. Mary was working as a surgeon at Epsom Hospital, south of London. The hospital was mainly used as an Army hospital during the War. Colin's mother, Agnes, was his only next of kin, and she was eventually informed of his death officially by the War office.

13/9/1916

Nothing doing. Football match against the 6th Field Ambulance today which we won.

14/9/1916

Nothing doing. It is beastly cold this morning.

15/9/1916

Repetition of yesterday; nothing much happening. A sports meeting was arranged for Sunday.

16/9/1916

Two football matches with the 6th Field Ambulance today. We won the Soccer but lost the Aussie Rules game. I am feeling very stiff tonight. I have heard tonight that we would be on the move again tomorrow.

17/9/1916

Moved to Renningghelst today; we have a kind of a Rest Station there. Mornings are getting beastly cold now.

(Renningghelst is near Poperinghe. It and the village of Wippenhoek nearby were billet camps for the Allies for the Ypres campaign.)

18/9/1916

It is raining heavily today. I wrote to Irwells asking them to forward me £5/-/-. In orders today it was announced that Kammerman had been awarded the Military Medal for Bravery. That is 5 now for the 7th Field Ambulance.

(Historical note:
Charles Kammerman, a Driver with the 7th Field Ambulance, was operating a horse-drawn ambulance near the front line on 29/8/16, and was awarded an MM for standing by his horses, calming them and returning them to the lines while under intense shelling from the Germans. It is interesting to compare the conferral of the MM on Charles with the conferral of the equivalent award to officers (MC) to Albert Jacka VC, MC and Bar, for his efforts at Pozieres. Essentially, Jacka, fighting with his battalion at Pozieres Heights, led his platoon out of a trench which had been bombed, into another and charged German troops. Every man in his party (including Jacka) was hit by bullets. They overcame the Germans, killing half and taking surrender from the others. A second melee ensued, and Jacka dived in

to help another platoon, killing a number of enemy and capturing a number of others. Eventually when the Germans surrendered, Jacka had single handedly killed 11 enemy and captured 14 prisoners, while sustaining serious bullet wounds in the fighting, Bean described it thus; "Jacka's counter-attack, which led directly to this result, stands as the most dramatic and effective act of individual audacity in the history of the AIF." Jacka was recommended for the VC, but his superior officer, with whom Jacka had several heated disagreements, refused to recommend a VC on the grounds that Jacka's sensational acts of individual bravery had not been witnessed by a superior officer. Several have argued that if any post-war honours are to be granted by the Army, Jacka ought to be the first to be granted a posthumous VC, which would have given him the honour of a VC and bar, having already earnt a VC in Gallipoli. Jacka was also conferred a bar to his MC in action in the Somme. Many argue his bravery on that occasion in capturing a machine gun post ought also have earnt him a VC.
(Bean, CEW, Vol III, P 718-720); Rule (1933); Lawriwsky (2007);(Ed)

19/9/1916.)
Finer today, but the past rain made sure there was plenty of mud about. I did a trip to Steenweerke.

20/9/1916

It was raining again today, and for most of the day. Having a slack time doing nothing more than reading, and writing letters.

21/9/1916

It is fining up a little today. We played another football match, this time against the 4th Field Ambulance, which we again lost. There was a big mail in today. I managed to get four letters, three of which were from home and one from K. Hawkes.

22/9/1916

Another small mail in today which brought two letters in to me, one from Ren Burnard and one from Uncle Clem enclosing 10/-. In all now I have received £3 from Uncle Clem. Our Soccer team played the 4th Field Ambulance today and we had a good win.

(Historical note:
I am guessing that Ren Burnard wrote to Ralph advising him he had enlisted in the AIF on 14/8/1916. He joined as a Captain, and Medical officer with the 7th Field Ambulance. I am sure Dr Burnard would have written Ralph to advise him of his enlistement. Uncle Clem was Elisha Clement DeGaris, who was from Mildura. Clem moved to Guernsey in 1916 to promote and manage the importing of dried fruits from Mildura to England and the Continent. He remained in Guernsey from 1916 to 1918, when his first wife Elizabeth died. Clem operated a comfort station for Australian servicemen, and during the war 'collected' a 'family' of 400 Australian servicemen with whom he corresponded by circular letters full of personal news and spiritual solace. See McCalman, Janet, 'De Garis, Elisha Clement (Elizee) (1851 - 1948)', Australian Dictionary of Biography, Volume 8, Melbourne University Press 1981, pp 270-271.)(Ed.))

23/9/1916

Preparations are being made for a move again today. We moved at midday and have taken up splendid quarters at Popperinghe. We are arranging to get a driver's mess.

24/9/1916

All drivers were at work today erecting our mess tent. I was elected President of the Drivers mess at the first meeting held this morning. Most of the Drivers attended the sports of the 7th and 6th Field Ambulances, but I stayed back on duty. I was detained for duty at about 3pm with the 5th Field Ambulance. Sent out to a quiet night at the main Dressing Station for the 5th Field Ambulance. *(This was* situated at Poperinghe, south of Ypres. See Butler, (1940) Vol II, P 135.(Ed.))

25/9/1916

A fairly busy day. Plenty of running around to do. I had a letter from Clemmie today telling me that she had heard of Colin's being killed but did not believe it. I sought special permission to write her from my O.C. They said I could write and give her the information I had about Colin. It was heartbreaking for me to write to dear Clemmie.

(Historical note:
Official notification was sent to Dr. Mary DeGaris dated September 15th 1916, advising her that her fiancée, Colin Thomson, was killed 6 weeks earlier, on the 4th August 1916. Ralph tried to write to Mary on 12/9/16, but was not permitted to do so. Clemmie wrote to Ralph on receiving the news of Colin's death. That letter reached Ralph on 25/9/16.(Ed.))
Official letters sent to Mrs Agnes Thomson, Colin's mother and next of kin, enclosed his personal effects. The handwritten note, "Seang Choon" records the ship on which the parcel was dispatched to Australia. "Seang Choon" was a P&O ship used as a troopship, and was mentioned as one of the ships unloaded by Ralph at Alexandria in August 1915.
Colin's body was not recovered immediately, and was not officially identified and formally buried until 1938.)(Ed.)

26/9/1916

I am here on duty as one of the Ambulances (car) was blown to billio last night, but the engine was not injured. One of the most marvelous things in the car world that I have ever seen. Told off for Advance Dressing Station work tonight.

(Historical note:
Between 25/9/16 and 30/9/16 there was a series of raids launched by the 4th Division and 2nd Division around Ypres, especially Oosthoek,

Ypres-Comines Canal, Picadilly Farm, Sanctuary Wood and Vierstraat. Ralph would have been operating outside of Ypres, most likely on the Menin Road, as the 2nd Division was south east of Ypres and south of the Menin Road.(Ed.))

27/9/1916

Going all last night, the roads are terribly bad, goodness knows what it will be like when the winter sets in. I am feeling particularly drained, and I am very tired today.

28/9/1916

Busy again today. I have been able to get very little sleep and have been feeling very tired. Still, thank goodness we have only three days in a stretch up here. The A.D.S's. are a good way out through Ypres. Ypres is the most severely bent place I have yet struck. It must have been a fine place before, but now it is a mass of ruins.

(The ADS's were east of Ypres, on the Menin Road.(Ed.))

29/9/1916

Another busy night, but I am not feeling so worn out today. There is a terrible amount of traffic on the roads at night and, of course, no lights are allowed to be used. We do the first trip at 10 pm and the second at 3 am and if any startling is doing on the lines, we have to do other trips. Our stay of A.D.S. work finishes for three days tonight. I got back to the Main Dress Station at 8pm.

30/9/1916

I went into the workshop today with differential trouble. They cannot get at it for a few days so I expect to be in Steenwerke for a time.

1/10/1916

Met Harry Lynn today and I got the surprise of my life when I saw the old lad with the D.C.M. stuck up. I was very pleased for him.

Historical note:
Sgt Harry Lynn's Official recommendation for the DCM, (Distinguished Conduct Medal) was for bravery at Pozieres Heights, August, 1916. Sgt Harry Cuthbert Lynn was a sergeant in the 27th Battalion. He was also an employee of DeGaris, Sons and Company Ltd, and ran the Penola office of that firm for many years.

I saw a great footy match between the 27th and the 28th Battalions. The former won. I spent night with Harry Lynn DCM. I also saw Nat Skuse and others.

2/10/1916

Received £5/-/- from Irwells in theirs of 25th last month. Acknowledged in mine of September 30th which was the day I received the amount. I bought a stove today. Much like the old Perfection, it is for use in the car in cold weather, which I expect plenty of in the next few months.

3/10/1916 to 19/10/1916

I have been in the workshops with car at Steenwoorke.

One of our Sections moved down here on the 10th. Luckily it was B Section, so Eric is down here with me. We have received a great mail from Australia. Since our car has been under repair, Callaghan and I have been billeted at Steenworke, and have a fine bed to sleep in. Johnny Walker whose car is also down, is with us, and together we knock out a very medium time.

(I reckon this is 2323 L/Cpl John Russell Walker, who originally was a driver with the 3rd Motor Transport Division. They would have

been operating in the same sector, and drivers were frequently posted between Divisions for varying lengths of time. (Ed.))

For days we were amusing ourselves painting the car, and now she is looking some car. Have had several letters from Uncle Clem and Clemmie and a great parcel from the latter, including books which kept me busy reading.

"The Sentimental Bloke" arrived from Luke, and I have had some good laughs reading it. Another 10/- note has come to light from Uncle Clem, and although so soon after the £5, it is very handy, as we have been very extravagant. At the French place at which we were billeted a son unexpectedly returned from the front after nine months without seeing his home people. The welcome was very amusing and very mild to what one would have expected.

The last night in the workshops we were working on the car very late to get her together.

19/10/1916

I returned to the Unit today, which had moved up here to Steenwoorke. A nice Australian mail came today bringing me five home letters.

20/10/1916

Another mail today had a couple of short runs, one to Ypres but otherwise nothing doing.

21/10/1916

We are on the move again today. We have been very busy, transporting sick. Expect to move in the morning. We have no idea as to where we are destined to be posted.

22/10/1916

Another busy day arising here (Tilques) very late tonight. I did several runs to St. Omer. We have heard that the boys entrain on Tuesday morning. The betting now is in favour of the Somme as our destination again.

23/10/1916

Left this morning at 8 am for Cassel to report for duty, and returned at dinner time. I did a trip to St. Omer this evening. Orders have been received for motors to leave at 7am tomorrow morning.

24/10/1916

Left at about 7 am this morning, after noticing that both Calley's and my kit were missing! We picked up the other Ambulances of the Division at Wizernes, and started steering South via Fruges, St. Pol, Frevent, and Doullens and reaching Vignacourt at about 6 pm where we stayed the night. Whether this last named town has appeared in this diary before or not, I don't know.

Football match between the 7th Field Ambulance and the 25th Battalion at Neuve Englise, just after the Battalion had come out of the line forward of Garter Point near Ypres. This photo was taken October 1917, later in the war. Photo: AWM

"The Mobile Rovers."
Soccer team of the 7th Field Ambulance, 1916. Eric Kidman is at back left. Photo; Courtesy Tania Shaw.

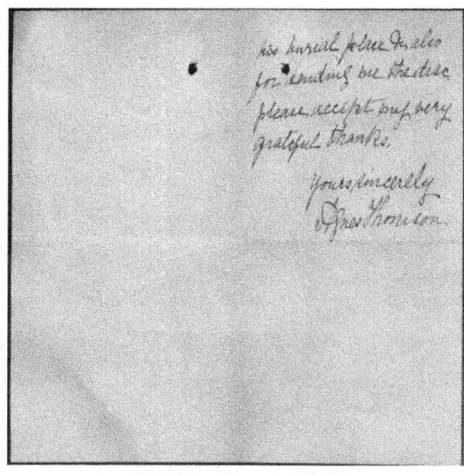

Letter written by Mrs Agnes Thomson, Colin's mother, acknowledging receipt of Colin's identity disc recovered at Pozieres in 1938, at the grave of an "unknown soldier." The body was formally identified as Colin's body by the discovery of his identity disc. Below, official advice of Goods returned.

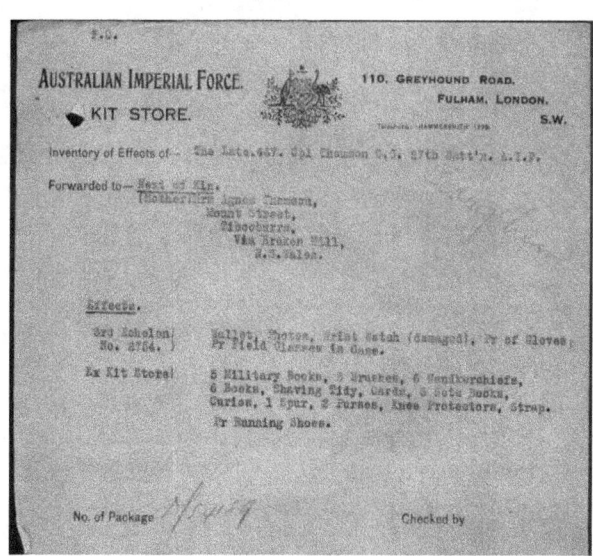

France, 1916: *Motor Ambulance with bomb damage, similar to that described by Ralph, near Ypres, 26/9/16. Photo; AWM.*

France, 1916:
This was an Advanced Dressing Station operated by the 6th Field Ambulance near the Menin Road, Ypres, Belgium (where Ralph was based in September 1916, and again in October 1917.) There are stretcher bearers tending to the wounded they have evacuated from the front line, after which the wounded are loaded onto the ambulance for evacuation. Note the 3 story bays in the motor ambulance. Ralph talks about driving with care, so as not to bump the top patient off his stretcher. Photo; AWM.

Eric Kidman: *Post 1918 War.*

Capt. Dr. Ren Burnard: Ralph's brother in law: (Cornwall 1917)

Chapter Eleven:
Winter back in the Somme Valley, 1916/17:

Historical note:
The 2nd Division had been "rested" at Ypres, Belgium for about 6 weeks. The Battles in the Somme Valley in 1916 were not yet completed. General Haig's policy was to break the Germans in the Spring of 1917. Part of his plan included a major assault towards Bapaume (continuing to gain ground won at Pozieres) then bed down for the winter. The battles at Flers and around the "Maze" were to witness the last of the Somme offensives. Winter rains started early, and the landscape, which had been decimated by constant shelling over the previous months, quickly turned into a cold, miserable gluepot of deep mud. Bean (1929) Vol III @ P 940, described the end of the Somme campaign thus;

> *"Thus ended a series of operations which, through the weather and the state*
> *of the ground, were undoubtedly the most difficult in which the A.I.F. was ever engaged."*

The ANZAC's were physically and mentally at a very low point, and many letters and diaries of this period show that they were utterly sick of the war, and did not want to fight again.

> *"There can be no question that the Australian force, reared in a land of almost continual sunshine and genial warmth, was, throughout this period being subjected to intense suffering...." (Bean, (1929)Vol III, P 941.)*

The conditions which were endured in this bleakest of European winters, is summed up well in this letter;

> *"Put him out of doors into the thick of a dirty European winter; march him ten miles through a bitter cold wind and driving rain, with--on his back--all the clothing, household furniture, utensils and even the only cover which he is allowed to take with him; dribble him in through mud up to his knees-sometimes up to his waist-along miles and miles of country that is nothing by broken tree stumps and endless shell holes-holes into which, if a man were to fall, he might lie for days before he were found, or even might never be found at all. At*

the end of it all put him to live there with what baggage he carried on his back and nothing more; put him in various depths of mud, to stay there all day in rain, wind, fog, hail, snowstorm-whatever weather comes-and to watch there during the endless winter nights, when the longed for dawn only means another day and another night out there in the mud ditch, without a shred of cover. And this is what our men had had to go through."
(Bean, CEW, "Letters from France" (1917) Pp.198-199.)

The Diary:

25/10/1916

We remained at Vignacourt all day. Nothing doing.

26/10/1916

I took an English Officer to a place the other side of Puchvillers today.

27/10/1916

We left Vignacourt at midday, and went as far as Heilly tonight.

(No. 38 Casualty Clearing Station was situated at Heilly.(Ed.))

28/10/1916

I joined the unit today at Dernancourt, near Albert. I have been going all day with patients.

29/10/1916

I went to workshop today near Heilly to get new tyres and have odd jobs done. The weather is getting chillier with each day.

30/10/1916

A long trip to Doullens today. It was beautiful scenery all the way. I took two Colonels and a Major. I did not get back till 2 am.

31/10/1916

Found the Battalions, and they were evacuating at Heilly. B Section went up to Becordel, which is very near to Becourt, and took over a Main Dressing Station today. Did letter writing for Christmas today. A few went over late tonight dropping bombs. The searchlights playing heavenwards were a very pretty sight.

1/11/1916

Nothing doing all day. Reported to the 5th Field Ambulance for advanced work. I went up to "Thistle Dump" Dressing Station which is through Mametz Wood, Montraut and Delville Wood. The road is in a fearful state and as a result our front axle is badly bent.

("Thistle Dump" was an ADS (Advanced Dressing Station) near Longueval.(Ed.))

2/11/1916

I had to go into workshops again today. I had the axle straightened, and back on duty at Becordel again tonight. I did not finish running till about 4 am on following morning. During the night's performance I got lost and found myself wandering into a German Prisoners Camp instead of a Hospital.

3/11/1916

Call on duty today so I had a sleep. The rest was very welcome.

4/11/1916

Rose very early this morning. I have to move up to Thistle Dump for permanent work today. After wandering about the country since midday, getting into bogs, we arrived at our destination at about 7 pm and I was immediately detailed to take a load down from the Thistle Dump.

5/11/1916

I arrived back from the trip at about 5am this morning, having had two blowouts. I was awakened at about 9 am by a sudden and terrific burst of artillery fire which lasted for about 15 minutes, ceased for about 5 minutes, and re-opened again. The blaze of fire just alongside us, across the flat, was a magnificent sight. At about 10 am we got the strength of the bombardment.

The 7th Brigade had charged and taken two lines of trenches. The fact that men by the score were being bogged between the trenches will give some idea of the conditions under which the charge was made.

Historical note:
The 7th Brigade who (like everyone else in the Somme valley) were exhausted by tramping through heavy mud and suffered from lack of sleep, engaged fresh troops of the German 4th Guard Division, who launched a blistering shelling attack against them.
General Rawlinson had inspected the front line, and agreed that the planned attack was impossible. General Haig refused to inspect the conditions, and ordered the Brigade to proceed in order to help the French to the south of the 2nd Division. (Pederson, Pp 180-181.)
The Australian 5th Brigade, which had relieved the 7th on 5/11/16, eventually took, and held The Maze, 0n 14/11/16, and were the only company to actually gain ground during this disastrous part of the campaign. (Bean, (1929) Vol III, Pp 900-917)
Until they were relieved on 5/11/16, the 7th Brigade had lost 819 men in the Flers campaign.
The Official Diary of the 8th Battalion of 8/1/16 records;
> *"Mud and more mud. Men cannot stand still long in one place without sinking up to their knees. Rations arrived but it was only with great difficulty they could be carried up."*

Bean notes Captain Morgan Jones of 20th Battalion, says he saw one of his troops standing up with his feet deep in the mud, his back against the trench wall, shaken by shivering fits from head to foot, but fast asleep. (Bean, (1929) Vol III, P. 919.)

Pedersen records the following remarkable observations made Captain Maxwell of part of the battle scene at the "Maze";
> *"Curiously enough their efforts were quite superfluous because the attacking troops sank up to their waists in the mire and could proceed no further than the centre of no mans land. The Huns did likewise and the absurd position was created of scores of attackers and defenders bogged up to their waists only a stones throw apart." (Pedersen (2007) P. 181.)*

As I expected, the front axle of the bus has gone again and we departed for the workshops once more. En route we got another blow out and as a result were stranded. After a few hours looking round and walking nearly knee deep in mud, we managed to strike a shop where we signed all sorts of documents, and made all sorts of promises, to get the loan of a tube which saw us safely into the workshops.

6/11/1916

I spent the day helping on the car and fixing up the axle and tubes. Have had the axle re-straightened, but do not expect it to last long, so they have sent for a new one in case this goes again.

7/11/1916

Back to Thistle Dump once again and all of us are hard at it. We are going continuously night and day. As we have no orderlies on the car it is necessary for both drivers to go together, as over such roads patients from the top stretcher are apt to fall off at any minute.

8/11/1916

We are still going strong. Both Callaghan and I are about worn out. We believe that they are trying to get us as orderlies, then we can work 24 hours alternatively.

9/11/1916

Orderlies are coming on tonight. Cal and I tossed as to who would be on duty tonight. Fortune was with me and gave me a night's sleep, which was entirely welcome.

10/11/1916

I relieved Cal this morning, and I have been kept fairly busy all day. I met Les Gurner and Barelow today.

(Leonard Gurner, (No 8781). Embarked Adelaide, 10/2/16, and served in the 3rd Field Ambulance.)

11/11/1916

Very heavy bombardment last night, but have heard of no local infantry action. The weather has been much clearer and the boys are expecting another stunt shooting.

(Planned actions and assaults were euphemistically called "stunts" by the ANZACs.(Ed.))

12/11/1916

Nothing startling, but have received a bonza Aust. mail. Also got a letter from Alec telling me that he had got a trip back to Australia. Eric and I are both delighted that Alec will see Australia and of course hope to join him there before long.

(Alec Blackwell went to Edinburgh War Hospital, Bangor, where he was operated on for appendicitis. His recovery was slow, and eventually he was repatriated to Australia. He sailed home on the "MT Wiltshire" 12/1/1916. Alec went back to the Mitcham AIF camp, but was not demobilised. He sailed back to France less than 2 weeks

later on the *"MT Militiades" (24/1/1917)*, disembarking at Devonport 27/3/1917. Co-incidentally, Ralph's brother in law, Dr Ren Burnard sailed for France on the same ship, on the same date. Alec was back in Etaples, France with the 2nd Division, 7th Field Ambulance Corp by 7/4/1917.(Ed.))

13/11/1916

Heard today that all along the 13 mile front our army had advanced. Our boys were in this, and of course, did well, but the conditions are playing the deuce with the men. Although the weather is picking up, the roads are still in a very bad condition and today I have had a wretched time with blowouts, bogs etc.

Historical note:
The Battle of the Somme ended after the actions at Flers, 13/11/16 to 16/11/16. The advance was stopped on November 19th. But the offensive launched 13-16th November at Flers really determined the action.
British casualties in the Somme had numbered nearly 432,000 men. British staff had estimated they would need to have that number "available for expenditure..." and "they were duly expended.." (Bean, CEW, (1929) Vol III, P. 943.)
The British and Dominion forces (including the Australians) had suffered their losses in advancing seven miles. This equates to one man per inch, over four and a half months. German losses opposite the British, were 230,000.
Field Marshall Haig was losing his men at twice the rate the Germans were losing their men.
However, the Allied commanders agreed on November 15th that the Germans had suffered 630,000 casualties on the Somme, compared with 485,000 for the French and British.
They were wrong. Subsequent historical analysis proves these figures incorrect.
The correct count for the Somme campaign would appear to be in to order of half a million German casualties, to 750,000 Allied casualties.

(Bean, CEW, (1929) Vol III, P 943-946; Butler, AG, Vol II, Pp 102-103.)

14/11/1916

I am still on the go. There is plenty of work to do. The wounded are coming in very quickly. I saw a tank today. This is the first I have seen.

Historical note:
Tanks were a new weapon, and were in the experimental stage at this time. The tank was actually an Australian invention.
They were first used in battle with Australian infantry at Bullecourt, April 1917. It was an absolute disaster for the Australian 1st Division, which suffered heavy losses as a result of the inefficacy of the tank battalion.
They were so ineffective, that Captain Albert Jacka VC, of the 14th Battalion, which suffered heavy losses at Bullecourt, had to be restrained from attacking and shooting one of the British tank commanders, as he thought he had cost his troop unnecessary lives.
Subsequently, in April 1917, Jacka wrote a report, (which was ignored), suggesting that tank battalions remain under the command of the infantry in the field. The report was countersigned by Colonel Peck and Colonel Drake-Brockman. General Gough, who was loathed by the ANZACs, shelved the report, never wanting to be reminded of the blood-bath he had presided over at Bullecourt. (Lawriwsky,(2007) Pp. 276-277.)
Jacka's suggestion was later adopted, with devastatingly successful military effect, by General Sir John Monash at Hamel. (Ed.)

15/11/1916

I have not been able to get down to Cal for relief so have to keep going. There are so many wounded coming in now, that we are entraining them closer up. After a heavy day, my differential went again tonight so have to wait up here for a lorry to tow me to the workshops.

16/11/1916

Fritz shelled this place fairly heavily last night, using shrapnel. I did not feel too comfortable in the car. The only casualty was a horse. Went over and saw Eric today at Green Dump and had a good feed. Fritz is dropping bombs very heavily this morning and he got a few chaps, but not Australians.

("Green Dump" was an RAP (Regimental Aid Post) near the lines, Eric was there with the Stretcher Bearers of the 7th Field Ambulance. They would deliver wounded from the front lines to the RAP's.(Ed.))

17/11/1916

A lorry arrived today at about noon. I had rather long and weary trip to the workshops which are only about 12 miles away. I did not arrive at the workshops until about 4 am this morning, at which hour it was snowing. While in tow, I had my radiator broken and lamps bashed in. Luckily, at that time, I was not driving, having given over to one of the workshop men in order that I could ride in the lorry to shown them the road.

Historical note:
The major offensives along the Somme Valley were now winding down. From now to the end of Winter, Ralph is clearly involved in repairs and maintenance to the ambulances. He is also driving with the Motor Transport Division. Just because there is a cessation in attacking the enemy lines does not mean a complete cessation in bombing, artillery action and the like. There is still a clear and present danger to all the ANZAC forces.(Ed.)

18/11/1916

There are about nine Daimlers in dock here now, all of which are going to the base at Paris, the first three to go tomorrow.

19/11/1916

There is a little snow lying about today; very cold, nothing doing.

20/11/1916

I spent most of the day cleaning up the old bus a bit. The water round the carburetor froze the other night bursting the carburetor jacket.

21/11/1916

There is nothing much doing. Fritz was over last night with his bombs.

22/11/1916

I walked into Heilly today, and had a good old bath. A badly needed one too. Orders are that we are to be ready to move tomorrow. Gave over a list of tools etc. today, which I think I will need.

23/11/1916

Two of us were towed to Albert Station today. The car that Pete Spence (my old mate) is on, is the other one.

24/11/1916

We are put on the rail trucks late tonight.

25/11/1916

We were moved out late tonight, and went as far as Romo camp.

26/11/1916

We did not move until very late tonight.

27/11/1916

We arrived in Abancourt early this morning, and have been here all day.

28/11/19116

We moved early this morning and were at Epluches when we went to bed.

29/11/1916

We arrived at Jennevillers (Gas works) this morning, but were not taken off the rail trucks. These gas works are immense. The Gas Works are said to be the largest in the world.

30/11/1916

We are eventually taken off the trucks and partially settled up today. We went to Epuray and had a good night. Two fine little places not far from the Gas Works.

1/12/1916

Left for St. Dennis, the engine repair part of the workshop, which is just near the gates of Paris. We went through a lot of signing papers etc. and were finally fixed up. We got a pay from the Adjutant and a pass to Paris this afternoon. We went to the Gay City, and had a splendid time. She undoubtedly is a splendid place.

2/12/1916

I am on fatigue work this morning. We get to go to Paris again this afternoon. Hired a taxi and had a splendid look round. Went to the Olympus, where there were a couple of Australian turns, which we were pleased to see. We got a free ticket given us by a chap who met us in the street. He turned out to be the "Mad Musician". I had seen him before at the Tivoli Theatre in Adelaide!

3/12/1916

In Paris again today and had a splendid time. Think it is a marvelous city and was terribly surprised at its cleanliness. Tipping is still a very big factor in that city.

4/12/1916

We caught the train at the Gare du Nord (Railway Station) in Paris at about 1.30 pm and left to rejoin our units. Up to very last minute thought we would have to go to Etaples, but fortunately these orders were changed. We arrived at Amiens at about 5.30 pm tonight after a very decent trip. We were waiting about on the platform all night for the train to Vignacourt, where we believed our visit to be.

(Historical note:
Ralph spent 2 days in Paris in December 1916 while his ambulance was being repaired. He wrote a letter home describing his 'adventure.' It is reproduced here in full;
"My dear all,
Well, here I find myself back and driving another Ambulance with the old Unit. There is no doubt we were very fortunate to get back to our units; most others get drafted to Base details, from where it is a difficult job to rejoin your own unit. Anyhow, here we are and feel like one returning to work after a holiday.
Last week has been a holiday. I had forgotten I was a member of the AIF.
The city itself (Paris) is marvellous really, no other word can express my feelings. The base workshops to which we had to take the car is an Imperial concern, and all officers and men were great to us. Three afternoons for 1pm until 9 pm we were given passes to the city, and being somewhere near the first Australians to visit the place, you can just imagine what a time we had. Laugh, why we never stopped laughing from the time we arrived there till the time of leaving.
The first tram we jumped aboard I became the cause of much laughter and subject of indelicate ridicule. The tram had pulled up and the chaps were hurriedly jumping aboard when I saw rather a nice looking young lady standing in the doorway while the others rushed passed her. Without giving another thought I caught hold of

one of my mates arms, who was just getting aboard, (badly formed sentence, but please excuse) saying, "One minute allow the lady to get out," and at the same time beckoning for the lady to get out.

You can perhaps imagine the laughter in which she, the conductress of the tram, joined.

One spoils ones experiences when he tries to commit them to paper, but I assure you I could keep you all laughing for hours if only I were with you in person to tell you all.

I felt mean that Eric was not with me to join in the fun. It would be impossible to enter that City in better dress than that of an Australian and will, I add, also as a private in that Army. One sees the place as it really is. We dined at a very nice quiet Hotel, the photo of which I enclose herewith, or possibly with the next letter.

We visited the Tony restaurants which all the authors are so fond of using; we saw most of the magnificent sights by taxi. We went in the Tube for the first time; we went to a couple of theatres and picture shows. All that in three afternoons, so now you have some conception of the time we had.

Fashions, why now I feel I am an authority in such, but will not try my descriptive talent in that respect.

All the French people there were good to us and at first we seemed to be quite the centre of attraction, or the 'Cynosure' (is that how it is spelt?) of neighbouring eyes.

The Australian hat, even our old one, like wine would cause the traffic of one of the main streets to come to a standstill. Most people took us for Canadians, but we rectified this at every opportunity. I have just read through what has been written so far, and feel very disappointed with it. What a pity I can't make these things not a little like they really were, but really the last few days have been great. The sights of the city are wonderful; the four of you who have visited the place will corroborate that.

The old car was in a fairly bad condition but not out of the usual run; the roads were absolutely the worst I have ever seen cars running continuously on.

A report as regards my car had to be sent in at the base; and to make that report (which as you will see was rather amusing) I had to answer the following questions and also the final part of the report, made up by the examining corporal.

    "The condition of:

>   *Your engine? -Carburettor jacket cracked.*
>   *Front axle, Springs? -Axle bent, springs sprung!*
>   *Radiator? -Broken.*
>   *Headlights and sidelights? -Damaged.*
>   *Differential? -Broken.*
>   *Cover to Ambulance? -Ripped and badly torn.*
>   *Otherwise the vehicle is in quite good condition!!"*

On arrival back was greeted by a great mail dated October 26th. I will deal with that mail tomorrow if I get a chance; if not I will answer it in the next week's letter.
Love to all
Yours lovingly
Ralph."
(Ed.))

The Diary:

5/12/1916

No train came till 6 o'clock this morning, so we spent a very cold night. On arrival at Vignacourt found our unit to be about 6 miles away. We arrived there about 10 am this morning, and reported for duty. We were put on to new cars and I am on with a Tommy now for a time.

6/12/1916

I am on duty today; clearing from the 2nd Division battalions, with plenty of work to keep one busy.

7/12/1916

Trip to Amiens with Eric today, had a good time.

8/12/1916

Differential in the new bus has gone today. This time the wheel and all have come off and naturally this gave me a bit of surprise.

10/12/1916

Nothing doing today; little snow this morning.

11/12/1916

Another day with nothing to report.

12/12/1916

My car is back today fixed up again, so I have been on duty.

13/12/1916

Eric and I spent the day at Amiens and had a good time. Went into town with a few other of the 7th Field Ambulance Unit, stretcher bearers and supply men.

14/12/1916

On battalion duty again all day.

15/12/1916

There is nothing much doing, but a bit of a mail today. They say a big Australian mail will be in tomorrow.

16/12/1916

The mail arrived today bringing the very letters I wanted.

17/12/1916

Noting doing except a very acceptable pay.

18/12/1916

On move today. Find ourselves in Buire tonight.

19/12/1916

On duty and heard that they are expecting the unit to move up the line again any day.

20/12/1916

Saw Val Giddings, Amos James and Bill Long. I have been pretty hard at it today.

21/12/1916

Late tonight, I was detailed in the 5th Field Ambulance. And now I find myself back at Bussey les Doaurs with the training Battalions. I have been going fairly hard all day, evacuating sick, getting drugs for the Medical officers, etc.

(The "training Battalions" were the replacement battalions for the front line battalions which had suffered heavy casualties.(Ed.))

22/12/1916

I have had a big letter writing day today, although have been kept fairly busy.

24/12/1916

A 5th Field Ambulance car came to relieve me tonight. I am to report back to the 7th Field Ambulance, which is now at an Advanced Dressing Station; so we spend Xmas near the front line, with the boys after all.

25/12/1916

I joined up with our boys at the A.D.S. at Bernafay Wood, not far from Thistle Dump, where we were the last time we were up in these parts. I spent a quiet Xmas day with Eric. Bill Graves was also down. I received a good Xmas parcel from Mrs Hawkes of Geelong.

26/12/1916

Another quiet day with very little doing. But it is cold and miserable, I can tell you.

27/12/1916

Repetition of yesterday as regards to work, but a few more shells of Fritz's flying about.

28/12/1916

Shells are lobbing rather too close to allow for a good night's spell. I did not get much rest last night. I did a couple of trips today. A couple of bombs dropped not far off today.

29/12/1916

I was detailed to the 5th Field Ambulance today. I reported to them at Becordel Advanced Dressing Station. Eric went up with the bearers yesterday.

30/12/1916

Left Becordel at about 10 o'clock this morning and took the Colonel of the 5th and two D.O.'s to Ribmont, Heilly, Bursey les Daours and finally to Amiens, where we had dinner and left for Becordel at about 5 o'clock. I arrived home in good time, but had misfortune to break both brakes en route. My Scottish mate was driving and got us home without any mishaps, and without any brakes!

31/12/1916

We went into the workshops with brakes today. I worked a little on car. Met Johnny Walker there; he is also in the shop with his Ford.

1/1/1917

Quiet New Year's Day. Workmen in the workshops are not working today.

2/1/1917

We just about completed her today.

3/1/1917

Out of the workshops today. I got back to the unit and found great Australian mail waiting for me. "Tres bonne!"

4/1/1917

Little work doing, but time mostly occupied by letter writing.

5/1/1917

A few shells over last night. Had a great dinner with Bill Graves tonight.

6/1/1917

Quiet day today; nothing doing. Bill came down tonight.

7/1/1917

An unusual occurrence in the form of Church Parade. Ironically, I was not able to attend.

8/1/1917

Another slack day.

9/1/1917

Little busier today. A few shells knocking around.

10/1/1917

There is a lot of talk about the English drivers, and the N.C.Os leaving us; but don't know if there is any truth therein.

11/1/1917

Fritz shelling during last night, some rather too close. It is snowing all morning and has commenced again tonight.

12/1/1917

All motor drivers, except Charlie Burrows, are transferred to A.S.C.M.T. 1st Division Supply. The Colonel, Tommy N.C.O.'s and men left us. A new Australian Sergeant has arrived for duty; I have been made a temporary Corporal, which is a great surprise to me.

13/1/1917

I am off the car today for first time since taking on driving. Re-assigned drivers had good old chat on old Gallipoli days. It is snowing here now.

14/1/1917

One of our drivers returned from England today. I am getting on well with Sgt. Stafford.

15/1/1917

Up early this morning, two cars detailed for duty away.

16/1/1917

Fritz sent a few over again last night. Sergeant and I busy on cars today.

17/1/1917

Snowing inches thick this morning, heaviest fall I have yet experienced. Great fun snow ball fighting. It is about the best fun we have had in weeks!

18/1/1917

Up early again this morning, and the snow is still lying thickly about, and falling slightly. We are on the move today and have taken over Becordel from 5th Field Ambulance. It is quite comfy, and we have a round a nice fire now. Another car detailed for duty is away today.

19/1/1917

Australian mail in today, but unfortunately did not get the ones I wanted, but am hoping for a few more tomorrow. Nothing startling doing.

20/1/1917

Most cars out on duty today, otherwise nothing doing.

21/1/1917

Very handy pay, but better allowed 70 francs now.

22/1/1917

Have been sleeping in an old shed, with nothing but rats for company last night. Another little rat in form of Donny Pace kept me company. Busy shifting camp, are taking over Rest Station in Albert. Slight fall of snow.

(Historical note:
Rats and vermin were a huge problem for the diggers in France.
Ralph only refers to them a couple of times, but they were a constant annoyance, and a constant unwelcome and uncomfortable companion to the diggers. One soldier recorded;
"Rats abound in thousands and are loathed if only because they feed on the corpses lying about. They are too surfeited very often to run."
(Kyle, R, (2005) P. 162.).
Don Pace was a 7th Field Ambulance driver with Ralph. (Ed.))

23/1/1917

Fritz shelled Albert nearly all last night; it was the coldest night yet experienced. Beautiful day; any amount of Taubes about. All the cars frozen up; two radiators and one carburetor burst. Blow lamp in action for starting.

I have had a busy day.

24/1/1917

Another very cold night and freezing all day, makes things very difficult for the drivers. Capt. Hamilton left us for Australia today. Shelling all round today with very big shells; supposed to be from 12 to 15 inches. Three of our chaps were wounded.

25/1/1917

Another very cold night; went round with one of the cars to take R.M.O's to Conference. Saw one of the 5th Field cars with the cylinder jacket burst out with the cold.

(Ralph records the freezing conditions. In fact, the 1916/17 winter in Europe was the coldest experienced for 40 years.)
26/1/1917

Just as cold again today. Another Officer's Conference, same as yesterday. Saw old Bill Graves today at Ribmont.

27/1/1917

Working at the room for our chaps today. The room is looking splendid and will be very comfy.

28/1/1917

Still excessively cold. Moved into new room tonight and are very comfy. Nice fire.

29/1/1917

Fritz shelling today. Not too pleasant. Met Ken McEwin and Jack Mehaffy today. Eric and I spent most of the evening with them. An Australian mail in today – Dec. 13th – Tres Bonne! Taubes over tonight in with bombs and machine guns, making things slightly too hot.

(Historical note:

No 3062 Sgt Kenneth John McEwin, 50th Battalion (formed from the original 27th Battalion. Sgt John Lamb Mehaffy, who served with the 50th Battalion (formed from the 27th). Killed in action less than 2 months later on 2/4/17.)

30/1/1917

Aust mail today; got 8 letters. Jack Mehaffy and Ken McEwin round here today. Had a good chat, both looking splendid and are on their way to England.

31/1/1917

Snow falling. Place inspected by General Smythe today.

1/2/1917

Anzac Corps gave us a splendid concert here tonight. Jack and Ken came with us. The MT boys were hard at it fixing the lighting.

2/2/1917

Jack and Ken over again today. Spent a good day fixing up our room. Had a good night with Eric, Ken and Jack.

3/2/1917

There was a good Australian mail today; but there was a big bombardment last night.

4/2/1917

Don Pace and I went to Amiens today; on duty with patients and it is very cold. Had grand bath and feed. Ken McEwin and Jack Mehaffy came in with us and spent the day. Temp today was 5 degrees Fahrenheit.

5/2/1917

Nothing much doing.

6/2/1917

Chestnuts issued today for the first time. Bombs dropped around last night.

7/2/1917

Fritz again around with his bombs last night.

8/2/1917

7th Bearers went up the line today. Eric was with them.

7ᵗʰ *Field Ambulance men:*

Corporal Eric Kidman, front seated, after he received his first "stripes," in November 1916. He is pictured here with (L to R) Jim Godfrey, Jack Dunn, Ken Dowding and Mortimer Bradshaw, all 7ᵗʰ Field Ambulance stretcher-bearers. Kidman, Godfrey, Dowding and Bradshaw all received a MM for bravery. Bradshaw died on 20/5/17 of wounds he received in the Bullecourt campaign.

France, Winter 1916.
A wounded soldier being loaded into an Australian Motor Ambulance at an Advanced Dressing Station outside Contalmaison, near Pozieres. Typical of the ambulance work Ralph was doing. (Photo; AWM. Winter 1916/17.)

Motor Cycles:
Alec Blackwell (R) at Amiens, motorcycling. Not sure if this was business or pleasure, but most likely it was not pleasure. As Drivers attached to 2nd Divisions Motor Transport Co., Alec and Ralph occasionally rode dispatch bikes. (Photo: Courtesty Margaret Wood.)

Sergeants of the 7th Field Ambulance, early May, 1916.
Eric Kidman was made Sergeant on 4th April and was wounded in action, (for a second time) on 5th May 1916. Eric has lost a lot of weight, and is noticeably thin and gaunt in this photo. Eric is in the centre of the back row. (Photo: Courtesy Tania Shaw.)

7th Field Ambulance, Xmas 1917.
Sgt. Ralph DeGaris is centre, middle row.

Ralph's first leave in Guernsey, May 1917.
(Above) Alec Blackwell, (left) and Ralph with Elizabeth DeGaris, first wife of EC DeGaris, (centre right.)
(Below) Alec, Elizabeth DeGaris, and Ralph. Guernsey, May 1917.

Chapter Twelve:
"Springtime" in the Somme Valley; Bullecourt, May 1917: The Diary:

9/2/1917

Very cold last night. One radiator burst in 28 places. Our infantry sapped the trenches last night and they are doing good work.

10/2/1917

Nothing doing. Artillery here was very active last night.

11/2/1917

Another quiet day. Our home is bonza and comfortable.

12/2/1917

Still very quiet only little running.

13/2/1917

One of our drivers returned from leave. It is warmer today.

14/2/1917

Very quiet here today, but this is what it is like. We seem to do nothing for days, then all hell breaks loose.

15/2/1917

Few repairs on car to keep us occupied.

(Historical note;
At this time, Europe was emerging from the coldest winter for 40 years. However, the war kept going! Many diaries report similar experiences to Ralph. Here, there has been a week of little activity. Then there will be a frantic week or two, when they virtually work around the clock, whether infantry, or support units such as the Field Ambulances.(Ed.))

16/2/1917

Taubes again over last night. Bombs are a little too handy to us. Capt. Stachan is back with us temporarily. Donny Pace and I went to Amiens with one of the Officers. We had a good feed. No lights to come home by, so it was rather a rough trip. Picked up two drunk officers and saw them to their billets. They threw the biggest tip to Donny that I have ever seen thrown; it was 100 francs.

17/2/1917

A day of arguments. Nothing doing.

18/2/1917

Two gramaphones have come in for repairs. We are rapidly becoming known as a workshop.

19/2/1917

Lovely weather again today.

20/2/1917

Still very quiet, but it is noticeable that the Artillery units are becoming more active.

21/2/1917

Sgt. Stafford went to Amiens today so I have been fairly busy.

22/2/1917

We have not returned one of the phonographs, so we are having music!

23/2/1917

Not much to do today.

24/2/1917

Repetition of yesterday, basically, waiting, waiting, waiting.

25/2/1917

Heard today that Fritz had retreated on this front. I hope it is true.

26/2/1917

Moved to Becordel today. Sorry to leave our old home.

27/2/1917

Started taking down the back axle on one of the cars today.

28/2/1917

Finished taking down the back axle today, and we are fitting up a new one as soon as we get one.

1/3/1917

Had a long trip today to Behencourt; Court Martial over a case where a driver was up for traveling against arrows. Roads here are in a wretched state.

(Historical note:
Courts Martial were not an insignificant part of life on the front. Men were constantly prosecuted for breaches of regulations. Penalties, such as prison and fines were carried into effect. The death penalty was passed on some 129 Australian soldiers in WW 1 (119 for desertion.) Carrying out of the death penalty required the consent of the Governor General (on advice from the Government of the day), which consent was constantly denied, the rationale being that the AIF was a volunteer force.
General Haigh tried to convince the Australian authorities to carry out the penalty, to enforce discipline on the troops, but was constantly rebuffed. The British Army, and other Dominion Armies, by contrast, carried out the sentence on 306 occasions. Offences carrying the death penalty included desertion and cowardice.
Possibly the most tragic, and one of the most celebrated Courts Martial of the first War involved Private John Leak, VC, a hero of the Pozieres campaign, but who deserted at Ypres, possibly due to the disabling effects of 'shell-shock.' He was convicted and given a suspended life sentence for desertion.
(Pederson, P. (2007), P 271.)(Ed.)

2/3/1917

Day passed quietly; gave evidence in case, held today; referred to in yesterday's portion (ie traveling against arrows). Australian mail in tonight; got seven letters, splendid news from home. Have been off colour all day.

3/3/1917

Spent day doing nothing except write a few letters.

4/3/1917

Busy working at back axle on one of our cars.

5/3/1917

Completed fitting new back axle in the car tonight. Parcel from Clemmie was received today. Also received a heap of Naracoorte Heralds today. Spent quiet night listening to our gramophone (the one which we have forgotten to return after repairing!!)

6/3/1917

Tried the car that we fixed up yesterday. I am on that car now. I did one short run this afternoon.

7/3/1917

Beastly windy day; spent most of it inside trying to make souvenirs.

(Historical note:
Ralph had several souvenirs he made, including salt and pepper shakers made of old ammunition shells. He also had two 50mm shells fired from ML 331 during the raid on Zeebrugge in May, 1915 made into a gong which his wife Betha presented to the Millicent RSL Club in memory of F/O William Sowden DeGaris who died in March 1945 in a raid over Germany during WW 2. (Ed.))

8/3/1917

Rather busy day. Left this morning for Behencourt. Car ran wretchedly, and I am having a deal of trouble on the road. Found our Ford stuck up at Behencourt, spent the best part of the afternoon helping him and arrived home late tonight.

(Behencourt is north-east of Amiens, between Amiens and Warloy (see the Amiens-Albert Map.(Ed.))

9/3/1917

Rather busy day. Slight trouble with one of the Fords this morning. Running bearers up line this evening.

10/3/1917

Ordinary day; little running.

11/3/1917

Beautiful day; I was working on car this morning. Part of the Australian mail came in tonight. I received a letter from home, and one from Alec. Eric and I think it wretched his having to leave so quickly. Things like that need ventilation.

12/3/1917

We were fairly busy today. Bill Graves came down to see us tonight.

13/3/1917

I spent the day again with Bill Graves. I wrote letters home tonight.

14/3/1917

Quite an ordinary day except that I did a little motor cycling. Roads are bad and it has been raining slightly. Spent night up at 5th Division's A.S.C. with some cobbers of the Sergeant.

15/3/1917

Another quiet day. Working on cars.

16/3/1917

Another fairly quiet day. Artillery kicking up a bit of a noise in the night.

17/3/1917

Australian mail closes tonight and I have got a few letters away by it. Heard tonight of the political crisis in Russia.

(Russian revolution, which occurred in 1917, towards the end of the war. Russia had suffered terribly in the war, and lost huge numbers of soldiers, and civilian, worse than most other nations. (Ed.))

18/3/1917

A beautiful day. Have been working on one of the cars all day. Had a couple of runs. Met Allan Janet in Albert tonight. Heard our boys had taken Bapaume.

19/3/1917

Slack day. Great talk today of the German retirement.

20/3/1917

Further good war news tonight. We will see home this year yet. Busy day on cars, and there is plenty of work.

(Historical note:
The German Army had withdrawn and retired from the front line at Bapaume. It moved back towards the strongholds which it established on the Hindenburg Line at Bullecourt.
The British and Australians had pushed the line from Pozieres through to Bapaume, and as a result, the Germans surprised the Allies by retreating towards the Hindenburg Line, about 8 Kms north of Bapaume. In March 1916, the front line was at Vaulx-Vracourt,

and the British plan was to push through the Hindenburg line at Bullecourt. (Bean, (1933) Vol IV, Chapter 4, Pp 60-111.)

This offensive occurred in May 1917, and was in human terms, another tragedy for ANZAC troops. In particular, it was a campaign which convinced many Australians, officers and ranks alike, that the British Generals were incompetent, poor planners, poor communicators, and worst of all, cared little about human life.

You note that Ralph is still hopeful of the war ending early. The retirement of the German Army however did not signal the impending defeat of the enemy, but a determination by them to reinforce their position, dig-in and re-group. (Ed.))

21/3/1917

Sgt. Stafford left here this morning for a test in answer to an application of his to the Australian Flying Corps. I have had a very busy day; electrician and all sorts. Was pulled out of bed at midnight to see about a car to be dispatched immediately to Bapaume.

22/3/1917

Sgt. Stafford is not back. I am very tired tonight as I have had another busy day. War news is good again tonight. Bill Graves came down again today.

23/3/1917

Trip to Amiens today. I had a good time, and had a splendid bath. Home to be at about 3am.

24/3/1917

Not so busy today; I am fixing up the electric light.

25/3/1917

Ford back axle fixed after I spent a full day at it. Splendid feed today. Time advanced 1 hour.

26/3/1917

Confirmation of my stripes through today. Had a few runs. Bill Graves was down to see us.

Historical note:
Ralph had been appointed Corporal in 11/1/17. This was confirmed officially 26/3/17.(Ed.))

27/3/1917

Nothing much doing; beautiful day. Bill Graves came down to see us again.

28/3/1917

All our cars, except the Ford reported back today. I did a few odd runs.

29/3/1917

There was plenty of work for drivers today. I did plenty of running around today.

30/3/1917

I have had another fairly busy day today. A couple of cars have gone a little crook. Bill Graves down again tonight.

31/3/1917

Fairly busy. Little Australian mail, but not much for me. I put in letter writing tonight.

1/4/1917

Nothing much doing for me. I did a little work on cars.

2/4/1917

Much same as yesterday.

3/4/1917

More Australian mail today, but I was stiff again and received nothing.

4/4/1917

Went into Albert tonight, but too late for the show. The French are beginning to come back to Albert. They look absolutely dead beat.

5/4/1917

I had a slow day. I had a letter from Alec telling of his arrival back in England. I got a great shock.

Ralph's notes:
"Alec had been repatriated to Australia because of his appendicitis, much to everyone's disappointment, but had sailed back to Europe on the "MT Militades" in January 1917. He arrived in Devonport, UK, in March and was back in the front by April!
Ren Burnard arrived in France early in April. Ren was immediately attached to the 2nd Field Hospital, at Wimereux, outside Boulogne."
[In fact, coincidentally, Alec and Ren had sailed to Europe together on the "Militidiades," In January 1917.](Ed.)

6/4/1917

Records from Uncle and Aunty for the Gramophone came today.

(EC DeGaris, (referred to by Ralph as "Uncle Clem"), and his first wife Elizabeth, operated a rest station for Australian Diggers on the island of Guernsey from 1916-1918. I reckon that it was they who sent the gramophone records to Ralph. Ralph visited them on Guernsey on three occasions during the war, all in 1917-18. The first visit was the leave Ralph took after the 2nd Division was relieved at Bullecourt, May 1917.(Ed.))

7/4/1917

Inoculated again today. Rather sore tonight.

8/4/1917

Church of England Service here today. First with unit for ages (years). I did not go.

9/4/1917

Part Australian mail came in today. No letters for me. Feel a bit isolated from everyone at the moment.

10/4/1917

Grand war news today. Very jubilant.

(Historical note:
The advances towards the Hindenburg Line were made by the 2nd Division north of Bapaume, and Vaulx-Vracourt, towards Bullecourt. The Germans had "retired," and the Allies advanced towards Bullecourt and Reincourt. The "jubilation" was short-lived. As set out in the Historical Note above, the Bullecourt campaign of April May turned out to be another disaster for the ANZAC's mainly due to the incompetence of the British Generals.(Ed.))

The Bullecourt campaigns, April-May 1917:

11/4/1917

Snowing today, and it is rather cold. Eric also had a letter from Alec.

(Historical note:
It was still bitterly cold 2 months before "high summer" in Europe. The coldest winter in 40 years extended through Spring, and nearly into summer.(Ed.))

12/4/1917

Busy day, but it is still snowing, and very cold. We are moving up towards the front tomorrow.

13/4/1917 to 12/5/1917

The past month has been the most crowded yet experienced. We moved from Becordel up to an Advanced Dressing Station just outside Vaulx.

The first excitement was that the Germans had broken through. But the depressing news is that 3 of our Unit were killed today, following on the loss of two other of our cobbers who died two days ago. Tim Healey and Willis were killed on the 3rd May, and today Roy Angel, Gallanty and Jarmain were all killed. There is general discontent that the British Generals are making mistake after mistake, and it is costing many lives unnecessarily. We just obey our orders, and try to get the job done.

(Historical note:
In March, as noted above, much to the surprise of the Allies, the German Army had retired from the area it had held around Bapaume and moved northwards and back to the fortified Hindenburg line.
The advances towards the Hindenburg Line were made by the 2nd Division north of Bapaume, and Vaulx-Vracourt, towards Bullecourt. The Germans had "retired," and the Allies advanced towards Bullecourt and Reincourt. Initially, there was much celebration of the retirement of the enemy, but this jubilation was short-lived.
The 2nd Division was involved in the First Bullecourt Battle, 11/4/17, which was a disaster for the ANZACS, and the English. It shook the confidence of the Australians in the British command. The errors made on 10-11/4/17 were obvious to all.
Tanks were used for the first time with infantry, and the result was appalling, both strategically, and in human terms for the Australians. General Gough said he was satisfied that ".....the ANZAC attack has been of great assistance...." (Bean, CEW, Vol IV, P. 349.) To this

point in time, the Allies were virtually chasing the Germans back to the Hindenburg Line.
Vaulx is about 4 kms south of Bullecourt. There was an Advanced Dressing Station just north of Vaulx. The Dressing Station was established as the ANZAC troops pushed northwards. The Motor Ambulances only worked at night here, as the roads lay open to German observers and snipers. The 7th Field Ambulance was in charge of this post. (Bean, CEW, Vol IV. Pp 474-475.)
German counter-attacks occurred on 5/5/17, (and again on 15/5/17, after the 2nd Division had been relieved), on the right flank of the Australians (east of Bullecourt) where the 2nd Division Brigades were operating (Bean, Vol IV, plan at P 526.)(Ed.))

At 5.30 in the morning we were all well awake watching the Artillery men getting back as quickly as possible with the sights of their guns being re-set as quickly as possible.

At about 8 o'clock the scene had changed, and our wounded were coming in greatly jubilant. The 2nd Division had saved the situation, capturing hundreds of prisoners and recapturing all guns and leaving 2,000 Germans dead on the field.

(Historical note:
This was on 6th May, 1917. The Australian Brigades of the 2nd Division were in the field from 14/4/17 until they were relieved by the 5th Division on May 10th, 1917 (Bean, CEW, Vol IV, P 527.) Ralph went on his first leave 2 days later.
The Hindenburg Line was the German defensive line, which the Germans reinforced as their last line of defence, after their initial invasions in 1914. Bullecourt was right on the Hindenburg Line, and Reincourt, a secondary objective, was just north of the Hindenburg Line, and north east of Bullecourt.
In the 2 Bullecourt campaigns, Ralph's 2nd Division suffered 3,798 casualties, markedly more than any other Australian Division. Total Australian casualties were about 10,000, with 3,000 at First Bullecourt and 7,000 at Second Bullecourt. (Bean, CEW, Vol IV, P. 543.)

The stretcher bearers suffered terribly, particularly in Ralph's unit. Colonel Black of the 7th Field Ambulance noted of his bearers;
> *"The morale of the stretcher-bearers was remarkable. Their casualties were very heavy but there was no hesitation. Heavy shelling tends to immobilise bearers, but this was not seen." (Butler, AG, (1940) Vol II, P 149.)(Ed.))*

For days after this we were expecting our boys to start the offensive on the Hindenberg line. Although the attack was held off for days, it did eventually come and was successful as far as our boys were concerned.

The wounded came in and our bearers suffered considerably. Apart from our cobbers killed, the men are exhausted in the conditions. They are working until they drop.

Historical note:
The ANZACs suffered terrible losses in the two Bullecourt battles in April 1917 and May 1917. The 4th Division achieved what most thought was not possible in the First Bullecourt on the 11th April, 1917. They broke through the Hindenburg line without artillery support. Subsequently, the German machine gunners closed a gate behind the ANZACS, who were then decimated. For example, the 4th Division suffered casualties of 2,339 out of 3,000 engaged (Bean, (1933) Vol IV, pp 341-344.). The 2nd Division also suffered awful casualties, as noted above.
The stretcher-bearers were operating at frenetic pace. With the number of wounded being transported, they would have been physically and mentally exhausted.(Ed.)

In the midst of all this Alec arrived back with us and we are having a grand time.

(Alec Blackwell arrives back to the Front, having been repatriated to Australia! Not too many diggers would have had the unusual

distinction of being repatriated home, then returned to the front-line. Alec had been away from his mates for 6 months.(Ed.))

The Australians have pierced the German grand line of defence, the Hindenburg Line; but all say it is impossible to hold the position. However, all the experts are beaten as our boys hang on and hold all gains, although counter-attacks are being delivered all the time by the Germans. 13 Counter-attacks were delivered in 24 hours, all of which failed, and when we were relieved, the position was still being held against the fiercest of attacks.

During this, Eric was wounded, and his work has been spoken most highly of. Although wounded he remained at work until proper relief came.

(Eric Kidman was wounded, for a second time, on 5/5/17, having been wounded previously in Gallipoli. He was repatriated to Rouen, where there was a field hospital. He was injured in the right leg, and was held in Rouen hospital until 2/6/17. Eric went on leave to the UK 7/7/17, and returned to the Unit, in the field 21/7/17.)

(Historical note:
The Hindenburg line was a heavily fortified defensive line running north-south from a point north of Arras, to just south of Vailly. Bapaume, which was behind the German lines, was destroyed by the Germans when they left the town, and retreated. (Bean, Vol IV, Chapter IV, P 60-111.)
The ANZACs faced terrible odds at Bullecourt. The enemy was well fortified, and the attacking ANZAC troops offered a tempting bait to the enemy. The Germans launched seven general counter-attacks, and perhaps a dozen minor counter-attacks. The fighting was fierce, as described by Ralph, and nobody thought the Australians would hold Bullecourt, but they did so against all odds.
Bean says that the Australian soldier won success by persistence through sheer quality of their mettle, and in the face of, and despite persistent tactical errors committed by the British Generals. He notes about the Second Bullecourt Battle (May 3-16th 1917), (which cost

tens of thousands of casualties on both sides, for no appreciable territorial gain,);

> "The Second Bullecourt was the most brilliant of these achievements, impressing enemy and friends alike; it was in some ways the stoutest achievement of the Australian soldier in France...." (Bean, (1933) Vol IV P. 545.)

However, Bean also noted;

> "Bullecourt, more than any other battle, shook the confidence of Australian soldiers in the capacity of the British command; the errors, particularly on April 10th and 11th, were obvious to almost everyone. As at Pozieres......results strategically important were clutched for by impossible tactics...." (Ed.)

12/5/17:

We are now at a quiet camp back at Bazantin. I saw Val Giddings yesterday. He is looking splendid.

(Valentine Giddings was from Naracoorte, and joined the 10th Battalion in 1915.(Ed.))

I expect to go on leave tomorrow, 13/5/17. It will be my first leave in Europe.

Epilogue to Part 1.

Part One of this record is now complete. Ralph's actual diary ends at this point of his journey in war-torn Europe.

Why does it end here? Because when Ralph returned to Australia in 1919, about one half of his diaries and letters were lost overboard when he was coming ashore. The handle on his case broke, and many of his treasured letters from home were lost. Tragically, his later diaries were also lost.

This explains why Part One finished so abruptly in May 1917.

However, this is not the end for our Innocent Crusaders.

This is the situation at this point, 13th May 1917.

Ralph takes his first official leave on 13/5/17. He has been in the field since arriving in France in March 1916, except for 2 days in Paris, December 1916. Ralph sails to Guernsey for his first leave, and spends his leave with his Uncle Clem and Aunty Elizabeth at La Hougue Farm. I believe Dr Mary DeGaris was there at the same time, on leave from Epsom Hospital, UK.

As to our other Innocent Crusaders;

Eric Kidman is in hospital in Rouen, recovering from shrapnel wounds he received in his right leg at Bullecourt on 5th May 1917. He returned to his Unit on 9th June 1917.

Alec Blackwell returned to the Western Front on 2nd May 1917. Having suffered appendicitis in June 1916, Alec was repatriated first to the UK, then to Australia in November 1916, and he arrived back in Europe 27th March 1917, on the same boat as Dr Ren Burnard.

Dr Renfrey Burnard was appointed to his first Field Hospital post at Wiseneaux, near Boulogne, on 13th April, 1917. He is diagnosed with tonsillitis on 12th May 1917, and is confined to hospital until ordered to take leave in the UK from 1st June 1917 to 22nd June 1917.

Harry Schinckel is in Tidworth, UK, training, and has not embarked to join the AIF at the Western Front. He eventually arrives in Le Havre on 2nd June 1917 to join the 15th Field Ambulance 8th June 1917. At his own request, he was transferred to the 7th Field Ambulance.

A number of their close friends have already been killed in action, or died of wounds received in action.

Up until the end of May 1917, some of the most desperate fighting on the Western Front has bedeviled the ANZACs around Armentieres, Ameins, Albert, Pozieres, Messines, Ypres, Fromelles, Bapaume, and lastly the hideous, but glorious victory at Bullecourt, on the Hindenburg line.

The 2nd Division was prominent in all of the above battles. Ralph, Eric and Alec have played their part in all of those awful tragedies.

From May 1917 we no longer have Ralph's eyewitness account to trace the movements of our Innocent Crusaders.

Fortunately there are still a number of valuable resources available which allow an accurate reconstruction of the remaining war years for our three Innocent Crusaders and their cobbers.

In Part 2 of this journey, we will join Ralph, Eric and Alec on the remainder of their World War 1 experiences.

They valiantly discharge their respective duties in the horrible events which eventually culminate in the finalization of the war. Having been at Bois Grenier, Pozieres, Ypres, and Bullecourt, one could be forgiven for thinking things could not get worse. But as the men continue to endure shocking living conditions, poor health, including the disabling trench-foot infection, and become increasingly susceptible to mental and psychiatric disorders, (then called "shell shock" today labeled "post traumatic stress disorder,") they continue to endure the savagery of trench warfare for example at Third Battle of Ypres, Hamel, and finally at Viller-Bretonneux, near Amiens.

They all serve valiantly, though progressively each has doubts about the reasons the war is proceeding at all. They are aware that Germany and the Allies are trying to broker a peace, using the United States, and newly re-elected US President Woodrow Wilson, as an independent mediator. Germany's demands are arrogant, and unrealistic, and the troops know, and expect, their peace offers will be rejected, which they are. The war is destined to rage on for another 15 months.

The three innocent crusaders endure further awful sights, sounds, smells, and tastes of war. Eric is recommended for, and receives a Military Medal for bravery at Ypres. Ralph receives the Meritorious Service Medal, also at Ypres, and is recommended for the Military Medal, which is not confirmed. Their cobbers in the 7th Field Ambulance, Jim Godfrey, Mortimer Bradshaw, Ken Dowding and

Bert Kammerman all receive the Military Medal for bravery in action. They lose many of their Unit cobbers killed in action, including Roy Angel, Mortimer Bradshaw, Bert Mallett, and Roy Bice. Others are wounded beyond recovery.

Further reinforcements arrive to bolster the flagging numbers in the various brigades and battalions. In the 7th Field Ambulance, Surgeon-Captain Ren Burnard arrived in France in April 1917. Harry Schinckel, who was rejected when the three men enlisted in 1915, is eventually accepted into the AIF, and arrived to join the 15th Field Ambulance in June 1917. He repeatedly requested a transfer to the 7th Field Ambulance, where Ralph and Eric and Alec are serving, and was granted his request in August, 1917.

Dr Ren Burnard, Eric, Harry, Alec, and eventually Ralph all spend time during the final months of the war in England, and particularly in Cornwall.

The second part of this story will alternately take the reader from the killing fields of France and Belgium to the quite and serene countryside of Cornwall. It will tell another tale of our Innocent Crusaders; one which was never envisaged by any of them, but which was to profoundly affect their future lives. It is the story of men at war, tired, hungry, dirty, desperate, exhausted, shell-shocked, sick, mentally tortured, and on the verge of losing both their religious faith and their faith in human nature, but who are each brought back emphatically to the reality of life's ultimate purpose.

Out of the most awful conditions imaginable, love touches three of our innocent crusaders, and their contact with love eventually triumphs over the evil of their war experiences in an incredible way. A set of remarkable coincidences culminates in Ralph, Eric and Harry meeting, and marrying three Cornish ladies, two sisters and one of the sister's best friends.

Their marriages, forged out of three whirl-wind romances, are to last a combined total of nearly 150 years.

Co-incidentally, when researching this story, I also researched my maternal grandfather Walter Reginald (Reg) Willson who also served in the first AIF. Reg saw action at Gallipoli and on the Western Front in the Provost Corp. He won the Military Medal in action on 20/9/17 to 23/9/17 in the Third Ypres battle, and was cited for bravery under heavy shell fire on the Birr-Menin road at Ypres.

Ralph won his Meritorious Service Medal for bravery displayed under heavy shell fire on the Birr- Menin Road at Ypres, from 2/10/17 to 11/10/17, in the Third Ypres battle. Reg also met his future wife, Daisy Herbert, while on leave in the UK. He married Daisy in England and brought his new bride home to Australia in 1919.

It is an irresistible notion that Ralph and Reg met each other somewhere in Belgium on, or near the Menin Road sometime in October 1917.

Bibliography.

Adam-Smith, Patsy, (1978). *"The Anzacs,"* Thomas Nelson Australia Pty Ltd.,

Bean C.E.W. (1946) *"Anzac to Amiens,"* Australian War Memorial,

Bean C.E.W. (1917) *"Letters from France,"* Cassell & Co Ltd., London,

Bean C.E.W. & Gullett H.S., (1923) *"Official History of Australia in the War, 1914-1918. An Annotated Photographic Record of the War."* Angus & Robertson,.

Bean C.E.W. (1921) *"Official History of Australia in the War, 1914-1918, Volume 1, 'The Story of Anzac,'* Angus & Robertson,

Bean C.E.W. (1924) *"Official History of Australia in the War, 1914-1918, Volume II, 'The Story of Anzac,'* Angus & Robertson,.

Bean C.E.W. (1929) *"Official History of Australia in the War, 1914-1918, Volume III, 'The AIF in France, 1916,'* Angus & Robertson,.

Bean C.E.W. (1933) *"Official History of Australia in the War, 1914-1918, Volume IV, 'The AIF in France, 1917,'* Angus & Robertson,.

Bean C.E.W. (1937) *"Official History of Australia in the War, 1914-1918, Volume V, 'The AIF in France, 1918,'* Angus & Robertson,

Bean C.E.W. (1942) *"Official History of Australia in the War, 1914-1918, Volume VI,, 'The AIF in France, 1918,'* Angus & Robertson,.

Bickersteth, J. (Editor). (1995) *"The Bickersteth Diaries,"* Leo Cooper, London,.

Brechtelsbauer, Clemens, *"His Imperial German Majesty's U Boats in World War 1"* http//uboat.net/history/wwi

Burness, Peter, (1996) *"The Nek,"* Kangaroo Press,.

Butler, A.G. (1933) *"Official History of the Australian Army Medical Services, 1914-1918, Volume 1, 'Gallipoli, Palestine and New Guinea,'* Australian War Memorial.

Butler, A.G. (1940) *"Official History of the Australian Army Medical Services, 1914-1918, Volume II, 'The Western Front,'* Australian War Memorial.

Butler, A.G. (1943) *"Official History of the Australian Army Medical Services, 1914-1918, Volume III, 'Problems and Services,'* Australian War Memorial,."

Carlyon, Les., (2002) *"Gallipoli,"* Pan Macmillan 2nd Edition.

Carlyon, Les., (2006) *"The Great War"* Pan Macmillan

Cassar, P.(1964) *"Medical History of Malta."* Wellcome Historical Library.: London,

DeGaris, R.E., OBE, MSM. *Typewritten Diary* (transcribed from the original war diaries kept by RE DeGaris.) These cover from May 1915 to May 1917 (Unpublished).

DeGaris, R.E., OBE, MSM. *Handwritten memoirs* reflecting on letters sent home, and other memoirs and records. (This is 77 pages long, handwritten, and covers a period from May 1915 to September 1916.) (Unpublished.)

Dunn, J.F.W., *"Souvenir to Commemorate the 50th Anniversary of the Formation of the Unit- 7th Field Ambulance-Gallipoli, France-Belgium"*

Gammage, B., (1974) *"The Broken Years-Australian Soldiers*

in the Great War." Penguin, Sydney.

Kearney, Robert, (2005) *"Silent Voices; The Story of the 10th Battalion AIF,"* New Holland Publishers, Sydney.

King, Jonathan, (2003) *"Gallipoli Diaries,"* Kangaroo Press, Melbourne.

Kyle, Roy, (2005) *"An ANZAC's Story, (Introduction by Bryce Courtney)"* Viking, Victoria.

Laffin, J., (1992) *"Guide to Australian Battlefields of the Western Front."* Kangaroo Press, Melbourne.

Lawriwsky, M. (2007) *"Hard Jacka"* Mira Books, Chatswood NSW.

Maxwell, J. VC., MC., DCM. (1939) *"Hells Bells and Mademoiselles,"* Angus & Robertson Sydney.

McCalman, Janet, (1981) *"De Garis, Elisha Clement (Elizee) (1851 - 1948)",* Australian Dictionary of Biography, Volume 8, Melbourne University Press, Pp 270-271.

Monash, Gen. Sir John, (1923) *"The Australian Victories in France, 1918."* 2nd Edition, Lothian Book Publishing Co., Melbourne.

Newbury, George, (1989) *"Mentioned in Despatches, Australians, World War I,"* Privately published by the author.

Nott, David, (1996) *"Somewhere in France"* Harper Perennial, Australia.

Pedersen, P.A, (2007) *"The Anzacs-Gallipoli to the Western Front,"* Viking, (Penguin Group Australia) Camberwell, Australia.

Rule, E.J. (1933) *"Jacka's Mob"* Angus & Robertson, Sydney.

Savona-Ventura, C. (2005) *"Military hospitals in Malta"* article published on the internet, at *www.geocities.com/hotsprings/2615/medhist.*

Schinckel, HB (2006) *"Diary 1916-1919"* unpublished.

Smith, Shane, (2007) *"Fighting Cavemen"* Self-published, (2007)

Scott, E., (1936) *"Official History of Australia in the War of 1914-1918"* Volume XI., Angus and Robertson, 1936.

Wallace, N.V. (1976) *"Bush Lawyer"* Rigby, Adelaide.

Australian War Memorial, Canberra:
I wish to recognize the help of the Australian War Memorial in Canberra for allowing the re-printing of the acknowledged photos used as illustrations in this book;

National Archives of Australia:
I also wish to recognize the valuable records held by the National Archives of Australia. All sources from the National Archives, including all individual service histories, battalion histories, and other historical documentation was sourced from the website at *http://naa.gov.au,* which I found most user friendly.

Index:

"SS Geelong", 10, 14
10th Battalion, 61, 105, 175, 180, 183, 246, 254
1st Division, 53, 170, 171, 176, 182, 184, 212, 222
20th Battalion, 139, 140, 208
28th Battalion, 139, 140, 161
2nd Division, xiv, 30, 32, 38, 41, 52, 54, 118, 125, 135, 164, 167, 171, 172, 173, 176, 178, 182, 190, 196, 205, 208, 211, 218, 240, 241, 242, 243, 244, 248
4th Field Ambulance, 53, 54, 194, 195
50th Battalion, 175, 226
5th Field Ambulance, 195, 207, 220, 221, 223
6th Field Ambulance, 47, 89, 132, 139, 192, 193, 203
7th Field Ambulance, vi, viii, ix, xii, xiv, 2, 38, 41, 42, 43, 53, 55, 69, 70, 71, 72, 80, 84, 103, 108, 109, 113, 119, 120, 121, 124, 125, 130, 143, 144, 145, 152, 163, 169, 172, 173, 176, 177, 178, 183, 184, 185, 188, 193, 195, 201, 211, 213, 219, 220, 224, 228, 230, 243, 248, 249, 250, 253
Abbassia, 22, 32, 39, 40, 45
Abbeville, 167
AIF, iii, iv, v, vi, viii, xii, 3, 21, 31, 41, 44, 104, 110, 111, 118, 125, 152, 162, 168, 170, 190, 194, 195, 210, 216, 234, 248, 250, 251, 252, 254
Albert, 165, 166, 169, 170, 171, 172, 175, 177, 178, 179, 180, 181, 182, 184, 186, 193, 206, 212, 214, 224, 236, 237, 240, 248
Alexandria, 2, 17, 32, 33, 34, 36, 37, 38, 39, 41, 47, 48, 52, 73, 74, 80, 86, 101, 102, 103, 113, 196
AMC Army Medical Corp, 24
Amiens, 165, 167, 168, 169, 170, 171, 185, 216, 218, 219, 221, 226, 229, 233, 236, 238, 249, 252
Andrews, Perce, 108
Angel, Roy,, 143, 160, 242, 250
ANZAC, 1, iv, v, xiv, 6, 48, 65, 103, 104, 109, 110, 118, 131, 144, 159, 167, 183, 186, 190, 205, 213, 238, 241, 242, 243, 245, 254
Armentieres, 2, 123, 124, 125, 126, 127, 128, 129, 131, 132, 134, 135, 139, 165, 167, 191, 248
Armentiers, 135, 137, 138, 140, 144, 145, 146, 158, 159, 160, 162
Bac St Maur, 123, 125, 132, 137, 155
Baillieu, 131
Bailluel, 146, 148, 149, 150, 153, 158, 160, 161, 165, 171
Bapaume, 166, 175, 205, 237, 238, 241, 242, 245, 248
Barclay, Charles, 61
Batt, Murray, 61, 182
Battle of the Wosser, 29
Bean, CEW,, viii, ix, x, 30, 31, 51, 54, 55, 61, 64, 65, 66, 105, 110, 111, 116, 118, 119, 120, 131, 132, 138, 139, 140, 141, 150, 159, 161, 167, 170, 171, 172, 176, 177, 178, 180, 182, 183, 184, 186, 190, 194, 205, 206, 208, 211, 212, 237, 242, 243, 244, 245, 246, 252
Beauval, 170, 171, 187
Becordel, 207, 221, 223, 234, 242
Becourt Wood, 176, 177, 181, 182, 183, 188
Behencourt, 234, 236
Bice, Roy, 73, 74, 80, 85, 90, 250
Bills, Ray, 28, 108
Blacket, John,, 161
Blackett, John, 5, 6, 60, 113
Blackwell, Alec, 2, v, xii, 1, 3, 9, 21, 24, 28, 32, 39, 42, 53, 55, 56, 57, 58, 63, 64, 65, 66, 67, 72, 74, 80, 86, 87, 90, 97, 102, 103, 104, 105, 107, 109, 110, 111, 113, 116, 120, 121, 122, 123, 124, 125, 126, 127, 128, 129, 130, 131, 132, 133, 134, 136, 137, 140, 143, 144, 145, 146, 147, 148, 152, 153, 154, 155, 173, 177, 210, 211, 229, 231, 236, 240, 241, 244, 247, 248, 249, 250, 260
Bois Grenier, 123, 125, 129, 131, 132, 137, 140, 147, 148, 152, 153, 154, 155, 156, 157, 158, 159, 164, 249

Borre, 165, 166
Brownell, H.P.,, 116, 120, 125, 127, 133, 136, 161, 162
Bullecourt, 2, 163, 212, 228, 232, 237, 240, 241, 242, 243, 244, 245, 246, 247, 248, 249
Burnard, Dr Renfrey G.,, ii, vi, 3, 84, 122, 195, 204, 211, 240, 248, 250, 260
Butler, Col AG,, iv, ix, 22, 31, 38, 39, 54, 55, 56, 67, 104, 110, 111, 114, 174, 184, 196, 212, 244, 253
Cairo, 2, 10, 11, 14, 15, 16, 17, 18, 19, 20, 22, 24, 25, 28, 29, 30, 31, 32, 34, 37, 38, 45, 52, 104, 106, 107, 108, 109, 111
Callagan, W.E.,, 178
Carlsson, A.F.,, 173
Chisholm, Donald, 61
Chunuk Bair, viii, 65
Citizens Military Force, ii, vi, 162
Courtenay, Bryce, iii
Davies, Geroge, 162
DeGaris, Beryl,, ii, 3, 130, 138, 144
DeGaris, C.J.,, 126
DeGaris, Dr Mary,, 76, 77, 111, 179, 196, 247, 259
DeGaris, E.C..
DeGaris, E.C.,, 126
DeGaris, Ralph, 1, 2, i, ii, iii, iv, v, vi, vii, viii, ix, x, xi, xii, xiii, xiv, xv, xvi, 1, 3, 5, 6, 9, 10, 11, 15, 18, 19, 21, 22, 23, 27, 28, 30, 31, 36, 38, 39, 42, 43, 44, 45, 50, 51, 52, 53, 54, 55, 56, 57, 58, 62, 63, 64, 65, 66, 67, 69, 72, 76, 77, 81, 82, 84, 87, 89, 92, 94, 96, 103, 106, 107, 108, 109, 111, 112, 113, 116, 117, 118, 119, 124, 125, 126, 128, 130, 131, 132, 136, 137, 140, 142, 143, 144, 145, 146, 149, 150, 151, 152, 155, 158, 160, 162, 164, 165, 166, 167, 172, 173, 175, 176, 178, 180, 181, 184, 185, 192, 195, 196, 197, 203, 204, 211, 213, 216, 218, 224, 225, 229, 230, 231, 232, 235, 238, 239, 240, 243, 245, 247, 248, 249, 250, 251, 259, 260
Dollman, Lt Col.,, 121
Doucourant Family,, 128, 129, 130, 131, 136
Doullens, 165, 171, 172, 186, 200, 206
Dourcourant Family, 134

Ducourant. *See* Doucourant Family
Dunn, Reginald,, 42, 113, 119, 228, 253
Ebblinghem, 166, 167
Egypt, 2, vi, x, 11, 17, 18, 20, 21, 23, 26, 31, 37, 40, 41, 43, 44, 45, 58, 66, 80, 83, 86, 93, 97, 98, 100, 101, 103, 104, 105, 109, 110, 113, 117, 130, 155, 175
Erquinghem, 131, 132, 137, 138, 166
Estaires, 125, 143, 148, 155, 157, 158
Fleurbaix, 125, 132, 137, 150
Fort Rompu, 123, 125, 137, 142, 149, 150, 158, 160
Fowler, Murray, 36, 61
Frommelles, 165, 168
Gallipoli, 1, 2, iv, vi, viii, ix, x, xi, 10, 11, 17, 32, 36, 39, 41, 45, 47, 49, 51, 52, 55, 56, 57, 60, 62, 64, 67, 68, 69, 70, 71, 72, 73, 79, 80, 81, 85, 86, 89, 101, 103, 105, 106, 110, 117, 130, 131, 176, 182, 194, 223, 245, 251, 253, 254
Ghain Tuffieha, 91, 92, 94, 95
Ghan Tuffieha. *See* Ghain Tuffieha.
Goddard, Jack, 61
Godfrey, Jim,, 103, 124, 136, 228, 249
Graves, Bill, 13, 29, 31, 34, 39, 40, 220, 222, 225, 236, 238, 239
Green Dump, 213
Haig, Sir Douglas,, 120, 205, 208, 211
Hatch, Roy,, 89, 90, 99
Hazebrouck, 118, 119, 120, 150
Heliopolis, 2, 11, 16, 17, 18, 20, 21, 22, 24, 32, 38, 43, 44, 45, 104
Hindenburg Line, 237, 241, 242, 243, 244
Hobbs, Sr Narelle,, 76, 82, 83, 85, 102
Hoggarth, Bill, 61, 175
Hughes, W.M.,, 149, 150, 164
Irwells, 119, 122, 127, 193, 198
Jacka, Albert, VC,, 193, 194, 212, 254
Jackson, Perce,, 161
Kammerman, C.,, 193, 250
Keast, Jim,, 124, 172
Kidman, Eric, v, xii, 1, 3, 9, 10, 11, 39, 42, 46, 49, 53, 54, 56, 60, 64, 65, 66, 67, 80, 86, 93, 97, 102, 103, 104, 108, 109, 110, 111, 113, 121, 122, 124, 127, 128, 129, 131, 132, 133, 134, 136, 140, 143, 145, 147, 148, 153, 155, 156, 160, 163, 171, 177,

178, 180, 182, 191, 198, 201, 204, 210, 213, 217, 218, 219, 220, 221, 225, 226, 227, 228, 230, 236, 241, 245, 247, 248, 249, 250, 251, 260
Kidman, Roy, ii, 3, 46, 93
King George V, 180
Kitchener, Lord,, 26, 117, 118, 155
Koster, Roy,, 142, 143
Lemnos, 48, 49, 53, 68, 73
Lynn, Harry, 168, 179, 198
Lyons, 117, 118
Mallet, Bert, 172, 180
Malta, 2, 66, 73, 74, 76, 77, 79, 80, 81, 83, 87, 88, 91, 93, 94, 96, 97, 98, 101, 102, 104, 113, 114, 171, 253, 255
Marseilles, 113, 114, 116, 118
McEwin, Ken, 175, 225, 226
Mehaffy, Jack,, 225, 226
Mitcham, v, 2, 8, 21, 23, 84, 210
Moascar, 110, 111, 112
Monash, John, xi, 212, 254
Morbecque, 119, 120, 123
Mouquet Farm, 180, 182, 183, 188
Naracoorte, i, ii, iii, v, xii, 5, 9, 28, 56, 84, 93, 104, 105, 109, 131, 146, 235, 246
Pace, Don,, 2, 224, 226, 233
Paris, 93, 117, 166, 214, 215, 216, 247
Pedersen, Peter, ix, 209, 254
Peninsula, 23, 32, 34, 50, 57, 63, 66, 67, 68, 74, 75, 77, 79, 81, 158
Picquigny, 167, 168
Polygon Camp, 22, 32
Popperinghe, 191, 195
Pozieres, 2, 165, 166, 169, 170, 172, 173, 174, 175, 176, 177, 178, 179, 180, 183, 188, 189, 190, 192, 193, 198, 202, 205, 229, 234, 237, 246, 248, 249, 259
Prince Alfred College

PAC, i, ii, 259
Puchevilliers, 170
Romarin, 159
Roper, Alex, 21, 22
Schinckel, Harry, vi, xii, 2, 3, 109, 181, 248, 250, 255
Schofield, Tom,, 96
Shrapnel Valley, 51, 52
Skuse. See Nat Skuse, Edward Skuse, Thomas Skuse.
Skuse, Edward,, 104
Skuse, Nathaniel,, 104
Skuse, Thomas,, 104
Somme, 2, 165, 184, 190, 194, 200, 205, 208, 211, 213, 232
Spence, Peter,, 2, 176, 179, 184, 214
St Andrew's Hospital, 82, 88, 91, 92, 94, 98
St David's, 76, 79, 80, 81, 82, 83, 85, 88, 96
St. Omer, 150, 154, 171, 200
Steele, Dr D.M.,, 107
Steenwerk, 125, 130, 147, 154
Streaky Bacon, 132, 133, 146, 147
Suez, 13, 14, 15, 33, 110, 111
Taubes, 181
Thistle Dump, 207, 209, 220
Thompson, Nicholas,, 179
Thomson, Colin, 76, 111, 178, 179, 181, 191, 192, 196
Tunstall, Bob,, 78, 80, 83, 85
Valletta, 74, 77, 78, 79, 80, 85, 87, 88, 90, 91, 92, 93, 94, 95, 96, 97, 98, 99
Vandencourt, 171, 172
West, David,, 185
White, Frank, 22, 24
Wosser. See "Battle of the Wosser"
Ypres, 2, 107, 125, 126, 135, 158, 178, 190, 191, 193, 196, 197, 199, 201, 203, 205, 234, 248, 249, 251

ABOUT THE AUTHOR:

Bill DeGaris is Ralph's grandson. Born in Millicent, where Ralph lived all his life after the Great War. Bill attended Millicent High School, Prince Alfred College in Adelaide, Staples School in Connecticut, USA, then the University of Adelaide, where he graduated with a Law degree in 1975. Bill practices law in Mount Gambier, the largest regional city in South Australia.

Bill and his wife Lyn have lived in the South East of South Australia for 40 years, and have 3 children and 5 grandchildren.

The interest in Ralph's adventures were sparked by the discovery of the primary documents referred to in the Preface. The gaps in the diary sparked Bill's interest to research the history of the events Ralph recorded. Initially produced for his family, there has been such wide inquiry for the book that it has been published and is available in both print and eBook form.

The diary ends in May 1917. However, Bill has researched the later period of the war, when, as the war effort demanded more and more troops in Europe, many of Ralph's mates joined the Innocent Crusaders.

Meantime, Ralph's cousin, Dr Mary DeGaris, who lost her fiancée at Pozieres, served as a field surgeon in Serbia. Mary and Ralph remained in close contact during the war.

Bill is working on completing a second book about the characters appearing in the Part 1 of "The Innocent Crusaders." Because of the lack of diary records for the period May 1917, the second volume is being written as an historical novel based on the later part of the war and the experiences of Ralph, Eric and Alec, and their mates. It also deals with remarkable Dr Mary DeGaris, and her adventures as an army field hospital surgeon in Serbia.

This second book traces the service of each of the boys on the Western Front. The book is based on the war records and actual experiences of the Innocent Crusaders in Europe. All 3 of our young men find love. Due to contacts made by Dr. Ren Burnard while he was recuperating in the UK, Ralph, Eric and Harry Schinckel all brought home Cornish brides. Ralph and Eric married sisters, and Harry married their best friend. They remained firm friends all their lives. Meantime, Alec and Mary both have different stories to tell.

www.ingramcontent.com/pod-product-compliance
Lightning Source LLC
Chambersburg PA
CBHW062153080426
42734CB00010B/1677